The Gift

Journey to the Self
Through Psychotherapy

The Gift

Journey to the Self
Through Psychotherapy

by
Kathleen B. Mountain, M.A.

With Afterword by
James P. Seymour, Ph.D.

Inner Passages Publishing
Garden Grove, California • Colorado Springs, Colorado

The Gift: Journey to the Self Through Psychotherapy.

Copyright © 1998 by Kathleen B. Mountain.

Printed and bound in the United States of America.

Although the author and publisher have exhaustively researched all sources to ensure the accuracy and completeness of the information contained in this book, we assume no responsibility for errors, inaccuracies, omissions or any other inconsistency herein. Any slights against people or organizations are unintentional.

Publisher's Cataloging-in-Publication
(Provided by Quality Books, Inc.)

Mountain, Kathleen B., 1961-
    The Gift: Journey to the Self Through Psychotherapy /
Kathleen B. Mountain.— 1st ed.
      p. cm.
      Preassigned LCCN: 98-70642
      ISBN: 0-9663271-0-1

    1. Mountain, Kathleen B.—Health. 2. Mountain, Kathleen B.
—Diaries. 3. Psychotherapy patients. 4. Depression, Mental
—Treatment. 5. Psychotherapy. I. Title.

RC464.M68 1998   616.89'17
QBI98-360

Cover design © 1998 by Cukjati Design
Colorado Springs, Colorado

For:

B.K.F. for her love, understanding, and patience.
P.J.S., my therapist, for his courage, commitment, and strength.
S.E.R., my physician, for his determination to start me on my road to healing.
F.L.C., my mentor, my fan, and above all, my friend.
My loving family, for without their patience, love, and support, my life would
not be possible.

Contents

The Gift

Preface

Are you searching for love in all its forms: the secrets to a wonderful relationship, acceptance by both others and yourself, and joy or happiness within your life? Although many claim to have the answer, most often, the answer to these questions must be learned through experience. Life's experience? Yes, but there is another, safer place to learn these lessons. These things can be learned within a simple relationship; the relationship known as psychotherapy. The first time I went into a therapist's office, I wasn't looking for all of these things, but in time, I would find there was so much I could gain from the therapeutic relationship.

People enter into psychotherapy for as many reasons as there are people. Each therapy experience is different. Sometimes the experiences are fruitful and the client walks away feeling "healed." Other times, the experience is frustrating and seemingly worthless. Psychotherapy can be one of the most powerful and life-changing experiences one can have. It is a relationship which has specific boundaries and rules. It is a relationship which is supposed to be about the client. It is a relationship which is supposed to be safe, nurturing, and supportive.

There have been many books written about psychotherapy. So why another? There are two principal reasons for this book. First, I believe there are many misconceptions as to what happens "on the couch." I want to give the public another look at what therapy can be. It isn't like the movies, where someone lies down on a couch and just jabbers on about odd and strange things, or where an inept and more neurotic therapist bumbles through someone else's life. It is a deep emotional commitment between two people in order to help the client discover and pursue a better life. I want to share the depths, struggles, pains, and triumphs which can be experienced through the process of psychotherapy. The second reason is, I hope that through this book, others who are in need of help, but are afraid of the therapeutic process, will gain a better understanding of what can happen and will pursue their own healing process.

This book is not so much about my journey as it is about the process of psychotherapy from the client's perspective. Granted, I will discuss my journey of discovery through therapy, but it will serve as a backdrop for the explanation of a therapeutic experience. I want to share as much of psychotherapy as I can bring to the printed page. I know each therapeutic relationship is unique to the individuals who participate, but there are some experiences which are common to most therapeutic relationships which explore the depths of the human psyche. This is the part of psychotherapy I want to share. I will briefly cover many topics to which other authors have devoted entire books. My discussions are meant to give a very brief introduction to topics associated with therapy, not a complete analysis. I want to describe what can happen in therapy, not all the theoretical aspects. Of course, many of my own personal opinions regarding psychotherapy, psychology, and life appear among these pages.

The psychotherapy experience I will describe covered a period of ten months, which is a very brief time for in-depth therapy. This therapeutic experience was preceded by two years and two months of previous therapeutic work with two other therapists.

I will discuss every aspect of the therapeutic experience from the initial session through to post-termination. In order to do this, I will include excerpts from my personal journal that deal specifically with my own therapy sessions and with my thoughts related to my self-discovery. These excerpts are accompanied by commentary on the significance of the content and further explanatory information to make my experiences more comprehensible and complete. Although I am a student of psychology, I keep the psychological jargon to an absolute minimum, and explain the terms as they are used.

The type of therapy discussed within these pages is a form of therapy which is becoming a thing of the past. I find this so unfortunate, for deep emotional healing should be a priority. When the ill are truly healed, the managed care companies would prosper and see their clients make fewer visits to their primary care physicians for diagnosable and non-diagnosable ailments. Headaches, ulcers, anxiety and discomfort would be greatly reduced. In the short run, therapy can be expensive; in the long run it can save not only money, but also lives and families.

All that is written within these pages are from one therapeutic relationship and do involve an actual client, myself, and a licensed clinical psychologist. In order to preserve the anonymity of both my family and the therapist, as well as other people in my life, the names have been changed.

Some of the entries have been tailored to include only the more relevant passages. There are some passages which do not speak to my therapy, but do lay the groundwork for future entries, and were, therefore, left intact and may not seem initially relevant.

In the Afterword of this book, Jim Seymour, Ph.D., the therapist who accompanied me on this journey, concludes this book with some of his thoughts, perspectives, and intentions regarding our therapy process. It provides a personal peek at the man who sat across from me all those ten months. I thank him for allowing me to talk candidly about what happened between us, for by doing this, he has shared many facets of himself also.

Kathleen B. Mountain

Prologue

Prior to August 1996

Throughout most of my life, I have been viewed by others, who didn't know me very well, as being self-confident, intelligent, conscientious, successful, and hard working. Those who thought they knew me best, thought I had my ups and downs, but could not guess or imagine the inner turmoil and pain I lived with most of my life. I led the seemingly "perfect" life.

I appeared to lead a happy and well-adjusted life at home with my mother and stepfather; we were a "model" family. I was a graduation speaker when I graduated from high school. I graduated from the United States Air Force Academy and became an aircraft maintenance officer in the United States Air Force. I was told, by my superiors, that I had one of the best set of military records they had ever seen for a junior officer. I was married to a wonderful man and had a beautiful daughter. I even lived in what many described as the perfect house. With all this perfection, how could there be anything wrong? In reality, my internal life did not match the illusion I created for the rest of the world to see.

I had lived with depression for most of the last eighteen years of my life. Unfortunately, I did not recognize, or maybe I denied, my depression with the exception of one brief period about fifteen years ago. My depression consisted of numerous symptoms: unexplained physical ailments, immediate anger, chronic fatigue, unreasonable irritability, emotional withdrawal and suicidal thoughts. As unbelievable as it may seem, I did not equate suicidal thoughts with depression. Now, looking back, it seems absurd not to have connected them.

My suicidal thoughts were constant and persistent. I saw suicidal potential in every bridge I crossed, every truck in on-coming traffic, every major pre-scription medication, every gun, and every other imaginable situation. Most people have hobbies such as stamp collecting, needlework, or auto repair; my hobby was collecting the means to kill myself. My intended suicide method had to comply with three criteria to be acceptable: 1) not appear to be a suicide, 2) be fatal, and 3) not leave a traumatic scene for anyone who might find me. At the time, it seemed unfortunate that I had not yet found a method of killing myself that fulfilled all three criteria.

I had a reason for each criterion. The reason for the first criterion was my mother had told me, many years ago, she would be terribly embarrassed if I ever committed suicide. I did not want to embarrass my mother. The second criterion was based on the notion that permanent disability was a fate worse than death. The third criterion was based on the thought that I did not want to psychologically harm anyone who would find me. My desire to die was based on one simple premise; I wanted my emotional pain to end, and the only way I could see that occurring was to die. I had no desire to "punish" anyone for my pain, nor did I desire to hurt anyone as a result of my death. Anyone who is familiar with the aftermath of suicide knows I would have failed, no matter how clever I might have been in devising my own death.

To provide a better understanding of my mental condition, I will describe how I relieved my day-to-day stress. Some people use cigarettes, food, or alcohol, I used the image of blowing my brains out with a handgun. In times of stress or agitation, which occurred numerous times a day, I would imagine each step in the process of placing a handgun to the side of my head, slowly pulling the trigger, the explosion and progress of the bullet, and the entry and exit of the bullet through my skull. This process became so automatic for me, I could imagine this whole process in a matter of seconds. From this mental image, I would derive a reduced sense of tension for at least a few minutes. There was a time when I did this twenty to thirty times a day. I did not see anything wrong with doing this. I thought using any means to survive the day was practical.

In May of 1994, I possessed a lethal dose of prescription medication and alcohol. I waged the battle of life or death. The emotional pain from which I suffered became so great I no longer cared if my means of suicide fulfilled the three criteria I had earlier devised. My only objective was to end my pain, agony, and suffering. I placed my daughter in front of the television with a snack and a drink. I knew there would be sufficient time before my husband would come home. I had the pills. I had the alcohol. I had the chair. I had chosen the place on our property; all I had to do was step off the deck. However, I stopped on the deck, sat down, and waged the battle for my life. The part of me which wanted to die screamed for my misery to end. The part of me which wished to live insisted that I stay on the deck long enough so there would not be enough time left for the pills to work before my husband arrived home from work. Slowly the hours passed. In the end, life won the battle, but the war was not yet won.

My trek through psychotherapy began at the demand of my family physician. At that time, he was the only person in whom I had implicit faith and trust. For the previous ten months, I had seen my family physician, Dr. Stephens, once every two weeks. I saw him for headaches, sore throats, general discomfort, back pain. This list goes on, but I no longer remember all my ailments. Dr. Stephens was the first person who ever told me I was depressed. I did not believe him then. I was to discover the truth only days later, when I contemplated suicide.

The day after I nearly attempted suicide, I had an appointment with Dr. Stephens. During this visit, I found the courage to tell him about the events of the previous day. He did not let me leave his office, and he made my first appointment with a therapist. Dr. Stephens set into motion a chain of events that would change my life over a period of three years. Since that day, I have seen a total of three therapists, including the one this book describes. All of the previous therapists were experienced clinicians and effective therapists; I achieved gains through my work with each. I came to realize I was a person who needed an unreasonable amount of control in my life. In my desire to take care of the lives of everyone around me, I did not take care of myself. I did not practice balance within my life. I finally admitted that I suffered from recurrent major depression and that to maintain and rehearse my suicidal thoughts was both unhealthy and abnormal.

Through therapy, I realized I lived my emotional life in a highly compartmentalized fashion. I divided my daily existence into what I called my Practical Self and my Personal Self. My daily interactions with people resided in my Practical Self. This part of me seemed to be normal, conscientious, intelligent, and successful. My self-evaluation and depressive episodes belonged to my Personal Self. This part of me was highly self-critical, prone to depression, and low in self-esteem. Despite the internal battles I waged, I was able to function very successfully in many jobs: in the United States Air Force, in major manufacturing positions, in clerical office positions and as a graduate student. The internal division and battles were hidden from everyone, including my closest friends and family. I maintained such strict self-control that no one could guess the agony and pain I endured.

Another result of therapy was my decision to pursue my childhood desire to help alleviate the emotional pain of others. I decided to pursue a career in psychology. However, before I could be effective in helping others, I knew I needed to heal myself using therapy.

I left the first therapist because I no longer needed the acute crisis care I required in the beginning. Also, he had succumbed to my talent for making people want to tell me about their lives. In the end, there were times when I wondered who should be paying whom. He was a good therapist, but I was very persuasive in my means of facilitating disclosure from others. I left my second therapist because I refused to sign a non-suicide contract with her and her supervisor. I could not willfully enter into an agreement I might not intend to uphold. I was unable to promise her that I was strong enough not to take my life. For a brief time, I was not in therapy.

In late August, 1996, I began my Master's program in Clinical Psychology. At this time I decided to return to therapy for several reasons. First, before I could heal anyone else, I had to find a way to heal myself. Second, I could not practice something I did not believe in; therefore, I needed to prove to myself that psychotherapy indeed could help cure psychological ailments. Third, I believed being involved in therapy during my Master's program would result in professional and personal development by seeing the practice of psychotherapy firsthand. Thus, I began my therapy with Jim Seymour, Ph.D.

1

❖

To Try Again

The process of finding a therapist and establishing a productive therapeutic relationship can be a most difficult task. The prospective client is faced with numerous questions: Whom do I call, will this therapist be the right one, how much will it cost, will my therapist's hours be compatible with my schedule, what will the therapist be like, what will therapy be like, etc.? The litany of questions and anxiety can increase with time and the length of the search. Going to several therapists, before finding the "right" therapist, is not an uncommon experience. As each therapist is ruled out, in many cases, the client becomes more aware of what is needed in the "right" therapist. Persistence in this endeavor can pay dividends much greater than any preconceived expectation.

Jim Seymour was recommended by a friend who knew him personally. At the time I began therapy with Jim, I was beginning to question whether or not therapy would work for me, or for that matter anyone. In a sense, this round of therapy was my last hope. Sometime in the beginning of August, 1996, I decided to try again.

September 15, 1996

I have been off my anti-depressants since June 28, 1996. I stopped taking everything I had been on for my depression and skin because I swelled up terribly.

In August, I started seeing Jim Seymour, Ph.D. He is very good. Our first session was an introductory session. He wanted to find out why I wanted to see him, and I wanted to find out what he was like.

I did not write about my first session with Jim because, in the beginning, I was skeptical about whether psychotherapy would work for me. Although I had made some gains during my previous therapeutic experiences, I still wondered if psychotherapy actually worked. I needed to know for myself. My attitude toward my third attempt with psychotherapy was one of extremely guarded hope with a huge side order of doubt. It was ironic that I thought I could use therapy to help others with their emotional pain, when I was doubtful about it being effective in treating my own depression.

Although I did not write much about my first meeting with Jim, I remember it well. The first time I laid eyes upon him was when he introduced himself to me in the waiting area. Jim appeared to be in his mid-forties, was of average height and build, and had a full-head of dark wavy hair. He did not have the imperious look of a television therapist, instead he appeared gentle, yet confident. He had an almost businesslike mood about him; this was as much an interview of me as it was of him. His office was typically void of family mementoes with the exception of one small picture of a young women, who I assumed was his daughter. Scattered throughout his office was an interesting mix of trinkets from other times and other places. The office was furnished with durable wooden furniture upholstered in emerald green velour. The expected academic diplomas and professional certificates were hung on the wall, but appeared as though they had not been touched since being hung. The atmosphere of the office was not dark and mysterious, but rather light and businesslike. He offered me a seat on the loveseat and he sat across from me in his accustomed desk chair, and then we began.

I told Jim I wanted to merge the two aspects of my "self," my Practical Self and my Personal Self. I also briefly told him of my previous therapeutic experiences. I told him what I did and did not like about my past therapists and their work. I did this so Jim would know what might help me and what I definitely did not want to see in our sessions. Jim would later tell me he appreciated my openness in this matter. In order to be fair, the reasons for terminating my previous therapeutic relationship were made clear. I would not sign a non-suicide contract. I could not promise to survive, I could only promise to make the *attempt* to survive. Another condition of our relationship was that Jim would not involuntarily hospitalize me for suicidal thoughts. My unspoken part of the bargain was to withhold the complete severity of my suicidal thoughts while I was in session. (It needs to be made clear that there are legal requirements for a therapist to secure the safety of an individual if there is serious concern about the client wanting to hurt him/herself or another. If I would have disclosed to Jim the current seriousness of my suicidal thoughts, he would have been obligated, by law, to protect me. I was very aware of his legal obligations; therefore I decided to withhold this information from him.)

In starting over for the third time, I had a vague sense of what I wanted from a therapist, but no specific requirements. I knew I wanted someone who truly listened to what I was feeling, not just to what I was saying. All too often, a thera-pist hears the factual content of what a client says but does not hear what else is being conveyed in the conversation. Since I knew one of my greatest weaknesses was not telling others what I wanted and what I really meant, it was very impor-tant for me to find someone who could hear the "entire" conversation; what was said, what was not said, what was implied, and what was felt.

Jim told me he was winding down his clinical practice and was frequently out of town and; therefore, would be unavailable to me for several days at a time. I easily consented to this condition of our relationship, which was surprising to me. Although I did not acknowledge my intuition about the relationship at the time, I felt this relationship would be different. He also made it clear he was being very selective in the cases he would accept. He did not elaborate on what this meant, but I did not question what it meant. I only wanted to know if he would take me on; for the time being, he agreed.

September 15, 1996 (continued)

> The second session went well. He put several things together for me. We talked about my relationship with my dad, and the sole memory I have of my dad, my mom, and me together: the one in which my dad is reading the newspaper, my mom is cooking, and I am riding my tricycle round and round. He pointed out this type of relationship still exists: my dad is still busy with work; my mom is still doing her own thing; and I am still left alone to take care of my own business. This made a lot of sense to me.

Jim's analysis of my early memory of my mother and father was very impressive for me. Until that time, there seemed to be no reason why I would remember this event, especially in light of the fact I have very few memories of my childhood. This condition continues into the present. Jim's insightful analysis of my memory gave me some confidence as to his therapeutic skill and intuition. I was hopeful, but remained extremely cautious.

The process of giving the client a "gift" during therapy is often recom-mended. What is meant by this is that the therapist should find some element of hope, or way of instilling confidence within the client that the current therapeutic experience will be effective. Many therapists believe this should be done on the first session, but in reality it may take several sessions for this to occur. The delay in helping the client achieve a heightened sense of confidence is not a reflection of the skill of the therapist; sometimes what the client brings to the first sessions is not the real objective of therapy. This may forestall the client's feeling of confidence in the therapist. Jim's analysis of my memory was the first of many "gifts" for me.

September 15, 1996 (continued)

> During the third session we talked about my Emotional Self and my Practical Self. He mentioned I discussed this sort of thing without much feeling. I realized I didn't have much of an idea as to what my Emotional Self was like. He asked me what I thought my life would be like once I was able to integrate my two selves. I told him I didn't think things would change much, and I really had no true idea. After all, this is the only way I know how to be.

The descriptions of the early visits were written from memory. They were emotionally cold and objective, and were almost written in the third person which is reflective of my lack of emotional connection with myself. I functioned in a day-to-day environment devoid of most of my emotions. To the outside world, I appeared to be well-controlled, conscientious, highly organized, and reserved. My internal world was laced with the self-doubt and criticism of my Personal Self. I interpreted every word and event as a direct reflection of something I had done or said. I viewed my internal world in an unforgiving and self-derogating manner, but saw the outside world with far more understanding and forgiveness.

September 15, 1996 (continued)

> Last Friday, I saw Jim for the fourth time. He was thrilled I displayed some emotion, even though I did let him know I already knew I would respond emotionally to the topics we discussed. In talking about my lack of childhood memories, he showed me it is in large part due to the fact I have suppressed and denied any emotive characteristics throughout my life, thus leaving my childhood almost an emotional wasteland. He used the phrase "a childhood of quiet desperation." I think that phrase applies to most of my life.

During the fourth session, I talked about my grandmother. In the third session, I told Jim I cried every time I talked of my grandmother. This time was no different. Although Jim was happy with some showing of emotion, for me it was almost as if on cue. I was emotionally disconnected from the reasons why I would cry when discussing my grandmother. I would not understand the ties which held me to my tears until much later. The phrase "a childhood of quiet desperation" found a direct connection with my Personal Self. The phrase seemed to succinctly describe how I had felt, but was unable to verbalize. The words "quiet desperation" rang out and reminded me of so much of what I had felt over the last twenty years. But why? The answer was to remain unknown for the time.

September 15, 1996 (continued)

> In thinking of the question Jim asked of me, "What is it that I need to explore?" I find it difficult to consider. It has taken many hours for me to allow myself access to those areas of myself which would be able to answer this question. I have allowed myself to speculate on the nature of my depression. I have been told several times my depression is related to a bio-chemical source. At this moment I question this notion.

Although I had worked *during* my sessions with my previous two therapists, this was the first time I worked on my healing *between* sessions in a constructive manner. Jim provided me with a question which would begin the inward journey. By asking this question, Jim gained an enormous amount of my trust and respect. I knew he was interested in working with me, and not just my symptoms or family relationships. Although relieving symptoms and understanding family relationships are important when working with a client; the client must gain the feeling the therapist is pursuing what the client really wants to know. For some clients, to gain symptom relief and to understand the family relationship are the key objectives, for me, I needed to meet and know my inner self. Jim's question reflected his understanding of my own goals in this therapeutic relationship.

The debate about the biochemical source of depression is long from decided. I was never satisfied with the biochemical answer as the total answer to my depression. Several knowledgeable clinicians had suggested I may be one of those people for whom medications may be a requirement for life. In my mind, there had to be more than just an imbalance of neurotransmitters (the brain chemicals which carry the "messages" throughout the brain). For a period of two and a half years, I had been on strong doses of anti-depressant medication. I had tried nearly all of the most widely prescribed Selective Serotonin Reuptake Inhibitor class of anti-depressant medications. Some symptom relief was achieved, but no lasting relief had resulted. The prospect of remaining on anti-depressant medications for the rest of my life was not an acceptable option at the time. I hated taking anti-depressants because I did not feel they were as effective for me as they should be, and they were also a sign of my ailment or, more accurately, my "defect." I could justify taking medications for life for "medical" problems, but I was not willing to do so for mental health reasons.

The Gift

Unfortunately, this attitude is very common. There are some individuals who could receive great benefit from anti-depressant medications, but due to this pervasive attitude, many do not take advantage of the medications available. It was hypocritical of me to disdain the notion of taking mental health medications which I would have recommended, without hesitation, for others.

September 15, 1996 (continued)

I have researched the issue of depression from many different aspects. I have heard the words hopeless, helplessness, and profound sorrow. In many of the typical renditions of what depression is, I have found difficulty in matching the cognitive characteristics listed with the ones which roam around my head. Instead, I have felt I am not hopeless, helpless, nor profoundly sad. I have a feeling of emotional oppression and affective pain. I am not sure it makes any sense.

The question of why I wanted to kill myself two years ago has remained a mystery to me until now. I feel I can finally answer this question. The answer is also intertwined with my own personal theory of why my depression exists, comes and goes, and how it may be controlled.

It is no secret that I am emotionally suppressed. The "whys and wherefors" are fairly clear to me now, but no longer are important. What remains important are the results. In my theory of my depression, I feel that over the years I have suppressed a major portion of my affective life. In doing so, I have maintained strict control of what and how I feel, therefore controlling how I act. Unfortunately, (or fortunately depending on one's view) the mind and body can only contain so much psychological waste. When my mind and body have exceeded their limits for containing my emotions, portions of the negative affect leak out into my everyday life in the form of mild depression. Since the feelings are diffuse and non-directive, they do not exert control over any one element in my life; instead, they darkly color all aspects. Yes, the depression does exert control, but it does not seem to be obvious enough for me or anyone else to notice. I was able to do all the things that were required of me, and do them quite well. Even my husband did not realize what I was going through.

So why the suicidal episode? Until May 1994, I had been under a lot of stress: school, work, marriage, job change, childbirth, relocation. Finally there came a time when there was nothing which needed to be done. For the first time in my life there appeared to be an extended period of stability. I think for many years, the stresses on my life were the capstones to my emotional storehouse. The stresses were no longer there; so, there was nothing to help me keep control of all the "affective junk" which I had stored for years.

In looking back, and reading my journals, I can see that over the course of a few days, the emotions stored for years came bursting forth. The emotional pain I felt was unlike anything I had ever felt before. I did not feel like that when my grandmother or Barney, my beloved dog, died. It was a pain I felt I did not want to endure. It had nothing to do with the thought that it would not go away; it was more of the thought that I didn't know how to deal with them, and I wanted to escape the pain. I was finally able to regain control over enough of the emotional pain so I could decide I did not need to kill myself. I think my obligations to my family helped me to stay.

Over the next three days [after the suicide attempt] I had anxiety attacks. I believe I now understand where they came from. I think my control over my emotions was quite weak, and again these emotions were overflowing my control.

By Friday, I was in bed and unable to do anything. I did not want to hear, see, or know any person was around. This included my family. I believe I felt this way because I knew any contact with other people would require an emotional cost. I could neither accept nor "dish out" any emotional payment at this time, no matter how small the cost. I remained in bed for three days.

So what does all this mean? In short, I know I am still emotionally suppressive. I have only a finite storage space available, and when that is exceeded, the excess spills over and manifests itself in the form of mild depression. I have learned to cope with the overall depressive feelings and find this preferable to dealing with the emotions of daily living as they occur. If for some reason I am able to contain more "emotional junk" than I can handle, and it is released in a short period of time; then I experience a major depressive episode. This is a situation I must avoid.

This passage may seem insightful. At first, I thought it was. In looking back on these thoughts, I find I was still mired in emotional disconnection. I felt coping with depressive feelings was preferable to dealing with my day-to-day emotions. This theory of depression made wonderful sense for a person who did not want to deal with the emotional aspects of daily human living. The theory was convenient and easy to accept. Unfortunately, it was far from accurate. What is interesting to note, is I never fully recognized the extent of my depression. I called what I was experiencing mild depression. Most people would not consider imagining blowing one's brains out, multiple times a day, as mild depression. Even after two years of therapy, I was not willing to admit the seriousness of my emotional condition.

September 15, 1996 (continued)

I don't think I will ever be able to live in the emotional here and now all the time. Therefore, I need to recognize and manage the emotional storehouse I have built and maintained over the years. I need to make sure I don't exceed critical mass. If I do, I am asking for emotional meltdown – major depression.

This paragraph from my journal emphasizes my inability or unwillingness to connect with my emotional life. By stating my doubt in connecting with my emotions, it gave me an escape from having to make the connection. This also allowed me to go about finding ways of maintaining my life much as it was prior to therapy. I was not yet ready to begin the real work ahead.

September 15, 1996 (continued)

Over the past two and a half months, I have been okay. I have had mild depressive episodes, but nothing major. I have not needed medication, but on the other hand, I don't think it ever worked very well for me anyway. I need to find ways of safely venting the emotions I keep, or better yet, find ways of dealing with my emotions and; therefore, not needing to store them.

I enjoy seeing Jim for more than personal reasons; I also enjoy him on a professional basis as well. I hope one day I will be able to be as effective a therapist as Jim. I can only hope.

The first four sessions were the initial steps in forming a therapeutic relationship with my therapist Jim. It is essential for the client to form a bond or relationship with the therapist. The bond must contain the foundations for trust, comfort, and openness. Seldom is this bond achieved quickly. The bond is developed over a course of sessions, and to some extent is built over the entire relationship.

Jim helped establish our relationship by his openness about his availability and case selection, the meaningful interpretation of my mentioned memory, his patient willingness to allow me to talk, and his ability to ask the right questions. In being open about his availability and case selection, he let me know that if he was not available or decided not to take me on as a client, the reasons would be more about him than me. If he had not been open, had not been available, or had decided not to take my case, I would have instantly assumed it was more about how disturbed I was rather than about what his schedule would allow. Personal rejection was one area in which I was terribly sensitive. I assumed every non-positive action was a result of me not doing something just right. I could conceive of other reasons why something could happen, but ultimately I decided it must have been my fault.

Jim's interpretation of my memory was important to me because it told me he had a fundamental understanding of my family as I had described them. This conveyed to me that he was actually hearing what I was saying and implying, not just listening to the words. My previous therapists were not as perceptive as Jim in perceiving the nuances of what I had said. Sometimes, they had simply not heard what was said. Throughout my life, I felt I was often not heard, in the deepest sense of the word. My family deeply respected my opinions and recommendations, but I felt they did not hear the emotional content of my life. Jim's ability to hear my words and emotions was a very powerful tool in building the trusting relationship I needed within which I could begin to heal.

Previously, I had been persuasive in making other people want to tell me their lives; I had elicited long dialogues from my previous therapists about their lives, families, and perspectives. This did not help heal me, but it shielded me from dealing with painful issues. I knew I needed a therapist who was strong enough not to succumb to my desire to hear him talk. Jim was such a therapist.

Anyone who spent a great deal of time with me had to be patient. I was very moody, defensive, and was stubborn about many things. I felt very comfortable that Jim would give me the latitude I needed to maintain enough control over the relationship, yet be able to help me find a way to heal.

The ability to ask the right questions in psychotherapy is part of the art. I needed someone who could push me to consider who I was and what I was about without putting me on the defensive. This was a difficult task. I was so sure I knew myself. I was so sure no one could understand me or what I needed. Jim would prove me wrong on all accounts.

Not everyone needs the same characteristics in a therapist. There are a few which are important for most people: the ability to trust the therapist, a level of comfort with the therapist, an aura of confidence in the therapist's abilities, and an appropriate personality compatibility. Most people do not itemize the positive and negative characteristics of the therapist in question: normally, people consider one of two things: 1) "It is easier to stay with the one I have," or 2) "What is my 'gut' level response to this therapist?" When faced with the decision to stay with a therapist or find a new one, it is important to go with your "gut" level response to the therapist. Maintaining the status quo, just because it is easier, is not a helpful reason to stay; this can often result in a disappointing and non-productive experience.

2

The Real First Step

Erroneously, clients sometime believe the therapist will "cure" their ills. For if they could cure themselves, the profession of psychotherapy would be useless. There may be those who can heal themselves, without the aid of a competent and intuitive therapist, but for many, the aid of the therapist is indispensable for beginning the difficult inward journey.

Oftentimes, friends and relatives criticize the ineptitude of their therapist, and in frustration have said, "I saw the therapist four or five times, and he didn't do a thing for me." Unfortunately, either the therapist did not convey to the client the necessity of the client having to do the real work, or the client did not hear this message. In either event, the result is the same – a failed attempt at psychotherapy.

Another erroneous thought by clients is, "I am the one who volunteered to come. It was my idea; therefore, I must be ready to heal myself." Healing ourselves and making the changes in our lives to do so is entirely different from wanting to do so. Most people have wanted to quit smoking, lose weight, or learn a foreign language. That is the easy part. How many have actually accomplished those desired goals, especially the most difficult and demanding ones? I venture to guess, not as many as I would like to think. The disparity between wanting to change, and having the will to change is profound. It is often the *want to* which brings the client to therapy, but it is the *will to* which brings the client to change.

After two years and two months of previous therapy, many would think I might have known this basic truth. I did not. I too believed my mere presence in therapy, all that time, should have resulted in my healing. I did achieve some gains and insights as a result of my previous therapy, but I did not attain any feeling of healing.

So when does healing begin? It begins when clients take the risks of facing the self, feeling the emotional pain and agony of life, and questioning the believed "truths" by which their lives are governed. Is that not what is done in therapy? Yes it is, but it can be done in an intellectual manner in which the client does not really risk, or it can be done in a manner in which clients risk everything – the Self.

The difference is not in the words spoken by clients, but rather from where the words originate - the mind or the soul. The words from the mind reflect events in an almost objective or observer position. The events are described in detail, as are possibly the emotions, but there is a detachment by clients from the event. Instead of change, clients are looking for explanation or affirmation of the self. The words from the soul speak of the experience using many if not all the same words as does the mind; the difference is that the words from the soul are truly open, ready for change, and to be challenged.

> September 27, 1996
>
> I went to see Jim today. It was a disappointing appointment. He was preoccupied with other things today. I don't feel like I got anywhere. A very superficial appointment.
>
> I am thinking about writing Jim a letter and telling him some things about me I find very difficult to bring up in session. Unfortunately, I won't have another session for another three weeks.

At this point in my therapy, I was beginning to feel frustrated that Jim was not "curing" me. I wanted something out of therapy, but did not know what specifically. Another feeling which was beginning to solidify for me was the belief in this relationship. There seemed to be something different about this therapeutic relationship which was entirely different from the previous ones. In Jim, I felt the same implicit trust I felt with my family physician, Dr. Stephens. I felt a sense of comfort and familiarity with Jim I had never before felt with another person in my life. At one moment, I felt safe and warm with Jim, in another I was terrified and uncomfortable with the way I felt. With the safety, would come my desire and willingness to disclose; I would have to risk everything.

> Dr. Seymour,   September 28, 1996
>
> Even though we just had a session, there are a few things I was unable to bring up. It is terribly difficult for me to face how I feel about myself. I feel like my Personal Self is not a worthwhile person. It doesn't matter how much I accomplish or am capable of; there is still an underlying sense I am just not good

enough. This is an area I really want to deal with, but have a tremendously difficult time bringing up during our sessions.

Since my opinion of my Personal Self is so low, I am very sensitive to the way people respond to me in a personal way. In everyday life I seem to weigh and balance every word and motion. During any personal interaction, I sense how much the other person wants to listen, if they are preoccupied, if they are happy, sad, etc. I respond to conversations rather than be a part of a conversation. I am most comfortable when listening to the lives of others, and have great difficulty in talking of my life.

I truly look forward to our sessions. The thought of dealing with my life is enjoyable until I get there, and then it is hard for me to talk to you about personal growth issues. It is easier to talk about other topics of casual interest, or issues I have dealt with before. When we do talk, I find myself weighing your reactions, comments, and actions. Building a solid therapeutic relationship with you is something a part of me wants desperately, yet there is another part who is too frightened to allow it to happen. I know I pay for your time; we are both there to gab about what my life has to offer me, and yet, it is so difficult for me to impose my own life on you.

To write this is almost torturous, but it is far easier to write it than say it. The hope is that through this letter, I will allow myself to venture where I need to go.

Sincerely,
Kathleen Mountain

At the time this letter was written, I did not fully appreciate what I was saying. What I was finally saying to Jim was that I was cracking the door open to my soul. I was taking the first steps in opening myself up to change and challenge. Had I known at that time what I was headed for during the coming months, I would not have sent the letter. Instead, I would have trudged through several more sessions and then would have given up, in every sense of the word.

October 16, 1996

I have survived the last three weeks. The first two weeks I managed through a bout of depression. I did send the letter. It took a great deal of agonizing. I thought he might think it stupid, but in the end, I decided I needed to deal with it.

There was a time when I would not have sent the letter for fear of being judged "stupid." I had finally reached a point in my journey in which I was willing to risk the judgment in hopes of a beginning of true healing. At the time of this entry, I was very detached from my depression. In looking back, I see my "bout" of depression was in response to my agony of sending or not sending the letter. My detachment was so severe I did not even make a cursory connection; that was impossible for me to even imagine.

October 16, 1996 (continued)

On October 13th, my mom fell off the roof of her house. [My mother sustained many injuries as a result. I will not elaborate, suffice it to say I was deeply concerned.]

Needless to say, all of this has caused me some emotional grief. Sunday night when I found out, I did okay. On Monday, I realized I was not dealing with my emotions and thoughts in a constructive way. When alone, I would cry, and fight the desire to just suppress all emotion. I called Ruth and got an appointment with Dr. Seymour for Tuesday at 12:00. Even though I would have to get my daughter out of school a little early, I took it anyway. I needed to get my brains in the right direction.

Although I mentioned my inability to deal with my emotional reaction to the injuries my mother had sustained, I felt I needed to see Dr. Seymour to put my "brains," not my emotions, in the right direction. Again, my detachment from my emotions allowed me to think I was not intellectually dealing with my mother's accident in the appropriate manner. There was no mention or consideration of my dealing with the emotions I was experiencing. This did not seem incongruent or odd to me at the time. I believed I had control over my thinking, but exercised no control over my emotions; therefore, there was no need to deal with something over which I had no control.

October 16, 1996 (continued)

On Tuesday, I was still not thinking and feeling in a constructive way. I was so glad I had the appointment. The first thing Jim mentioned was the letter. He was pleased I had written and sent the letter. We also talked about my mom's accident. He helped me sort out what I needed to deal with in terms of going to see her. Since this is not currently a life threatening situation, I should decide to go or stay based on what is best for me, not what I ought to do for anyone else. At the time, it was hard for me to know what I should do; as the afternoon progressed, I realized it was best for me to stay for now.

Part of my problem with the notion of to go or to stay was how hurt I was that my mom did not want me to be there. Forget the fact she was only looking out for what was best for me; I was feeling hurt and rejected. It was so good to be able to admit that to Jim. It isn't enough to be able to intellectualize these thoughts and feelings. There is something about being able to verbalize them to someone else.

This paragraph was the first time I was able to verbally express what I was feeling, without censoring my thoughts with the "oughts and shoulds" of my life's belief system. This was also the first glimpse into what psychotherapy could be about for me. My admission of feeling hurt and rejected was a tremendous step. Prior to this time, I would have pushed aside those thoughts because I "should" have known my mother was not rejecting me, but rather looking out for my own well-being. The rejection of my feelings and emotions was an integral part of my life. I did not recognize it at the time, but I believed what I felt was not as important or relevant as what I "should" or "ought" to feel and think.

October 16, 1996 (continued)

During this discussion, he tied in the idea of my thoughts of worthlessness. He helped me realize that part of my inner turmoil was over the difficulty of trying to decide what to do; what I ought to do, versus what I choose to do. I wonder if this theme is going to be life long? I hope I get a grasp of it soon. I imagine it will come with time.

The most important part of our session dealt with the letter. He read the letter to me and then asked how I felt after hearing my words. I told him I could have read the letter from memory, because I had read it so many times myself. I also said I felt uncomfortable, but relieved. At the time, I did not realize how relieved I would really be. He tried to help me determine why I have the feeling of personal worthlessness. He asked who felt that I was special. I told him my grandmother and Barney, of course. He wasn't surprised. I then told him everyone who meant something special to me either died, left, or betrayed me. I also told him over time I have withdrawn from forming close friend relationships. It caused too much pain when they ended. I admitted I really only have acquaintances, no real friends.

It felt so good to openly say these things. I even got to tell Jim I thought it was a sad commentary on my state of relationships that I have to pay someone $2.11 per minute just to listen to me. He tried to tell me it wasn't all negative; since I was doing it, I was doing something positive.

In admitting my feelings of worthlessness, it felt like a weight has been lifted off of me. It has been so liberating, a lightness, a freedom. The feeling is so wonderful. For the first time since I can remember, it is as though I am at peace with myself to some degree. I am not "cured," but I am on the road to a healthy self. There is no other feeling quite like it. I can only equate it to falling in love. No, I do not have any romantic feelings for Jim, only gratitude that he is my therapist. Thank God. I just wish I could convey in words all I feel and have felt since yesterday. It is truly one of the most marvelous experiences of my life. Thank you, Jim!

Jim seemed very pleased I wanted our therapeutic relationship and had written the letter. He seems very committed to me now. It made me feel so good to see the sparkle in his eyes, and the enthusiasm for where we were headed. He gave me a sense that we can build a relationship unlike any I have had before, one in which there is total trust and it will be only about me. WOW! I have never experienced this before.

In thinking about my relationship with Jim, I noticed this is the first time in a long time in which I have spent this much time with a person, and not know much more about him than

on the day we met. For once, I think I finally have the therapeutic relationship I have been seeking. I don't even care that
I don't know anything about him. It feels so good to know
when I go to session, the session will be about me, not him. I
hope there will come a time when I will be able to thank Jim
for all he has done. In times and situations like this, money
doesn't seem appropriate compensation.

The best thing that has happened to me in a long time is that
Jim is my therapist. It is so hard to describe the progress I feel
I have made in better understanding myself, and how my
internal feelings affect my life. Although I knew myself well
before, I only really understood my Practical Self. I knew so
little about my Personal Self. This has been a wonderful
journey of self-discovery.

I want to leave today's entry with the thought that this is the
first time in my life in which I feel a sense of serenity. Even
though I feel tired both mentally and physically, I feel at peace
with myself. The best part is this is just an everyday thing; I
am not escaping from anything. I am just me.

This journal entry reflected my first step in my healing process. During previous times in my life, I had discarded many of the "oughts" and "shoulds" of
my belief system. I had discarded many false beliefs about what to do, but not
how to feel. I unknowingly held onto the "oughts" and "shoulds" about my feelings and emotions.

The belief that therapists tell clients what is wrong with them is a popular
misconception. There are therapists who believe this is how therapy should be
done; however, clients' self-revelation is more productive. This is not to say
therapists would not point out what clients are doing which may be counter-productive. What I am saying is, if clients arrive at their own conclusions about their
own counter-productive behavior, then the likelihood of lasting change within
clients are greatly increased.

I do not refer to experimental proof in making this observation, but rather, I
ask you to look at your own experiences. How many times have others told you
there was something about you which was not quite right? Did you wholeheart-
edly believe the person? Probably not, perhaps you became angry or at least a
little indignant. Now, look back to a time when you decided there was something
about yourself you were not as happy with as you had been previously. Were you
in disbelief or angry with yourself in making this observation? Probably not. You

were far more likely to take your own comments constructively, rather than the comments of someone else. This holds true in therapy as well.

When clients go to therapy, they often want the therapist to tell them what is wrong with themselves, and how to fix the problem. If the therapist obliges, often times, the client is angry or disbelieving. Many times, the therapy is cut short. Instead, most therapists risk aggravating the client a little by not giving the answers, but rather help clients to arrive at their own answers.

The second common misconception about what happens in therapy is that the therapist will tell clients how to fix their problems. It is far more effective for clients to find their own solutions to life problems than for the therapist to provide a solution. There are some additional reasons for this approach. First, therapists may not know the answer to the problem. Although therapists are experienced in the process of therapy, they do not know all the answers to all of life's problems. Clients are the only real experts on their own lives. They know their lives and perceptions best. Even though clients tell therapists each and every detail of every memory from their lives, some aspects of their lives will be inexplicable. There are non-spoken influences that have molded and shaped the clients' perceptions and thoughts. Only clients will be able to find the answers for their lives which will be of true value in the healing process.

Since infancy, we have been conditioned by listening and reacting to our mothers and fathers, or other primary care-givers. As children, we listened and reacted to what the school system required and expected. As adults, we listen and react to what our society and employers require and expect. It is no wonder we want our therapist to tell us how to "fix" our lives.

Part of therapy teaches clients how to think about themselves for themselves. Mistakenly, most believe their self-esteem is not dependent on the opinion of others or the outside environment. To answer this: "Who am I?" Most people would give their name, occupation, relationships, hobbies, or religious affiliations. This does not tell us who they are, but rather it tells about them. To answer: "How do I know I am doing a good job?" Most would say they have accomplished the intended goals, or someone has told them they have done a good job. The typical responses to these questions are not wrong, but rather they indicate a dependence on outside sources of information. Clients must really come to know about themselves and how well they are doing in relationship to themselves and only themselves? For most, this is foreign territory. For most, this territory is explored with the guidance of a psychotherapist.

Psychotherapy is fundamentally a problem-solving process. A goal of the process is to help clients learn how to solve their own life problems. If this is not part of the goal, then clients become dependent on therapists to solve the problems of their lives; this is definitely not the goal of therapy. The end result of psychotherapy is for clients to live an autonomous life in which they can face the challenges of life and not only survive, but flourish and live.

Psychotherapy is a journey through the self, about the self, using the self. No one else can tell clients exactly where they are, how to get to where they need to go, nor where it is they need to go. The therapist and client are partners on this journey. The therapist is just more experienced in undertaking such a journey and has accompanied many others on such a journey. Therapists cannot give clients the answers, but rather help them undertake the journey to find the answers.

October 17, 1996

Before I see Jim again, I am trying to understand the nature of my feelings toward him. I do not have romantic feelings, but there are some strange feelings I do have. I find I almost obsess about him. I seem to constantly bring him into my thoughts. I find I want to be in session again and again. If I could, I would be there right now. Why do I have these feelings? Why am I clinging to him as though he were a life preserver? I keep telling myself he is my sanity.

I feel like being in session with Jim is so safe. I feel it is somehow a key to my survival. In reality, it is not. I think it is my Personal Self who is craving him. But to what purpose and why in such an obsessive way? I wonder if it isn't a set up. I will want him, and then he will disappoint me. I will again validate my feelings that I am just not worth it, even to someone I pay. Is this the point to wanting an unreasonable relationship?

In the best of all possible worlds, I would like to spend several days just talking about me and anything I want to talk about. I would love to walk and talk. This would be so wonderful to me. But why? I am not sure.

I have been trying to deal with this. I want to be able to put into words what I am feeling, and what is going on in my head. I cannot understand this. In trying to clarify my thoughts and wishes, I asked myself, "If I could get from this relationship whatever I wanted, what would it be?" I want him to care for me. I want him to be there for me. I want unconditional acceptance from him. I want him to love me for the person I am, not what I appear to be (but not in the romantic sense, but as a person). I want him to support me emotionally when I need it.

I want to be as special to him as I was to my grandmother. I know this cannot and will not be. I miss that relationship so much. I wonder why I don't feel that special connection with my daughter. I want to, but it is not there. I know I am perpetuating my misery. I have to find a way to stop it. I should never have had a child until I was whole, but I didn't realize I was so fragile and broken.

My relationship with Jim is very important to me. I need to use it to help me heal. Although I do not feel depressed, I do feel tired and fragile. I wish I still had my appointment with Jim tomorrow. I wish I had the money to see him whenever I felt I needed to. I think he can help me. I hope I am right.

I wonder why I don't trust anyone with "me." I am so afraid they will break me or hurt me. I am afraid they will laugh at me and ridicule me. I know the logical response is maybe they won't or what is the worst thing that could happen if they do? I am afraid they will validate that I am not a good person. I hurt. Where do these feelings come from? I can't figure it out. Maybe I will never know. I need to find the courage to bring up these two topics to Jim. I don't know if I can.

The American Heritage Dictionary, Third Edition, defines courage as: "The quality of mind that enables one to face danger with self-possession, confidence, and resolution; bravery." I do not intend to challenge the American Heritage Dictionary, but instead I propose there may be other ways of being courageous, but not necessarily be grounded in self-possession, confidence, and resolution. I see courage as the personal fortitude an individual displays in facing not only danger, but also personal fear, despite the desire to flee. This is the courage I perceive as necessary to undertake the journey of self-discovery. To visit the self I am not steadfastly self-possessed, confident, or resolute; instead I am rightfully timid, scared, unsure, and at times ready to flee. True courage is seen in those people who stay, knowing they may face the scariest thing in life – the true self.

Self Divided

Trying to describe what I felt like inside, was an extremely difficult thing to do. An even more difficult task was trying to explain to others what I was feeling inside when I felt as though I lived my life from within two different places. This story is not about Dissociative Identity Disorder (better known as Multiple Personality Disorder). What it is about is trying to find the self and to heal the self. I will admit I might have been diagnosed as Dissociative Identity Disorder (DID), Not Otherwise Specified, Subcategory One.[1] I do not know whether or not Dr. Seymour made this formal diagnosis or not. Although this chapter does talk about my two selves, the important aspect of this passage is to describe my struggle to define myself, to convey what I felt, and to risk being who I felt I really was with a stranger. Fully admitting the nature of my Practical and Personal Selves was exceedingly difficult and one of the most scary things I have ever done.

October 19, 1996

I have decided to do something in my next session with Jim. I took the Coolidge Axis II Inventory[2] (CATI) twice last night. Once as my Practical Self, and again as my Personal Self. It was interesting to see the results.

Taking the CATI twice took many hours. The first time I completed the inventory, I took it as my Practical Self. This was easy because I spent most of my time as my Practical Self. It took several hours for me to bring out my feelings and ability to answer the questions as my Personal Self. I had to concentrate on how I felt as my Personal Self. Once I was able to feel the beginnings of my

Personal Self become more evident, I took the CATI again. I did not want to spend too much time dwelling on my Personal Self. If I did, I feared I would enter into a deeper state of depression.

Although I am extremely familiar with the CATI and each of the questions, I sincerely believe I responded to each question in an honest fashion as both my Practical and Personal Self. The scores on the validity scales support my assertion.

October 19, 1996 (continued)

As "Practical" all three of the validity scales were fine, the Look good/bad scale was a .88 z score and the Tendency to Deny Blatant Pathology (TDBP) was a -.50 z score. I showed significant elevations in Obsessive-Compulsive and Schizoid scales for Axis II [personality disorders], and Apathy in the Other category. All other scales were within the normal range. Although within the normal range, I scored a t-score of 59 on Schizotypal [personality disorder] and Apathetic scales, and a t-score of 58 on the Withdrawal scale.

The scores were not important. What this information indicated was I was not trying to look too good or too bad by the way I answered the questions. Basically, the report suggested the Practical Self was perfectionistic, obsessively worried about various things, was socially withdrawn, preferred not to be with people, and had some unusual thought patterns.

October 19, 1996 (continued)

As "Personal" all three of the validity scales were fine, the Look good/bad scale was a .00 z score and the TDBP was a .12 z score. My elevations were extensive: Axis II [personality disorder scales]: Avoidant, Depressive, Obsessive-Compulsive, Paranoid, Self-defeating, Schizotypal; Axis I [mental disorders]: Anxiety, PTSD, Depression, Withdrawal, Schizophrenia; and Emotional Labile. Although in the normal range, I showed a t score of 59 in Maladjustment.

These scores indicated I was not trying to look too good or too bad, as my Personal Self. The report suggested I had a lot of problems. In addition to those tendencies listed for Practical Self, Personal had tendencies to avoid others for fear of ridicule, suspects others were negatively evaluating her, was not confident, was anxious much of the time, was depressed, was socially isolated and had wide swings in emotions.

October 19, 1996 (continued)

I think the dramatic difference between the two profiles truly illustrates the extent of the difference between my two selves. I intend to show Jim the Practical Self first, and then show him the Personal Self last. Once he has a chance to look at both of them, I will illustrate to him how I live my lives. I will overlap the Practical Self over the Personal Self and explain that is how I live 90% of the time. I will then pull the Personal Self out so that 15 - 20% of it shows from underneath and tell him that when I am alone, this is how I am. I will further explain the more Personal Self is exposed, the more I have depressive symptoms, but I am not sure which is causal.

I hope this will help to explain to him the world I live in. It is so hard for my therapists to grasp what it is I am trying to say to them, especially since they do not have an idea what my Personal Self is like. I am hoping the contrast of the two CATIs will make it painfully obvious I live in a conflicted world, but do a damn fine job of hiding it.

I would also like to bring up the subject of my obsessive thoughts about Jim. I have been obsessively mulling it over, but I have not yet settled on a way to talk about it.

I am still doing well, I have had some dips into depressive thinking and feeling, but very mild. Overall, I feel I have retained the improved feeling I alluded to in previous days.

As pointed out in the CATI reports, I had the strong tendency to obsess about various things, one of which became Jim. I constantly thought about Jim and therapy. I would try and remember every detail of every session and relive each session again and again. Once I had tired of reliving the session, I would start constructing my next session mentally. I did not feel I could go to a session without being thoroughly prepared. I did not know how to be spontaneous in therapy, nor in most aspects of my life.

Spending time doing mental therapy is not all bad. In fact, this highlights the fourth major misconception about therapy. Most people believe the work is done in session with the therapist. In reality, clients do most of the work outside of therapy, whether it be thinking about the self or practicing new skills. What each session provides the clients is a catalyst for change. Each session should illuminate various beliefs and behaviors which the clients may or may not be aware. Then clients are able to consider whether or not the beliefs and behaviors are conducive to the type of life desired. Therapy also gives the clients an opportunity to try out and risk new beliefs and behaviors. The bulk of the contemplative work is done between each session.

Dear Dr. Seymour,   October 25, 1996

Originally, I wrote the accompanying note in case I could not bring my Personal Self to therapy. The more I think about bringing my Personal Self to therapy, the more I fear I will not allow it to happen. I neither have the time or money to wait until I feel ready spontaneously. Therefore, I am sending this note before our next session in hopes it will force me to bring my Personal Self into therapy. At least this way I know you will already have an idea as to what I may say.

As you read the sample of what goes on inside, you should know that even though these comments are representative of my thoughts, the comments are somewhat tempered in intensity.

I am horribly embarrassed and pained to the core by what is written. To send this has been an agonizing decision. My hope is that by exposing the other half of my life to you, it will diminish the power of these thoughts.

In allowing you to see these thoughts, I have made several assumptions. First, your confidentiality. I will be paying for these upcoming sessions out of pocket. Therefore, my insurance carrier has no right to this letter and note, nor to the contents of the sessions for which I will pay. Second, my faith and trust are well placed. I am placing my complete faith and trust into your hands. This is horrendously scary. I do not relinquish control of any part of my life without serious forethought and requirement for change. I feel that in our relationship I have a chance to make myself whole. Without that, I cannot proceed with my future intentions of pursuing my Ph.D. It would not be ethically or morally fair to my potential clients. Finally, I assume you will not be shocked or surprised by anything I say. I maintain strict physical control of my impulses. I will never do anything that might jeopardize what we have. I cannot afford to lose this relationship. I neither have the desire or the strength to find someone new.

If for any reason these assumptions are faulty, I need to know before we start our next session.

To help me during our next session, please ask about anything you deem important.

'Til Friday,
Kathleen Mountain

Even though I have talked about my Practical and Personal Selves, the personalities expressed in the accompanying notes are neither my Practical or Personal selves. The personalities expressed were not given any identifying labels. They will be discussed again, but much later in the book. At the time I wrote this note, I thought it was my Personal Self, but I was mistaken. Many months later I would recognize from where these thoughts originated.

[Accompanying note]

In case kathleen doesn't have the strength to summon her personal self to this session, I thought I'd write this note to let you know some of what I think about.

Other people: I don't understand why she keeps helping other people. She has this desire, but in the end, other people only come to her when they need help. They take from her without giving back. There isn't anyone that just wants her for her. I get so angry to see these people take advantage of her.

Therapy: Yes, I also believe you are in the same boat. You really don't care about her either. This is a great way for you to get $95 for 45 minutes. What can you really do for her? She believes you will help her get rid of me. I will always be here, and the only one who will always be there.

It is a good thing she wants to become a therapist. At least she will finally get something back from all the people she helps. I've watched her help keep a "friend" from committing suicide, with barely a thank you. At least when she is done, she will get paid.

You: I know it sounds like I take care of her, but that is not always the case. Sometimes I like to make her miserable. She wants you to help her, but I don't want you to. So I think about you in ways that make her uncomfortable. My goal is to make her want to leave you. How? She is so committed to her marriage and family, she would leave your care if she thought her feelings were beyond what they should be for you. So, when she thinks about therapy, which is all the time, I make other thoughts arise. Sometimes, I am successful in making her wonder if she is falling in love with you. It would please me to no end to be successful in terminating her therapy with you because she thinks she loves you. I would win and remain, and she would agonize over you and what she has lost.

It feels so good to be able to tell you what is on my mind, not just hers. There have been so many times I have wanted to do or say something that would be awful to her, but she won't let me. She has only let me come out in her journals and this letter.

I think you would enjoy my company in session. I am much less inhibited than she.

Do you really think you can help her or is this a good ride for you? Will your personal self answer, or your public self? We shall see!

[A different self writes]

What I want: I want to feel special to someone like I did with my grandmother. I know she loved me better than any other. She told me and made me feel that way. I felt so safe with her. I felt serenity, almost immortality with her. I want that feeling again.

I want you to care about me. I feel so fragile sometimes. In a way, you are my sanity. Knowing I will have another session with you is what keeps me together. I hate that I have become dependent on you. I know you will go away like everybody else. I keep my husband and daughter at a distance so they won't leave me. I know you won't stay, but I wish you would. I hurt.

I don't want to hurt anymore. That is why I want to die. Then my hurt will stop. She keeps me here with all her fancy obligations. I wish she could let us go, the hurt would stop. Can you make it stop? I don't think so. I wish you could.

I wish you really cared about me. I wish someone did, someone who didn't want anything from me. I g....

There are so many difficult aspects to therapy. For me, one of the most difficult was finding the courage to reveal my true self to Jim. This may be a gross assumption, but I feel thc most difficult task any of us may face is to reveal the true self. Not the self we show to the world, but the self we hear in our thoughts and self-doubts, the self we face each morning and evening in the semi-dream like state, just before waking or falling asleep. For many of us, we ourselves do not know our true selves. We often define ourselves by our professions, relationships, or hobbies. We seldom define ourselves by the beliefs and self-thoughts we live by, rather than the ones we would like to say we live by.

How can the true self be discovered? One way is to examine the uncensored thoughts which flow from the self. There are various ways to capture the thoughts which describe the self: writing in a journal, speaking into a tape recorder, or talking with a close and loving friend or therapist. For me, it was through the process of writing. Within my journals I would write the thoughts and feelings that emerged as the words began to flow. I did not give myself time to censor the thoughts. I wrote whatever came to mind. Do not be deceived as to the seemingly simple nature of this task. It can be difficult. I was so accustomed to censoring what I said day-to-day that committing my uncensored thoughts to paper actually took some practice. I found using a computer is easier than hand-writing. The reason is that I could type faster than I could write. If I wrote by hand, I found I had more time to censor my thoughts. As the words flowed through my fingertips, onto the keyboard, and finally onto the electronic page, my thoughts would coalesce, find form, and mirror me. Once the words were committed to paper, I would reread what I had written. In facing the thoughts I had written, I finally met the real me. There would come times when I did not like the person I was discovering, but that is yet to come.

Over time, I learned that by writing my thoughts it diminished the power my thoughts had over me. In keeping my thoughts hidden and secret, they seemed to take on a power of their own. Oftentimes, they seemed to become hideous and scary. They loomed larger than was reasonable. They became shameful and horrid. In committing the thoughts to paper, I could see the thoughts for what they were, neither ugly, horrid, nor powerful. They were merely part of who I was. In recognizing them, I found the beauty in who I am, and the fault in my logic. They returned to being just my thoughts, not my masters.

4

❖

Love and Fear

The process of psychotherapy can evoke so many feelings; some are well-known, others have only been met in passing. An important part of my therapeutic process was learning what emotions I had and how to deal with them. Through the preceding years, I had slowly shelved all my emotions except anger toward myself, frustration with things, and casual amusement. In the coming sessions, I would relearn emotional fear, anger toward others, love of all kinds, as well as many other emotions.

So often, many of us have learned incongruent or inappropriate emotional responses to the world around us. We became angry at inanimate objects in our paths, when it was us who walked into them; or we love our cars when they are only possessions. What is it that truly matters within our lives? One of the most fulfilling parts of life lies within our relationships. Consider these questions: In my deepest pain and agony, do I search out and desire contact with those things I deem important? Or did I desire the warmth and love of human contact? For most, being loved and needed by another human being is one of the most important feelings of acceptance. For most, loving and caring for another human being is one of the most wondrous feelings which give deep meaning to living. What gives life true meaning?

November 2, 1996

Yesterday's session with Jim brought out so much emotion from me. In fact, I sat in the van for twenty minutes, after the session, just feeling experiencing, and healing. So what happened?

Where to begin. Let me start by laying the groundwork for what has happened. Jim challenged me to bring my Personal Self to therapy. Over the last month, I have been trying to comply with this. I am unable to make my Personal Self come and go. When my Personal Self is present, she stays.

In the beginning, I was able to maintain a part of my Personal Self and maintain control of my depressive feelings; for they come hand-in-hand. As the days passed, unknowingly, I began to lose my hold of my Personal Self. By my last visit with Jim only a few remnants remained of my Practical Self, and I was in a full-blown state of depression. When I am fully run by my Personal Self, I am a bundle of emotions. I can feel, but I am not able to articulate what I feel, or little of what I think.

I went to the session as me. I left my Practical Self in the van. I allowed my Personal Self to feel the pain of my depression. I could not bring my ambivalent feelings, but I could bring the raw agony and pain. I didn't sit in the usual spot. I sat farther away from Jim. I was huddled on his love seat. I wanted to melt into the fabric and disappear.

Jim acknowledged that I had left my Practical Self elsewhere. He acknowledged he could feel my raw pain and agony. It seemed to permeate the room. He mentioned he received but had not closely read my letter. I was disappointed. I do think he did quickly read it. He read the introductory letter with me there, but I could not allow him to read my personal thoughts with me present. I wasn't ready for that yet.

He told me my assumptions about our relationship were correct. He said it was also scary for him that I was placing my complete trust and faith in him. I find that hard to believe. I am sure hundreds of people have, or maybe it is scary because he knows the journey we have begun will be long and difficult.

He told me an assumption he was making of me was I did not need to be called every night to make sure I was okay, and I could endure the fact he is frequently out of town. He said he felt I was strong and stable enough so I wouldn't need him everyday. I told him I could. Inside, a part of me wanted to

scream out, NO! don't go! The rest of me knew we would be
okay.

We talked about the way in which I chose to deal with my suicidal thoughts, and how I would potentially react if I was
forced into a hospital. I reiterated my view of hospitalization
and suicide: If he forced me into hospitalization, he would further increase the likelihood I would successfully commit the
act because I was pushed into a corner. I let Jim know my
choice of whether to live or to die was my responsibility, not
his or anyone else's. His response was he was not surprised and
it was what he expected. He said he would be sad if I chose to
die, but would not feel responsible. He said he had lost a few
patients in the past, and could deal with the loss if I chose to
die.

While reading these passages, it has occurred to me there is an important element which is missing. Because my suicidal thoughts were constant, I gave them
little mention within the journal. To mention my suicidal thoughts was as unnecessary as mentioning the sun rose this morning and the sun set this evening.
There did not seem to be any reason to state the obvious; therefore, it is strangely
absent in print.

I had two different types of suicidal thoughts. The first type consisted of generally wanting to be dead and constantly searching for the means for my death.
Each night before I fell asleep, I hoped I would not awake in the morning; and
when I did, I was disappointed. Each time I became ill, I hoped it would be fatal.
Although I did not actively pursue my own death, I spent numerous hours each
day thinking about death and dying. I found death in bridges, in on-coming vehi-
cles, and in any illness I might have.

The second type was extremely serious and potentially lethal. These
thoughts consisted of actual, viable plans to end my life. I kept an accurate inventory of the medications in the house. I spent considerable energy thinking about
and designing plans which might look as though my death was accidental. I will
not speak of any of my plans lest I might help someone else take the last fatal
step; this I will not do. Although the plans are not mentioned in the journal
entries, they were with me constantly, unless specifically mentioned otherwise.

November 2, 1996 (continued)

Jim told me he had read an article about depression which
mentioned two types of depression. One of isolation; not
wanting to endure the hopelessness and pain of being alone.

The other of achievement; the result of not feeling like one is good enough is an over attempt at perfection and achievement. I readily admitted I fit the achievement model of depression. He agreed.

He asked me if I believed in reincarnation. I cannot recall if I answered or not. He then brought up the notion that if one believed in reliving life's struggle, suicide results in having to go through this struggle again in another life. I don't believe that.

As homework, Jim gave me an interesting book to read. It is called *The Drama of the Gifted Child*, by Alice Miller. It is about how a painful childhood can affect the life of a person. Jim gave me this book to read after he again asked me if I suffered abuse in my childhood. After reading the book, I could see why Jim would ask. I exhibit many of the symptoms of a person who has suffered some type of childhood abuse. Although I have read this book, I still cannot find any memory of anything which would resemble abuse.

On his way back from the book shelf, he let his guard down; he let me inside of him. He said "When I face dep...." He stopped and rephrased the statement to remove himself from it. It was too late. He let me walk around inside him. He quickly shut me out.

Next, Jim spoke of a chapter in the book *Beowolf*, which talks about the exploration of the self. In *Beowolf*, apparently there is a deer which is chased to the edge of a lake by a pack of wolves. The deer's fear of the water is so intense it cannot jump into the water to save itself. Instead, the deer is devoured by the wolves at the edge of the lake. He likened my journey to wholeness to the plight of the deer. In so many words, he said to save myself, I must take the plunge into the lake and take the risk of the unknown, or I would be devoured by the wolves of depression. Little known to Jim, the lake proved to be a powerful metaphor. He does not know I nearly drowned twice. In a way, it made the power of the fear of the deer even more vivid.

We spoke further of my taking the plunge into the lake of self-discovery. I told him it is a scary proposition, and letting go of the edge is not a task I found appealing, but did understand the necessity.

I told him how difficult it had been for me to bring myself to the session. He wanted to know why I had come. I said I knew I needed to be here to resurrect my life.

For the second time, he asked me if I believed in reincarnation and destiny. I told him my belief in not one destiny for each life, but rather a lot of potentials, and with each choice we make, in everyday life, we open and close doors to each possibility. I said I didn't believe in reincarnation. Although I don't believe in it, in the classical sense, I believe the essence or spirit of each person comes and goes through time. I believe there are some spiritual connections we make which are safe, comfortable, and meant to be, the ultimate reason for which is unknown to me. I couldn't tell him these thoughts because I had not been previously challenged to articulate the thoughts.

Again Jim asked me if I believed in reincarnation. I told him I did not, but did say at least death would give a momentary respite from the pain. Then he went on to say something to me I have known for quite sometime, but did not know he felt the same way. He said he felt there was something in our relationship. It felt as though it was meant to be. He then said he was not "bullshitting " me. I do believe him. I am not sure if it is because I too feel the same way and hope he really does feel that way, or because I know he does feel that way. I have known for a long time our relationship is one in which I have the possibility to become whole and find the serenity I long for. I also know, in a karmic sense, we have known each other before, but not in the standard reincarnation way. I know our spiritual essences have been intertwined before in a warm and loving relationship, one which was very different than this one. I want to tell Jim this, but I am unsure how he will take it.

He told me he would be there for me on this journey. He would be my strength. He would swim the lake with me. He wouldn't let me drown. With those words, I began to cry. How did he know the very words I needed to hear? It was as though he truly knew what I needed. Maybe he does. At the time, I knew what I felt, but could not verbalize it. If I could have, Jim would have known the trouble for which I was headed. Since I could not, he could only say: "It is good to see you cry."

I cannot remember a relationship in which I have ever felt this way. In Jim I feel safe, warm, and comfortable. It is a comfort of familiarity. One which I have never before known. I feel our connection almost transcends time. I take comfort in it. I feel the serenity and security I thought would never come. And yet I fear it for two reasons: 1) I know it can't last forever, and 2) it has changed what I want from my husband. I want to feel a connection with my husband I do not currently feel. I fear I am walking beyond my marriage. We do have a bond, but now it is not the one I want; it is too aloof, free, and detached. I hope it will be enough.

I both love him and fear him. [Jim]

Jim is the second person whom I have met who has the strength to withstand my destructive emotional force. He was able to remain fortified against my ability to walk around inside him, until yesterday. For some reason, he let me in briefly twice. I think once was partially intentional. He did it to let me know he does in fact have the strength to sustain both of us. But why the second time? It was through a distant glance that he let me in, unknowingly. Why?

These past three sessions have been almost unreal. It seems as though the entire dance has been orchestrated from afar. It was as if we were players, but truly living the parts; as if we had danced this dance before. The feeling is beyond my limited abilities to articulate.

-later-

I don't know what is going on inside my head. I am feeling all kinds of emotions and feelings, mostly toward Jim. At one moment I think he is so wonderful, the next I think he despises me and thinks I am pathetic. All these emotions are tearing me up inside. When will they subside? I hope it is soon.

I feel like I need an emotional break from all this. I don t think I'll be getting one soon.

November 9, 1996

During the three days after my last appointment, I ruminated about the four comments: I will be your strength, I will not let you drown, I will swim with you, and this relationship is meant to be. I could feel I wanted Jim more and more. Not in a romantic sense, more out of desperation and pain. I wanted a safe pace to be emotionally, and I thought being with Jim would provide that. I must remind myself my Personal Self was in full control of my life. I was only able to feel and not artic-ulate. I was in the deepest, non-suicidal, depression since my near suicide attempt two and a half years ago. I was getting closer and closer to the vegetative state. My thoughts were becoming extreme, obsessive, and losing basis in reality.

On Sunday, I went to see Wil (my best friend - the dead guy). I poured out my words to him. It did not matter if they made sense or not. I was finally able to start articulating what was going on inside. I really cannot remember anything I talked about. It was good to release all that was going on. It was enough to allow me to start my statistics homework which was looming on the horizon.

My best friend during this time was a man named Wilhelm Stern. In 1983, he died in an aircraft accident. He was on final approach during his solo flight when his aircraft sank to the ground. I referred to Wil as the dead guy because he is in fact deceased. I made comment on his death because I felt it was so unfair that Wil should have died, and I should live. Wil was a wonderful man who loved life and was pursuing his dream to fly. I can still remember his warm and infec-tious smile. I will always love and miss Wil. Both in life and death he has been my friend.

November 9, 1996 (continued)

Monday through Tuesday morning only brought on a deeper depression. By Tuesday morning, I was seriously considering not going to class. I drove to the university, but had serious doubt about going to class. I went to Rick's [my professor, Rick Lawrence] office and called Ruth to see if Jim had any cancellations for the week. I could not understand what she was saying. I could hear her, but had no idea what she was telling me. She finally said she would have Jim talk to me. I told Ruth it was not needed since I knew he was busy. Then she said, apparently again, he had a cancellation for the current time slot and Jim could talk to me. I hesitated, and then she said she would put Jim on the phone. At this point, she didn't care what I had to say in protest.

When Jim got on the phone, his voice was distant and cool. He asked me why I was so depressed. I told him I wasn't sure. I thought maybe it was something about the book. He said he felt I should go back onto meds [medication] and talk to the people who love me.

I was so crushed. I wanted to hear him say, "Come and see me." I wanted him to take care of me. He made it clear he would not. Luckily, my Practical Self was there enough to hear the implied message: "It is you who must be your strength, you must not let yourself drown, and you will be the only one which will always be there." The last bit of strength my Practical Self had was used to force me into the classroom.

I state the message was implied because I do not know if Jim had any underlying message to what he was saying, or was just saying exactly what he intended. He has never mentioned if there was an implied message.

November 9, 1996 (continued)

By Tuesday night, I was feeling devastated. I could not believe the one relationship I had so much hope in was ending up just like the rest. I finally knew what I had been wanting so badly all these years is for someone like Jim to be my strength. I wanted someone to figuratively bundle me up in their arms and rock me. I wanted that person to tell me they would keep me safe and secure. They would always be there for me. All the things Jim implied in our last session. Oddly, it seemed a relief I finally knew what the underlying pain was all about. It seemed all had come to a crescendo, to a head, to a convergence the bringing of my Personal Self and depression to the forefront, Jim's words in session, the reading of the book; and the rejection on the phone. My thoughts exploded into a thick cloud of clarity.

When Wednesday came, I was angry. How could this relationship end up like all the rest I thought therapy relationships were supposed to be different. I thought this relationship would bring the caring and understanding I really wanted. How could it end up like all the rest?

I was still hurt. I then asked myself, why am I letting him off the hook? I really began to verbalize the hurt feelings. I was never going back to Jim. Then I realized this is my one chance to tell the person who hurt me what they did to me. It really wouldn't matter what it did to him. I let myself be angry and feel all those angry feelings be projected onto another real person, not me. I was then able to be angry that my mom wasn't there for me, my dad wasn't there for me, Ken [a man with whom I had a relationship before my marriage] wasn't who I thought he was, my grandmother died when I needed her, and of course at Jim. It felt okay to be angry. Nothing terrible happened. I didn't have to carry around the hurt any more. Why couldn't I let go of the anger before? I guess I did not know just how much anger there was. By Wednesday night I was spent.

Thursday morning I felt good. I thought all was well, and it was, until the afternoon. In Psychotherapy Seminar, I volunteered for an undefined exercise. It was to role play a therapist. I did not do well. When I look back on it, it was because I had reboxed my Personal Self and put it on a higher shelf. I was not in touch with my emotions. I felt uncomfortable during the role play because I could not tap into the feelings of the client. It was evident Dr. Bennett knew the role well, and I should have been able to grasp what was going on. But I could not.

Later, during the same class, we had an exercise in which we were to get to know a real client through a psychological assessment. Initially, Christine was asked to role play the client. She did very well. I let my Personal Self out of the box so I could find and feel the client. Dr. Bennett asked Christine what the client's relationship was between her and her professor. Christine could not come up with an answer. So I volunteered. I let my Personal Self build and find the client we read about, and I answered as the client. Apparently, I did well. Dr. Bennett said, "OOOO, I'm getting goose bumps." I didn't know it at the time, but the answer I gave was almost verbatim to what the actual client said. This experience was very powerful.

This experience was indeed powerful. Through it, I found I needed to have my Personal Self to understand the clients I would meet in the future. I finally began to realize I needed to make myself whole. I could not discard the bits and pieces of who I am which make me uncomfortable. Instead, I would have to learn to integrate, appreciate, and use all of my selves.

November 9, 1996 (continued)

Thursday night, I realized I was again feeling the depression coming on. Even though I gave it great effort, I could not make my Practical Self control my Personal Self. After everyone went to bed, I sat down and decided it was time to confront my Personal Self, with my Practical Self. Initially, my Practical Self felt frightened and out of control, but then I realized this was giving my Personal Self the power to escalate the depression, and this would only make things worse. So I decided to try something new. I decided to have my Practical Self confront my Personal Self in a calm, accepting manner. At first, it was difficult, but soon I was able to engage both halves of me in a conversation.

Practical assured Personal all that was wanted was a better understanding of the how Personal felt, and what it was Personal wanted. Slowly it came out. The feeling of wanting to be held, kept safe, and cared for. Personal let Practical know that is what she wanted from Jim. Once the full picture of what Personal was feeling became evident, Practical began responding to Personal in the way in which she had hoped Jim would respond to her. Practical told Personal only Practical had the strength to keep her safe. Only she could always be there for her, and do all the things she wanted Jim to do for her.

I think the conversation lasted for about an hour and a half to two hours. In the end, Personal felt safe. She no longer felt she had to use depression as a way of trying to get someone to notice what it was she wanted. It doesn't mean she won't use it again, because it is the only way she knows to get Practical's attention. Personal and Practical both wanted Me to become a therapist. They both agreed I have something to offer the world, and Practical finally realized she could not be a therapist without Personal. Personal now knows she is no longer at odds with Practical, and that she too is important in my life, and is necessary for my future happiness and success.

I know it sounds as though I am a done deal. I really think I am still somewhere in the beginning, but at a good place to continue the journey to wholeness and serenity. I will again see Jim on Monday. With each passing day, I can both see and feel the healing which is taking place within me.

This was a long winded way of telling the story of discovering part of who I was. It was at this point the depth of my problems became evident to Jim. Even though I spoke of my different selves in the third person, I truly did not appreciate or understand the fine edge I walked. I was getting close to the point of reaching a full diagnosis of DID. Unknown to me, Jim was deeply concerned he could not provide the level of care necessary to help me. A person with DID needs a lot of care; in some cases, daily. The effort is tremendous for both the therapist and client to bring the client back to an integrated state; sometimes, this cannot be done. If full integration cannot be achieved, then finding a way to help the client live a life of compromise between all the personalities is the objective. Jim did not want to engage in a battle of attrition, with his strength against my needs, if I was a fully diagnosed case of DID.

Oftentimes, throughout the therapy process, the client reaches understandings and enlightenment. These periods are both healing and dangerous. They are healing because they provide the client with insights into the self and give directions for personal improvement. They are dangerous in that they may provide the client with a false sense of "doneness." Although the client is often the one who determines the termination of therapy, unless ruled by managed care, the client may be the least-knowledgeable person to make that decision. Instead of knowing I was at the beginning, I could have felt enough healing to think I was complete enough to quit.

I want to address the comment I made of loving Jim. Because I am a woman and Jim is a man, there may be concern and confusion as to the meaning of this statement. Unfortunately, the English language is not one of emotional expression. We are left with one word to express a deep and wide range of human emotions. There is love for one's mother, brother, sister, friend, lover, pet, and others in general. How can one word truly suffice for all the levels of love there seems to be? Maybe this is one of the reasons why our society seems to be closed emotionally. Our language does not provide a means to convey all we are capable of feeling.

Yes, I did and still do love Jim. He has helped me to achieve so much within my life. How can I not love a person who has given me the greatest gift of all, the gift of life? Without our relationship, I know I would not have seen my fortieth birthday. My will to live was coming to an end. How can I not love a person who has found the strength to risk such a difficult relationship, despite not initially wanting to involve himself in a relationship requiring so much. Jim elected to stay with me, despite knowing the possibility of me committing suicide was very great. How could I not love a person who took the time and love to find out the true nature of who I am and to what depths my pain and agony reached? How could I not love a person who has tread a journey possibly not much different from my own? How could I not love a person who trusted me more than I trusted myself?

The flavor of my love for Jim was also swirled with deep respect and gratitude. I find it difficult, even now, to describe the love relationship I feel we had. I have found another author, more gifted than myself, who can describe to some degree, the feelings a client and therapist share. Dr. M. Scott Peck's book, *The Road Less Traveled*, has a wonderful section which describes the love between a therapist and client.[1]

Those who seek a therapist of the same gender, should not feel they will be missing the loving relationship. If the therapist is of sufficient temperament and strength, they can experience a truly loving relationship between two people. This is the true essence of therapy. Unfortunately, many therapists and authors on therapy refuse to deal with this issue. Many are frightened of the implications of a loving relationship. The fear of the therapist and client engaging in a sexual relationship is a real and serious consideration. However, if therapists have done their own work on the self, and retain the proper focus on what the relationship is about, then the therapist can refrain from crossing the line. The basic point of the therapeutic relationship is for the therapist to engage in a relationship in which the client can heal the self and find a more contented life. This thought should be in the forefront no matter what the therapist decides to do with the client, whether it be a sexual relationship or the use of a technique. If the welfare of the client can be maintained as the paramount concern, then the therapist can see clearly to make the best possible decisions for the effective treatment of the client.

Love within the therapeutic relationship is often an essential part of the healing process. So many of us have been hurt within a "loving" relationship.

Oftentimes, we must relearn to trust and love within a relationship, and to relinquish it without destroying our self-image and lives. Although these two points may seem to be so basic to human existence, they are often not learned as a part of growing-up. Without knowing how to have, enjoy, and appreciate a loving relationship, how can anyone truly enjoy all there is in life? If we have not learned how to say good-bye to a truly loving relationship, how can we go on with our lives. For many, learning these two lessons in life is the key to a fulfilling and happy life. For many, not learning these two lessons is the root of the pain and agony with which we exist.

Do you really know how to live within a loving relationship in which you truly trust your loving partner? One way to know is to examine your answers to these questions: "Does my loving partner know how I feel because I have articulated my feelings? Can I tolerate correction and feedback from this person without feeling rejected or betrayed? Can I tell my loving partner my deepest secrets and desires without censoring what I feel and think? Can I trust my loving partner to love me even after I may have hurt my partner? Can I maintain my individuality despite the similarities between me and my loving partner? Do I really know how to forgive? Have I learned how to say good-bye to someone whom I have loved? Do I know how to grieve the loss of my loving partner? After a loving relationship is over, do I look back with love, fondness, regret, anger, or despair? How well have I learned the lessons of love?"

Through the experience of psychotherapy, one can learn how to effectively answer all these questions. Through therapy, we can learn how to improve the way we interacted with those we love. In doing so, we can became more loving towards the people we love and to those we did not know. Learning how to love and let go is not an intellectual task. It cannot be done by asking the therapist each of the above questions and getting an answer. These lessons are learned through experience. By experiencing all the facets of a loving relationship in the safe environment of psychotherapy, we can experiment and try new ways of interacting and responding to those around us.

The old saying, "You can't love someone else until you learn to love yourself," is so true. Most would say "I do love myself." I had to challenge my own notion about this. I asked myself: "Do I really love myself?" What is the most important thing in my life? Is it my occupation, spouse, or child? Whom do I take care of without fail? Is it my spouse, friends, or child? Altruism may suggest others, but how could I really care for others if I have not taken care of myself? How could I help heal others if I am ailing? How could I teach my daughter to care for herself, if I did not care for myself?"

Many people enter the field of psychology to heal themselves. I was no different. I too sought to heal myself. The important aspect is that therapists do work to heal themselves, before attempting to assist clients. As a client, I found the issues of the therapist can and do creep into the sessions. If the therapist has an area in need of work, it often is projected onto the client, whether or not the client needs help in the same area. So, how does the client know the therapist is "okay?" Often times it may be difficult to know. One way is to ask if the therapist has ever been in long term psychotherapy. The reasons for the therapist's therapy are not of importance to the healing of the client. If the therapist has not, the client might be concerned. No one should dispense such an intense and often painful method of recovery if one is unwilling to experience the personal transformation too.

This is not to suggest that all therapists have serious psychological ailments, but everyone has areas which could be improved. It would be wise and morally appropriate for each therapist to undergo the therapy experience. Empathy for what the client is experiencing is difficult if the therapist has not undergone the same struggle. Most of the truly effective therapists that I have known have been on the "couch." I have not yet met one who has not.

I also stated I feared Jim. But why? As each session passed, Jim was discovering the real me. I found letting someone really know me was a frightening experience. To have someone know nearly all my secrets, no matter how great or trivial, was a prospect I feared. I felt if someone knew all there was to know about me, what motivated me, what I feared, what was important, etc., then that person could exert so much power and influence over me. Not only would they know my secrets, what if they saw the real me and recoiled in horror? What if Jim found out I was terribly broken and felt I was not going to be healed enough to ever practice therapy? What if Jim saw me as a miserable person? What if Jim decided I was not worth his time and effort? What if Jim saw the real me and decided he did not want to help me?

For me, the other aspect of fear was the dependency I was beginning to feel toward Jim. I feared he would leave me as all the other people whom I relied on emotionally had done. My most basic fear was that Jim would hurt me deeply; this I could not tolerate. As the relationship deepened, my dependency deepened, and so did all my feelings. Logically, I knew my fear of Jim hurting me was not rational. After all, he was in this relationship to help me heal. There were specific rules and boundaries which specify this relationship. This relationship was built to help me overcome these fears, and yet I was still terrified.

We Begin

Usually, most people consider the beginning of therapy as the first session. Therapy actually begins when there was a true commitment by both the therapist and the client to commence the journey of healing. During the early sessions, the client and therapist start to learn about each other: what are the motivations, ailments, likes, dislikes, and styles? The therapist and client may both say they are committed to the relationship, but this may be only cursory. The real commitment is not usually realized until much later. Until the time when both the client and the therapist have made the solid commitment to the relationship, there may be a series of steps both toward and away from the relationship. It may be the client or the therapist who may doubt the utility of the relationship. Each will feel the other pull away and question the commitment. Each will wonder if the correct decision was made. Each will long for some certainty about the outcome of the relationship. Only time will tell if the relationship will endure.

November 15, 1996

Last Monday I finally had my appointment with Jim. I did tell him a very abbreviated version of my last entry. I also outlined for him my spiritual beliefs. Just before I left, I told him I found him interesting in that he has been fairly impervious to my intuition.

The session itself had a strange, sterile quality to it. It really bothered me. To start with, he started our appointment fifteen minutes late, which was highly unusual. Then, he was very uncomfortable and distant with me. In fact, he spent a good portion of the time with his body facing away from me. He sounded so clinical and withdrawn. After I mentioned my inability to get inside him, he made a strange comment. He said: "I deal with therapists in therapy different. I am more distant because therapists are good at sucking each other into taking care of each other too much." During the session, I could feel it, but was unable to connect with what I was feeling and respond to it. It wasn't until after the session that I was able to sort out all I felt.

I was left with such a feeling of uncertainty. I wondered if I had done something to bring this on. I couldn't understand what had happened, why he would pull away so drastically. I thought maybe it had been the contents of the letter I had given him. [The letter dated 25 October 1996, see Chapter 3.] There were some things in the letter that could be unnerving and even considered confrontational.

I agonized for the four days as to what to do. I seriously considered confronting him, or even not returning to the next session. I was filled with mixed feelings: hurt, anger, uncertainty, fear, and confusion. I was convinced I was going to confront him first in the session and be quite direct. I even wanted to put some negative feelings and blame on him for some of the decisions I wanted to make [suicide]. But Wednesday night, I had a dream that seemingly had nothing to do with this situation, yet in analyzing the dream further, I found it had everything to do with what was going on.

The dream was quite simple. It started out I was walking up a hill in a city, like San Francisco, with a man I don't know, but in the dream we were quite enamored with each other. The walk was very pleasant and loving. We then entered a bar. We sat on a bench which was next to a wall, with some tables around. While we were sitting there, more of his friends showed up, including female ones. One woman in particular kept vying for the attention and affection of the man I was with, and she was becoming quite successful. She finally was able to get him to hold her hand in front of me. I became very angry. I decided to get out of the situation, so I told him I had to call some friends about a get-together I had promised to go to on the same night. He made some comment, but now I cannot remember it. I went to the phone and called, but found

I could not reach them by phone. On the way back to the table, a man yelled out to the man I had been with that I was on my way back and was going to leave. The man I was with made no attempt to keep me from going. So I left. The next part of my dream was in the present. I was miserable, and fighting with my daughter. (One of the few times she has been in one of my dreams.)

So what does this have to do with my therapy? I believe the man in my dream was Jim and our therapeutic relationship. The walk up the hill symbolized the difficult nature of the work I have been doing in therapy. The pleasantness of the experience symbolized my pleasure in the gains I feel I am making in therapy, and my enjoyment of my relationship with Jim. I think the bar was what was to come, our next session. The pretty woman who distracted the man was whatever it was that caused Jim to be so uncomfortable with me. The anger I felt in my dream directly relates to how I was feeling toward Jim. The whole part of me getting up to leave was about my desire to run from therapy because I didn't know what was going on. The part about my return and the other man yelling at the man I was with about my intentions to leave was Jim's conscience. I think he knew what happened in our last session could have had adverse effects after it had happened. I think he became cognizant when I brought up the inaccessibility issue, and he made that comment to me. I also believe the man in the dream not making any effort to keep me at the bar would have been exactly the same reaction Jim would have had on my announcing my leaving. It wouldn't matter what he felt or wanted; he would have let me go without one word otherwise. The remainder of the dream was a very overt way of telling me not to leave therapy; I would go back to the life I had before.

It took a while to piece all this together, but once I did, I tried to understand what it is I should do. I was so afraid I was losing the only relationship I have had in years in which I felt comfortable and cared about, with so much trust. I kept going back to the dream, what should I have done in the dream to get the man's attention back to me? I knew the man in the dream cared about me and was sincerely interested in me. It finally came to me this morning on my drive to Jim's office. All I needed to do was to put my hand on his arm, look him in the eye and give him a small loving smile.

In the short drive to the office, I realized anything harsh was not needed. What was needed was to give him room, give him trust, and I needn't be angry.

The dream described in the previous passage may have had no meaning whatsoever. Then again, it may have been the metaphor I perceived. Dreams can be a tool to help people understand and solve their problems. Dreams are the product of the power, imagination, and intuition the mind possesses. Many cultures, both ancient and modern, have looked to dreams as a key to unlocking the knowledge within and to solving life's dilemmas.[1] When looking for some guidance about life, we need only look within ourselves, and our dreams. I ask myself: "How are my dreams similar to my current life situations? Is the emotional or situational content similar? Was there a lesson to be learned in the dream? Was the action or inaction of the characters in the dream appropriate to my situation now?"

November 15, 1996 (continued)

When I got to the office, I still wasn't completely sure how all this would translate to my actions in session. When Jim came up to greet me, he was so gentle and warm. It caught me off guard. I hadn't expected it. I waited in his office, and jotted a few notes in my other journal. He came down and sat across from me. He sat in his usual spot, at the usual distance. It was the Jim I knew and yet he was different too. The things we talked about were not as important as the feelings I had during the session.

The change from Monday was incredible. I felt he was more present, caring, and open with me than any time before. The experience of all the unsaid things was almost overwhelming. I can't remember a relationship in which I felt so accepted, worthwhile, and genuinely cared for.

He gave to me what I have been wanting. I truly felt as though he figuratively took me up in his arms, cradled me, and took care of me. This feeling was not a result of the words we spoke, but rather all the nonverbal emotional feelings I could feel from him.

I felt all the warmth, caring, and concern I have so desperately
wanted from this and other relationships. The very feelings he
told me he could not provide, and yet on the very next session
he did. I could feel the nurturance and acceptance I have
craved all these years. I felt he genuinely cared for me, like no
one else. Although it is too difficult to specifically explain, he
conveyed to me he truly understood and knew what I was
about. In fact, at one point, he said I was so finely tuned into
the reactions and feelings of others, he had to be careful about
what he did in session, because he knew I would take what he
did personally. It was as if he knew the struggle I had faced
over the past four days. I hadn't even brought it up. At that
point, I did bring up his discomfort on Monday. I thought he
would deny it, but he did not. He did not even ask me why I
thought that; he just agreed and said he was. He told me he
was concerned I would need more care than he could provide.
I might need someone who could be there daily. I really don't
believe that was all of it. He said one of his goals for us was to
be as authentic as possible, and we would need to continually
check on the state of our relationship. I could not believe it. I
really feel he is the second person I have ever met who could
walk around inside of me. It was such a strange and comforting
feeling.

I told him about my ability to walk around inside of people,
and my inability to do that with him. He did not seemed surprised or skeptical. In fact, it was as though he knew exactly
what I was talking about, like he does it himself. I now think
it is good that I can't read Jim. I told him that as well. I feel
this because if I could read him or walk around inside him, I
would start tailoring my comments and actions to be comple-
mentary to what he would feel comfortable with and what he
would want me to do. As it is now, I am flying blind and feel I
can say anything. It is so wonderful.

What I meant by "walking around inside of people" is I feel that I have
the ability to perceive many of the feelings and emotions of other people. It is not
mind reading or anything like that. It is being empathetic and being cognizant of
it.

November 15, 1996 (continued)

I was able to talk freely with Jim about things I could not tell anyone else. I told him I still feared his rejection. I wondered if he believed what I said. I thought part of my depression was a mechanism to make other people take me seriously. I talked openly about how I felt people don't care about me, and they don't listen to me. He commented that I took a lot of risks today in session. If I would have been with anyone else, they would have been risks, but with Jim, it is not a risk. It is a blessing to be able to say exactly what I think and feel.

At the end of our session, the strangest thing happened. Jim and I locked eyes twice. I can't remember a time when I locked eyes with someone in which I felt so much energy, power (in a positive sense), caring, and consumption. The first time we locked eyes I couldn't and didn't want to look away. It was incredible. Then the thought came through my mind that I loved him (not romantically, but as a person with a gift). He then quickly looked away, almost as if he could hear me. The second time we locked eyes the intensity, power, and consuming of my being was too much for me. I have never felt that way before in my life. I was literally overwhelmed by the power of his eyes. I can still feel remnants of the feeling. I can still see his eyes in my mind. I wish I could convey in words all that I felt and still feel. It was as if he could see every corner of my mind, and he was searching for the key to my depression, and he was able to see who and what I really am. I felt like he was taking me all in and giving me strength, love, and hope. It was truly beyond words.

I now know he is truly committed to my healing. I believe I am a challenge to all his therapeutic skill. I think he recognizes this and is finally prepared to confront the challenge that lay before us. I also believe we both feel this relationship is meant to be. I don't know what will come of all of this in the long run. I do believe when I am done with therapy with Jim, our relationship will not come to an end; there is too much connectedness between us. No, I do not believe we will be together and my marriage is over or any of that. I think we will be important to each other in another way, yet to be determined and formed.

> I love Jim as a person. I have no desire for him in a romantic
> sense. I feel a connection with him. I think we share many of
> the same abilities, intuitiveness, and beliefs. I truly believe we
> were spiritually connected before, and will be again at some
> other point in time. I also believe he feels the same way. It is
> so indescribable.

I can think of nothing more powerful than the feeling of being accepted and loved. It is one of the most basic human yearnings. Without this need fulfilled, we stumble through life looking for just that. Finding acceptance and love has been the driving force for so many of us. In many cases, we are not even aware of the strength of the desire to fulfill our need for belonging. We join gangs, clubs, companies, and religions, or sometimes we just wander. If we find the acceptance, we cling to the source as though our very existence depends on it. In evolutionary theory, some suggest our survival may depend on our finding acceptance and belonging within a group, any group.

One way to recognize the "right" relationship is that it is possible, even necessary, to freely disclose our thoughts and feelings which we might feel uncomfortable to share with anyone else, and feel no threat or risk in doing so. Not only is this true of the therapeutic relationship, but also friendships and other loving relationships. Establishing and developing this type of relationship is often both rare and difficult. The risks include not only perceptions about the self and others, but also the emotions about and feelings of connectedness with the conversational partner. How many times have you honestly told another person how you felt about that person in a loving and nurturing way, to include apprehensions, worries, and possibly some not so flattering concerns? This was a very scary thing to do, especially with the people we cared about most. Most of us have not learned the art of speaking honestly, openly, constructively, and lovingly all at once. One of the lessons in life we can take from therapy is doing just that. It takes practice, just like any new task. The therapist is an excellent person with whom to practice because, even a therapist needs honest, open, constructive, and loving feedback now and again.

A truly authentic relationship can be very difficult because, it requires both persons to trust one another emotionally. It requires strength for both persons to speak openly, honestly, and constructively. The authentic relationship is based on an openness to accept criticism and decide whether or not to act on the criticism given. It demands deep emotional caring and tolerance to accept the other person whether or not there is agreement on many issues. It requires work to maintain and develop the relationship. The relationship demands the patience to listen to the other person, whether or not there is agreement. An authentic relationship grows over time, even if it is a difficult one to establish and maintain. Even though I had tremendous trust and respect for Jim, I was not able to maintain a truly authentic relationship with him. I was too afraid to tell him all I felt and wanted to express. This would remain true until the end. I could tell him almost anything. I just could not tell him everything.

A very important issue is the belief by the client in the therapist's commitment to the client. If there exists any doubt by the client, then the client will probably not fully disclose or trust the therapist. Of course this only stands to reason; however, the client often does not confront the therapist or search for a new therapist. Many times, the client will stick with the therapist and feel the relationship is good enough. Unfortunately, good enough is usually not good enough. If the doubt exists this can, and oftentimes does, undermine the therapeutic process. The client does not learn or experience a truly trusting relationship. The client is not able to bring the full extent of life's turmoil into session. Since the client does not fully trust the therapist's commitment, the client may not fully trust the process. Part of what makes any curing intervention work (whether medical or psychotherapeutic) is the client's belief that the curing interventions will work. This belief will put into motion the emotional commitment to the intervention. Personal belief is a powerful tool in helping a client to heal. If both the client and the therapist believe, then there is a synergistic effect. I am not saying a cure will inevitably come about, but rather it greatly increases the likelihood the intervention will promote some level of healing.

6

❖

Beginning to Feel

I was one of those who thought I knew what I was feeling, but in reality, I had no real idea. If my feelings were counter to how I thought I "should" feel, the feelings were ignored and suppressed. The feelings were never expressed, confronted, or acknowledged, only buried and thought to be forgotten. As I would find out, all the suppressed feelings I had were not forgotten, instead they were eating away at the very foundations of my life.

At this point in my therapy, my emotions were finding their way to the surface, I was finding the strength to begin to feel and to face them. For so many years I had stored away all I had felt. The emotions that were coming forth were new, scary, and confusing. It was difficult to claim ownership to feelings and emotions which were counter to what I thought they "should" be. How could I account for and answer to the thoughts I was having. What I felt was not mirroring the person I thought I "should" be or the way I "should" feel. Some of what was being felt was so new, I could not articulate what was has going on, nor could I identify what was being felt. This was very new and frightening for me.

If it was not for knowing Jim was there for me, I would have tried to stuff all these new emotions back inside and would have run from therapy. My trust in Jim was the only thing which allowed me to keep myself in therapy. If it was not for the implicit faith and trust I had for Jim and for our relationship, I would not have allowed the confusion and the pain to come forth and remain.

For me, learning to feel and to acknowledge these feelings was part of my healing process. In accepting my feelings, I would be accepting of myself. This acceptance was a long and painful process. In the beginning, it was easier to reject both my feelings and myself, that was the lifelong habit I was starting to discard.

November 16, 1996

Today I have felt out of sorts. I was kind of depressed, but in an unsettled way. I know right now I am wrestling with my feelings of ambivalence with my family life. The feelings have intensified over the last week. I have finally admitted to myself I am avoiding my family. In some ways, I really don't want to be a part of this family. I am wrestling with all the ramifications of feeling this way: the guilt, the confusion, and the anxiety.

I cannot believe the complexity and diversity of all that I feel. It seems to be a torrent of emotions which threatens to overwhelm me at the next turn. I find I am consumed with the internal issues I face, to the near detriment of all else I must do. How will I keep my head above water to make it? I don't know.

I saw Greg G. for the first time in months. After the Theodore Millon Seminar today we talked. It felt so nice to talk to Greg again. Greg asked me to wait for him so we could talk for a few moments. The first thing he asked me was how I was doing. I guess it was obvious I was not my usual self. In fact, Monica asked me the same thing earlier. We talked at some length about what is going on in my life; I could not bring myself to be too specific, after all we were just standing in the hallway. I also don't want to take advantage of him emotionally. I only hinted at what lay beneath my turmoil. I think he could guess at what I was feeling. I could finally sense in someone else a sense of caring for me.

I realized, for the first time in a long time, that there are people who do care about me. It hit me like a ton of bricks. I was never able to allow myself to feel the extent to which some people care about me. I was so touched with the revelation. I don't know why I was never able to feel it before. It is such a warm feeling, a self-verifying feeling, a feeling which truly reaches the humanity within me. I was overwhelmed by it. On the drive home today I cried.

Feeling, for the first time, the warmth and caring another person had for me was a tremendous feeling. I was overcome by sheer emotion. At the time, I did not realize it, but through the therapeutic process, I was not only beginning to have trust and faith in Jim, but also in myself. Until this time, I did not care enough about myself to allow myself to feel the care other people had for me. If I did not care for myself, how could I honestly believe anyone would care for me? I did not believe it was possible. To know it intellectually is not to believe it emotionally, that is completely separate.

For me, learning to believe, care, and love the self was a long and torturous process. I did not arrive at this point in my life in just three months of therapy. It could not have happened, had I not also gone through the previous therapy over the past two and a half years. All the time spent with the previous therapists helped lay the groundwork for me to be able to learn to care about myself. It took this relationship with Jim to complete the process. Even though two and a half years may sound like a long time, for many it takes even longer, and still for others it never occurs.

November 19, 1996

Last Saturday night I finally told my husband almost everything which has been going on. Throughout the hour and a
half all he said was the following six comments:

1. What am I supposed to say?
2. I never knew it was this bad.
3. I can't believe that I have known you for thirteen
   years, we have been married for eleven years,
   and now I find out that I don't really know any
   thing about you. You know everything there is
   to know about me.
4. You know my track record, our daughter and I
   aren't going anywhere.
5. You are a good mother.
6. I think it's time to go to bed.

Well, at least he knows. Whatever happens won't be much of
a surprise. He couldn't even tell me how he felt about what I
had to say. I guess he is just as screwed up as I am. Oh well...

This conversation with my husband was very disappointing and painful for me. I had rather hoped more would have been accomplished; what specifically, I had no idea. What was disappointing was the lack of interest, concern, and response I felt. What was painful was the emerging thought that my marriage was ending.

Maintaining my marriage for the length of my life was of utmost importance. In fact, its importance overshadowed my relationship with my daughter. I would not tell my daughter she was the most important person in my life. I could only tell her both she and my husband were important. I was fearful my husband would feel slighted, not feel important; therefore, might seek to end this marriage. My marriage was so important, I would let go of anything which seemed to threaten its integrity. I would have left the university, had I believed it would have jeopardized our marriage. This point was made clear to my professors. My marriage was fundamental, and possibly the most important part of my life. I tried to suppress my emerging doubts about my marriage. Fortunately, they would resurface again and again, whether I wanted them to or not.

One of the many concerns of a client in therapy is, "What if I don't get deal with one of my important issues?" Even if the therapist does not tackle an issue the first time it is brought up, the client will almost always find a way to bring it up again, without even trying. The truly important issues of life find a way of creeping into the sessions over and over again. When they no longer come back they have been dealt with satisfactorily.

November 19, 1996 (continued)

It is hard for me to describe just how I feel. I feel amorphous. I know I am still me, but I have no idea who I am, or what I am about. I mean this in a self-knowledge sense. I can only describe my current state using imagery. This is strange, because in the past I have never used imagery. So here goes.

In considering the question of who I am, I can only say this. In my mind I am someplace outside. It is light but there is no sun, no moon, no lamp, only diffused light. There is no substance to my surroundings. When I look to the ground, I see broken parts of me. I can recognize it is both my Practical Self and my Personal Self. So I ask myself, what is there left of me? I do not know the answer to this question. There are no shadows, so I cannot guess. There are no mirrors or reflective surfaces, so I cannot see any reflections. I look about and only know I am sitting and waiting. I can see no part of myself; I only feel I am sitting, and I exist.

In considering the question of what I am about, I can see water, like a lake. It is barely light out. There is mist and clouds, so I can't tell how big the lake is. It is raining, so I see no reflections in the water. I can't tell if the water is clear or muddy, blue or green, deep or shallow. All I see is the ringlets left by the raindrops.

I am not angry, fearful, impatient, or worried. I am. I exist.

Introspection into the nature of the true self may be one of the hallmarks of psychotherapy, but how it comes about is unique to each person. I was not accustomed to using imagery to explain anything, let alone myself. It was a unique experience to feel myself through a visual sense. It wasn't that I saw what I described, it was more that I felt what I described. This may be confusing and difficult to understand, but it is also difficult to explain.

Using another method to describe what I felt was a positive experience. It allowed me to view myself in a new and interesting way. It began to reopen expressive avenues which had been closed for far too many years. As I have reread these passages, those which use imagery as an explanation evoke the most emotion, even now.

November 19, 1996 (continued)

Sadly, I find I am married to a man I love only as a person. I enjoy his company as a companion. I am not in love with him as I remember I once was. I feel as though we are cohabitating, and doing a good job of that. But I feel nothing more. I will not leave, because it is important to me that my daughter grow up with her mother and father. We will lead the life she now knows. I think this will quite do. When she leaves the house, I will consider what I will do. I am saddened that all the passions I am capable of will languish alone, untouched. I only pray no man will be able to remind me of their existence, for the pain will be too much to bear. It will bring back my depression.

I am thankful Jim is my therapist. He has given me the strength to make it through this. When I need strength, I only have to think about the look in his eyes and the warmth of his presence, these are enough. I will see Jim again on Friday. I wonder what the next session will bring. I hope it will bring a new sense of who I am.

Jim had become the anchor in my life. Sadly, it was not my husband. Emotionally, I held onto Jim so tightly. If I did not, I was afraid I would emotionally drown and be lost. Jim had become my strength, sanity, and sanctuary.

As hard as I tried to remain independent of him, I was beginning to depend on him emotionally, more and more. Feeling my dependency on this relationship was so scary. I prized my emotional independence. I felt it kept me safe from being hurt again. What I did not realize was that feeling an emotional interdependence was part of what makes life worth living; that was yet to come.

Emotional dependence on another person was something I had not done for fourteen years. After my relationship with Ken (the last person I had emotionally let into my life and had deeply loved) ended, I promised myself to never allow myself to get into a position of emotional dependence again. As each session progressed, I was allowing myself to be more emotionally dependent on Jim. This dependence did not occur without a fight from my Personal Self. I would find ways of trying to sabotage my relationship.

[An unsent letter]

Dear Jim,   November 19, 1996

I wish I could convey to you all that I feel. I wish I had the expressive ability to make myself understood to you. At this moment, I lack the command of our language which would allow me to convey my feelings and emotions.

I wish the English language had the appropriate words to convey love of each type and variety. To say, "I love you," brings the wrong connotations to mind, but to not say it leaves so much unsaid. I love you because you have the gift of penetrable presence. It is as though you are able to walk around inside of me. I know what I mean by this, because I do it so often with other people. I have never before felt the strength of presence as I do with you. In session, I feel your presence come and go from me at your will. I do not find it intrusive; for me it is a relief. It is as though I know you know some things about me without me having to say a word. By your words and actions in session, I know it is true.

The strength and familiarity of your presence makes me wonder if reincarnation isn't true, in the way others view it. I feel we have spent a lifetime together in another time. If it were true, the relationship was loving, warm, and devoted. I feel the strength of that love resonate through the relationship we have today. I feel a commitment which goes beyond just strangers thrown together by chance.

I feel as though we could sit together in the same room and not say a word, but would still know the emotions and feelings of the other. Even though I cannot penetrate the wall you have erected against my intuition, I know some of what you feel. I know it is similar to what I feel.

I do not ask for anything. I only wanted to have the chance to tell you what I feel. It is unfortunate this letter will never be sent. Maybe one day I will be able to speak these words. I can only hope.

> With great affection,
> Kathleen

There were so many things I wanted to tell Jim, but I could not find the strength nor confidence to do so. Instead, I wrote several letters trying to tell Jim what I felt; these letters were never sent. There would come a time I would allow him to see them, but it would not be for many more months.

Writing these letters proved to be beneficial in giving me the opportunity to learn how to express my feelings about another person to that person. This was something I had not learned to do. I had always been too afraid to put my feelings out in the open. I was terrified of rejection and humiliation. Learning to trust another enough to tell someone I loved them and in what ways was a long struggle. I could tell my daughter and husband that I loved them, but it was more out of custom, rather than truth of emotion.

Sometimes, it can be difficult to tell someone how much they are loved and why. One way to do this is to start with letter writing. For some, it is easier to send the letter than say it face-to-face. Although this can alleviate some of the anxiety, in the end strength and confidence are needed to say the words in person. There are few things more powerful than telling someone, "I love you because...." By adding the because, it adds what is special about the person. It adds depth of meaning, rather than leaving it to sound like a custom or habit. Many people think it is unnecessary to explain their love to those who are loved. I believe we should tell the people we love how special and wonderful they are, and why. Hearing why we are special to other people, and the feeling of being loved is glorious.

November 21, 1996

I have my next appointment with Jim tomorrow. I have no idea what I will say. I am not even sure I will tell him about this past week. I am not sure why this is. I am tired. Of what?

Many things. I think I need a break from all that is going on. I just can't see how I will get to Christmas from here. I am overwhelmed with so much work at school, stuff to do at home, and thoughts upstairs.

I wish I could take off my brain for a while and relax. It seems everything is crashing this week: me, the school computer system, my data........

I am not even sure why I am going to see Jim tomorrow. I really don't like to go without an agenda in mind. Maybe tomorrow I will just be spontaneous. Yeah right.

Maybe I need to see what I feel like right now.......I am tired. My brain is saying: "Enough!" Why does everybody depend on me? Why do I have to feel like I hold the kettle? I guess I need to ask the question, "Do I?" Logically, I know the answer is no. I need to let go of the feeling, "I am so responsible." I do not need to be responsible for everything and everyone - only myself. It sure makes it easy for everybody else because I feel this way. I need to let go and let others take on the responsibility for their own lives and projects. I have reached my limit.

This last paragraph was the beginning of my admission as to my true feelings about my Self, my relationship with my family, and what it was I felt I needed to do. Not only was I beginning to feel, I was beginning to heal.

Heaven

Within the process of therapy, lie both great and intense pain, and also, great and intense joy. In learning to feel and accept the consequences of feeling, I learned to feel hurt, care, love, and joy, just to name a few. Feeling joy for the first time was a wondrous experience. I try to carry the feeling with me; sometimes it is difficult. When joy is difficult to find within my life, I come back to this journal entry and the following letter.

November 22, 1996

I have just come in from sitting outside. This afternoon, I sat in the very spot in which I had planned to die, just two and a half years ago. I chose that spot because it was from there I wanted to depart from this life. And this afternoon, I now feel as though it is the spot from which I will begin living. It is hard to explain the notion that I will begin living at age thirty-five, but in essence I feel it is true.

Until now, I have never felt such a sense of wholeness, serenity and calmness. I feel an exceptional feeling of clarity. In no one way do I feel these things, but through every atom of my existence. It is as though for the first time I am living. I have always known of my spiritual self, but now I feel I am my spiritual self. I am whole; I am in harmony with my self.

While sitting outside, it was as though every sense was bristling with life, existence, and clarity. A wondrous feeling.

Joseph Campbell[1] was right. Heaven is here. It is not elsewhere, not after death, not to be earned, but to be experienced. I have been in hell; now I too have been in heaven.

How I wish I could have shared this moment with Jim. There is no one who deserves to share this moment with me more than he. It is true. He has been my strength. He has not let me drown. He has swum the journey with me. I know the journey is not yet over. I wonder where it will take me from here.

This morning, Jim gave me the best advice. He told me about when he moved from California to Northern Utah and the winter arrived. He talked about the cold and how he was so uncomfortable. He spoke of the suggestion someone had given him. He was told not to be uncomfortable with the cold, but instead to experience it. This past week I have been fighting these emotions and feelings. This afternoon, I decided to experience them. Each experience of emotion is a new experience in life for me. I have never been to where I am now. I should enjoy this part of the journey; I should not be afraid. I am experiencing this, feeling it, living this moment.

While I sat out on the property, I picked a stalk of grass. I sat and marveled at its simple beauty. I experienced all the awakening feelings of life coming into being, and could only share it with this stalk of grass. I have kept it. I will give it to Jim as a gift. I have to find a way of conveying the feelings and emotions I felt this afternoon. I do not want to lose the feeling of coming alive. I hope I will be able to keep it alive within me. The strength, power, sensuality, and totality of that moment was truly a gift from God.

This moment was sheer joy. I cannot tell you completely what the experience brought to my life. This was the first time I had experienced the true joy of living. The joy was not a result of achieving something, or getting away from something. The joy was a result of being there for that moment, and allowing my mind to linger on the moment, not race ahead in time, nor ruminate about past transgressions. This was experiencing the here and now.[2] So few times in my life had I actually done this, probably not since childhood. To sit and experience only what is happening in that moment, without worrying about yesterday or tomorrow has to happen daily, continuously.

To talk of heaven on Earth may offend or may contradict your religious beliefs, but it best describes the joy and contentment I felt in that moment. It is not that I do not believe in "Heaven" after death, for I do believe the soul is eternal. I also believe we can make this life a living hell or heaven, depending on what choices we make. My beliefs also include the ability for us to enjoy and treasure this lifetime; for within this lifetime, we learn the lessons of humanity and love. Without those lessons, what then is the point?

Dear Jim,   November 22, 1996

This stalk of grass is my gift to you. I know it seems a strange gift, but one I want you to have. Here is why.

This afternoon I had the luxury of not having my daughter for a few hours, so I went out to the very spot on which I had planned to take my life two and a half years ago, and sat. I went out there as if called. While I was out there, I allowed myself to experience my life, as you had recommended. During this time I realized for the first time in my life I am living my life.

While out there I felt sensations beyond description. It was like a focusing of all that I am. I cannot say with certainty who I am or what I am about yet, but a feeling of wholeness, certainty, and centeredness. A sense of clarity filled me. It is beyond description what I felt and experienced out there.

So what of this stalk of grass? While out there, I picked this stalk of grass and examined it from top to bottom. As all the feelings came and went, I saw how it changed the way in which I saw this stalk. I loved, for that moment, all the simple beauty of its being. It was through this simple piece of nature that I feel as though I have been to what some might call heaven... calmness, hope, clarity, certainty, wholeness, peace, centeredness, strength, experiencing, love, and serenity.

My only thought is I wish you could have been there to experience it with me. I know it would not have happened if I had not been alone, but I wish you could know what I felt, because without you, this would not have been.

I want you to have this stalk of grass, for it is the only remnant of the moment, besides what is left within me. I cannot fully share that, so I give you this. I do not intend that you need to keep this grass, but instead I wanted to give you a gift which symbolizes my journey, for this moment.

Thank you for your strength, commitment, caring, and love.

In serenity,
Kathleen

Because I had spent so much time unloading my pain, frustration, and agony on Jim, I felt it was only fair for him to also hear my joys as well. It gave me great pleasure to share this experience with the one person who helped me get to this point. In addition, I think I wanted to give Jim a sense I was making some progress. I worried he would tire of my depression; I had hoped this would help sustain him on my journey.

I was still care-taking. This is a lifelong habit, whether or not the situation required my help. Even within this relationship, my desire to remain the care-taker was not relieved. I knew Jim did not need me to take care of him, but there were some deeply ingrained reasons behind my care-taking. I just had not yet faced them.

Feeling this joy, no matter how brief, was something I could use to help sustain me through the rest of my healing journey. When things became bleak and painful, returning to this moment would give me hope for a better life. I knew this joy would not be a constant state, but would possibly return if I stayed the course. All the external support in the world could not help me if I could not allow myself to hope. This moment gave me the hope to find a better life.

November 23, 1996

Today, I am still feeling emotionally well; physically it is a different story. I am learning how to get along without so much tension in my neck and shoulders, and it is tough. My neck and shoulders have been so sore. I guess it is because they are used to being so tense, and now I am forcing them to relax. I think I have reminded myself a thousand times today.

I reread the letter I brought to Jim's office yesterday. I wondered if it would sound strange or kind of stupid. Instead it brought tears to my eyes again. I could remember the feeling and the gratitude I felt for Jim's help. I hope he gets a sense of what I feel. I venture to guess he already knows.

In thinking about the things Jim has said to me, I think he has been where I am. He said, "When I face my dep..." and, "People like you, intelligent and interested in psychology, are often drawn to the field because they are looking for emotional connectedness." Also because of the glimpses of himself he allowed me to have a couple of sessions ago, and the intense interest he has shown for me and my case. I do not believe many of the people who are interested in psychology come barging through his door; I rather think he was speaking from the reference point of his own personal experience and from the experience of a few therapists he has counseled before.

I went to see Wil today. I thought it was about time I pay him a visit without being completely miserable. I told him how good it felt to be alive. I thanked Wil for his support, love, and caring. I thought I heard him say he knew I would be okay all along. I just started crying. I am brought to tears even now. I guess Wil had more confidence in my healing than I ever did. I can't thank Wil's spirit enough for his patience. I always felt like he cared about me and knew how I felt. I don't know how I could have made it this far without him. I wish I could have given him a hug and kiss. He means so much to me, and he always will. Thanks, Wil.

Over the past three years, I went to see Wil many times. He was the only person I could talk to about wanting to die. In the past, I had begged Wil to trade places with me. There were times I felt it so unfair he was the one to have died. Wil loved life and living. Wil had so much to look forward to in the future. I felt there was nothing but pain in my life and future; why should it have been Wil to die? It should have been me. The only positive aspect to Wil's death was he was there for me throughout this process. I only wish I could thank him in person. Short of that, I hope Wil's family will learn of the wonderful gift of love, support, and friendship he has given me throughout the most difficult years of my life. I love you Wil.

There have been times when I needed someone to talk to about my life and feelings. Sometimes the things I have wanted to say seemed too outlandish or morbid for living ears to hear. When this happened, I turned to the people I have loved, and who have loved me; those from the past which are no longer with me.

Their love is still with me. Their love still strengthens me. Their love carries me when there seems to be no other way to make it through life. I let their love sustain me, whether or not they know it. If they did know, they would want me to trust them, lean on them, and let them be there for me. Whether or not the ones I have loved were still living, they would want to be there for me. I let them.

8

❖

Their Anger,
My Anger

During the process of discovering the self and its motivations, a time arrived when I felt I must confront my emotions. What I felt and my perceptions of the past were not necessarily what actually happened. Actual events were not as important as the way in which I interpreted what I thought happened. My perceptions of reality were what changed, influenced, and molded me, not what actually happened. For many of my childhood years, I had been angry about my life. I was not abused or mistreated. I sincerely believe my parents did the best they could. This does not justify everything that happened; nor does it make the past and how I perceive it any easier to take. It is simply the way life was for me.

There are some therapeutic styles which require the child to confront the parents and tell them their thoughts, perceptions, and angers about their lives. I do not subscribe to this method. My therapeutic belief is it is enough to recognize and acknowledge the emotions and perceptions about the past, and then find ways of working through the past. If confrontation is required, then I ask the question: "If the parents are deceased, is there no hope for recovery?" I think not. Sometimes, the confrontation leads to additional problems: hurt feelings, anger, and confusion of other family members. What is perceived about the past by one member of the family may be quite differently perceived by another member of the same family.

Until this time in therapy, I had been angry with my family off and on, but with no direct reason or cause. I kept this anger hidden and even denied its existence on more than one occasion; however, I was finally starting to face the anger of my past. I did not confront my parents about what happened in the past. I did not feel it necessary. What was necessary was my ability to feel, acknowledge, and work through the anger.

Prior to the publication of this book, I gave my parents a copy of the manuscript and sat down and talked with them about what they might encounter. In our conversation, I tried to convey to them my basic philosophy of the importance of the coming entries, the confrontation of my own anger and the self-permission to feel anger. The importance of the past does not lie in what they did or did not do. I attempted to make them understand it was not my intent to hurt them, or make them feel guilty for my perceptions of my youth. They did what they had to, at the time; I did what I had to do. My daughter will have memories of my depression and anger; they may not be pleasant memories, but this is her reality. My family gave me life. Without their love, patience, and nurturance this journey would not have been possible. I was and am grateful.

November 24, 1996

Today, I just had to get out of the house. I knew I could not stand another moment within the confines of my family. I was getting anxious, irritable, and withdrawn. I just wanted to bail out. Within twenty minutes of leaving the house I felt so much better. It was such a relief. I wondered about why this is so. I also wondered why my relationship with Jim is having the effect it does. Why do I have an automatic suppression or squashing impulse when people around me are angry? Why Why Why?

I felt like there was an underlying current or theme to all these thoughts, but it took a while to distill the common thread. Through rambling self-talk, I realized I take responsibility for the happiness and well-being of those closest to me, my mom, dad, husband, daughter, therapist. I also realized I internalized this reaction from my interactions with my parents as a child. They led me to believe that what I did was responsible for the way they felt, and the way they felt directly affected whether or not they loved me. If I did everything to make them happy, then they would love me because I did what I was supposed to do, and only in that condition could they love me. OUCH! In distilling all that down, I realized why it was I was such a good girl. I understand why it is I go to the Nth degree in everything I do. I know why it is I perform so well for Jim. Why it is, right now, I do not want to be with my family.

I was a good girl so my parents would love me.

I go the Nth degree so others will value me.

I perform for Jim because I want him to value me, care for me, and want to put effort into me. I want to prove to him I am worthy of his attention and care.

I don't want to be with my family because I am tired of them hanging their lives on me. I am tired of them wanting me to do their living for them. I am tired of them wanting me to mediate their arguments. I am tired of them wanting me to plan their lives. I am tired of them expecting me to make their lives easier, happier, better. I feel like they are sucking the life out of me; that is why I want to run.

About a half hour ago, I was feeling the onset of depression. I could not understand why I was feeling that way. I was trying to search around to find the source, but was unsuccessful. A few minutes ago, walking through the halls of the psychology department, I felt the quiet twinges of being angry. My first instinct was to suppress the feeling, but I fought it and allowed my anger to rise. I sat down and told myself it was okay for me to be angry. There is no reason why I am not allowed to be angry. I have the God-given right to be angry just like everybody else. The anger welled up. At first, the source of the anger was not apparent. Slowly, I began to formulate the causes.

I am angry at my parents for laying their marital problems on my life. I am angry because I feel they used me to take responsibility for their happiness. I hate the way they made me responsible for choosing what we would see, what we should eat, what we would do, so they would not have to enter the battlegrounds themselves. They made me decide so it would not be their issue. I was the one who chose; therefore, I was the one who decided who would be happy and who would not.

I am angry because I let this go on for so many years, eight to be exact. I was too young. I should never have been given the responsibility for the happiness of their lives. I did not deserve to bear the burden of their weakness for what they could not or did not want to face. I was given the burden to keep the resentment and anger for them because they could not deal with the day-to-day mechanics of living together. I am angry because of their weakness. I am angry because they assuaged their anger and anxiety by placing the burden on me, a child. They robbed me of being who I wanted to be. They robbed me of feeling what I wanted to feel. They robbed me of my childhood, which I will never have back. I can never have those feelings of what I want for me without the burden of my family. I am so angry. I thought they loved me. If they loved me, then why did they take from me the only thing I had, my childhood?

Once I left home and was on my own, I always wondered why I felt like they abandoned me. They never called, wrote, or came to see me. It was as if they had no use for me. They didn't. Once I left home, they finally had to deal with each other, and found out they could. Since they could deal with each other, they did not need me anymore as intermediary, so I was discarded. Consequently, the only time they come around is when they need to feel like parents and grandparents.

So, what about my relationship with my family and with Jim? I really do not know. I now know I must extract myself from the current triangulation which exists. I no longer will be responsible for what emotionally happens to our family. I must convey to both husband and daughter it is they who are responsible for their lives, happiness, and sadness. They need to take responsibility for how they feel, not me.

I guess I will just tell Jim why it is I have responded to him the way I have. I have tried to take responsibility for the way in which he responds to me. I have done everything within my power to ensure he will want to help me and care about me. That is why I take everything he does so personally. I respond to his expectations so he will be happy with me. If he is happy with me, then he will care for me. If he cares for me, I have a reason to live.

I see this will be a very difficult message for me to convey. It will also be extremely difficult for me to change the way I behave and think. Many of my reactions are so automatic. I must now pay attention to everything I do. Even when I feel extremely uncomfortable, I must ask myself, "Am I doing this

because I am uncomfortable and I am taking responsibility for their lives, or am I doing what is best for me?"
I wish I were seeing Jim soon. I wish I could take the easiest of the steps by explaining this to him first. I guess I will just have to wait. Always I wait.

I feel much better now. I am glad I have this journal to turn to. It helps me clarify and articulate my thoughts and feelings. It allows me to pour forth what is inside without having to censor myself. I don't know what I would do without it. At least I have the foundations for my internal work which lies ahead. I also have a week to further consider what and how I will say what I need to say to Jim. I just wish it weren't a week. Maybe I will call Ruth tomorrow.

WOW! What a revealing day. I feel emotionally drained. I feel as though all I can do is sit. I have so much to do yet. I guess I better make the attempt.

In today's world, many people talk about their "dysfunctional families." Since our parents are human beings each family is most likely dysfunctional on some level. It is time we recognize and acknowledge the past, but also let it go. We cannot undo what has been, but we can change who and what we have become. Although we are a product of genetic inheritance and the environment, both past and present, this does not require that we spend the rest of our lives being less than whatever our potential gives us room to be.

We must start with ourselves. We cannot change our family, but we can change ourselves. We must look within, find what the origins of our behaviors and thoughts are. Then ask ourselves, "Is this still true today?" If not, then we must let our hatred, anger, and frustration go. There are some things in this world which cannot be changed. So we must either let it go, work through and accept it as it is, or walk away. This process does not have to be done alone, this is what psychotherapy is all about, working through the past and present in order to have a better tomorrow.

The past is gone, today will be the past, and what we do today will influence the future. "If only" and "what was" are oftentimes excuses to remain the same. Horrendous things can and do happen; nonetheless, courage, strength, and the determination to pursue self-discovery begins the healing process.

November 25, 1996

Late last night I thought more about all that stuff. I was angry at Jim. I felt like he knew all this about me, and then he used it to his own benefit. I thought he used it to make himself feel like he was doing me some good, making him feel as though he is some great therapist. I was angry because I felt like he used me.

It took a while, but I came to realize the truth; it was I who used Jim. Once I realized that, I felt so terrible. I had no idea everything I did in therapy was so I could manipulate Jim into wanting to help me. I wanted him to feel like I was making progress so he would want to stay with me. I wanted him to feel like he was doing me some good so he would care about me more. I wanted him to feel like I was someone special. I wanted him to care about me more than any of his other clients. I needed to be special to him so I could feel important, loved, and cared about. I used Jim for everything I wanted from him, not to get better. Although I may have become better in the process, I feel so ashamed about using Jim. I feel so terrible that everything I have done has not been to help myself get better, but instead to get the feeling of being special, and the caring and love I did not get when I was a kid. Jim, I am so sorry.

I have an appointment with Jim on Wednesday. I am going to apologize for everything I have done. I am so afraid he will turn me away, be angry, won't care, and won't want to see me anymore. I will be devastated if that happens, but I am also ready to accept the consequences of what I have done.

I remember several sessions ago he said "Therapists in therapy can easily suck each other into caring for each other too much," or something like that. I wonder now if he knew then what I have just discovered about myself. If he did, then he was angry with me. I wonder why he stayed with me.

I feel so lost. I am finding out I am nowhere near the person I thought I was. I am so lost and don't know where to start in finding out who I am. I cannot believe I am further dismantled than I was last week. What is left? Is there anything worthwhile left? All that I thought I was seems to be a sham. So what is the point? I just feel like giving up. I am so broken. I am so alone. I could walk out of Wednesday's session without Jim. As scary as that may seem, I must prepare myself for the possibility. How could he ever forgive me? I can't even forgive myself for what I have done.

I just feel so broken, lost, alone, and without hope.

If Jim does keep me, what then? I am so afraid that each thing I do is for all the wrong reasons. I don't trust myself anymore. If I can't trust me, then who can I trust? I'm not sure. So, what is the point? Am I any better off now than before? At least before I could function to some degree, at least with a false pretense of certainty. Right now, it would be so easy to just quit everything. I question everything I am, I want, I dream about. I see everything as constructs of some false reality. If all that has been a false reality, what then is my true reality? I am further from answering that question than at any other time in my life. I never imagined I could ever feel this way. I feel like I am sitting on a little saucer out in black space and the saucer is spinning around and around and just flying through the blackness. I have no control and no idea where I am going. I just want to stop and get off anywhere. I wish there were someone who could help me, but I know I am the only one who can. I am the only one who can stop the saucer and find a way to some version of reality. I hurt. I am scared to be so alone. Neither Jim nor anyone else can really help me. What would be the point in going back to see Jim after Wednesday?

How can I go from such a wonderful experience on Friday to such bleakness on Monday? Was Friday just an illusion? Was it just a way to endear myself to Jim? Was it just a strange joke I played on myself, and myself alone. I want so desperately for it to have been real. I need for it to have been real. I need to have that to hang on to, especially now.

A trend in today's society is to blame everyone and everything else for life's misfortunes and pains. It is time each of us took responsibility for and owned our part in our lives. We are not idle bystanders in our lives, but rather active participants. We have allowed our lives to become what they are. Each of us must challenge ourselves to carefully look at our lives and honestly examine what role we have played. In youth, many of the events which took place were out of our control, but in adulthood, we have to make more intelligent choices, find a way to accept and love ourselves, and love those around us. All this sounds easy and simple. It is not. It will be a lifetime struggle and journey.

Therapy can help us to heal and to give us tools to better equip ourselves to achieve our goals. These goals are not to be reached in a single session of therapy, but to be pursued with courage, love, and perseverance over an entire lifetime. We may or may not reach each of our goals, what is important is the attempt, the struggle, the journey itself.

In accepting the responsibility for our lives and our choices, we will be far less angry. We will do far less finger pointing and incorrectly displacing our anger onto others. Each time we lay our poor choices and mistakes at the feet of another, we give away our ability to take control of our lives. In giving away this control, we say: "I am helpless." Instead of standing up and trying to change what can be changed, oftentimes, we sit idly by and wish for a different world. We settle for the world we have, believing there was little we can do. We have the ability to affect change within the world we live. We do not have to be helpless.

9

❖

Admitting My Truth

To admit my own shortcomings to anyone was frightening and it opened me up to ridicule and rejection. I felt I could admit many of my shortcomings to Jim, because this relationship was built on trust, caring, love, and faith. Although I felt my relationship with Jim was constructed this way, at times I still had my doubts. These doubts were not based on anything Jim had said or done. The doubts were based on my own self-doubt. How could I trust Jim if I did not trust myself? Through learning to trust Jim, and Jim trusting and believing in me, I would learn to trust myself.

November 26, 1996

Tomorrow, I face Jim with what I have to say. I am scared. I have little idea as to how he will react. I hope he will be accepting and open, but I do have my fears that he will be angry and rejecting. I guess I will find out soon. I really do not look forward to tomorrow. I guess it is fear which lets me know I will be doing the right thing.

Earlier today, I felt myself talking to myself in an objective way. I was trying to fragment in order to cope with my fears and anxiety. I was able to stop the process before it got out of hand. I am relieved.

I wish myself luck.

I have done and said things which have caused me great fear, but there has been nothing in the past which could compare to the fear I felt in admitting the truth I had learned about myself. Throughout my life, I feared rejection more than anything else, including failure. Now, I faced the prospect of admitting that I felt I had manipulated Jim, and faced the consequences. Although logically I felt Jim would not reject me; emotionally there was no doubt in my mind that he would refuse to see me again.

As I sat waiting to see Jim, it never occurred to me that I had changed. There was a time when I would not have risked the loss of the most important relationship I had. There was a time when I would have hidden the truth in order to maintain the status quo. I felt an obligation to admit my folly and ask for forgiveness, despite the potential loss. Even if therapy ended right then and there, I knew I would end up a better person for just facing and admitting to myself and another the motivation for much of what I had done. For whatever the reason, I can not remember if there was even an articulated reason, I knew I had to tell Jim the truth, no matter the risk. There seemed to be more at stake in not telling him, than in telling him.

November 27, 1996

It is a relief to have told someone.

It is a relief to have had the appointment before Monday. I think I would have been a complete wreck if I had had to wait. I told Jim all I had to say. He neither acknowledged that he already knew nor indicated that it was news to him. This is the reaction I was hoping for.

I was so scared waiting for Jim. I wanted to run from the office and pretend I was never there. I did not want to tell him about what I had discovered about myself, and that I felt I had been manipulating him. In the end I did.

I really do not remember much from our session, other than the intense fear at the start, and the feeling of relief at the end. He did say he would never tell me not to come back. I hope he is telling the truth. In one sense I know he is, but in another way I find it hard to believe.

I think he really believes I suffer from a mild form of dissociative identity disorder. I don't blame him. Although I am aware of all my aspects [personalities], the way in which they present themselves, at times, leads me to think I do have DID.

Ever since my appointment, I am emotionally busted. I am so tired and worn down. I wish I could just find a hole to crawl in and not come out for a week.

Jim thinks I should confront my husband about the way I feel about our marriage – the feeling I have that I do everything. I am just not ready for any type of confrontation right now. I just want to run away. I told Jim I was ready to pull the plug on everything. He asked me what I would do if I did. I suppose he has to consider I might, and wants to know how serious I am.

Jim asked me if I had any friends. I told him no, I don't have any friends, except Wil - the dead guy. But I am a friend to a lot of people. He nodded his head like that was the answer he expected. I am sure it was.

I feel so numb. It is extremely hard to quantify or explain. I just feel numb. In a way I feel like I am loose inside of who I am. There is a nebulous quality to it. Again, amorphous fits. I wonder what is happening to me. I feel like I am not solid. If Jim were to put out his hand to touch me, it would pass right through me. A very strange feeling.

Right now, I am very tied to Jim. I can't imagine my life without him. I would be more devastated, than would be expected, if he were unable to care for me. It is as if he is my lifeline to reality. I feel I have such a tenuous grasp of the here and now, if he were to leave me, I would be lost within my mind. In a way, it is so comforting to have him, and yet I don't like the fact I am so dependent on him. I need to find the strength to back away from him, but I don't know how.

This time, I have described my state of being in terms of a physical feeling. With each passing day, I slowly learned how I felt and what I felt. My emotions were not returning in a way in which I could easily sense. My emotions were creeping back, ever so slowly, almost imperceptibly.

Some might say that feeling numb and amorphous would be akin to my difficulty with dissociation. I do not believe this was true. The numbness had more to do with not knowing myself, being uncertain as to where I was headed, and the uncertainty about my self-identity. I had just admitted to Jim I was a manipulative person, just what I hate most in other people. The pain and confusion of this admission were overwhelming. The fear of the possibility of Jim's rejection was terrifying. So much emotion was packed into such a short period of time. I was not sure how to process or work through all my feelings. I was floundering in my sea of emotions, unsure if I would drown or survive.

❖

10

To Endure

As with any difficult task, finding the courage, strength, and stamina to stay the course can be difficult. Many times throughout the process of therapy I wanted to quit. There were times I wondered if I was deriving any benefit; at other times I was simply tired. Sometimes, I feared Jim and the process. I remember telling Jim: "This isn't a good time for me to be doing this type of therapy." I reconsidered my statement almost as quickly as I spoke, and followed with, "Then again, I suppose there is no real good time to do this type of therapy." Jim simply nodded his head in agreement.

People can be so creative in finding ways to not do things. Psychotherapy is one of those things many people avoid, myself included. Dr. Stephens had recommended counseling to me prior to my most serious suicidal episode more than two years earlier. I found wonderful excuses to not be available: my daughter, the money, the time. Looking back, I nearly killed myself because I found too many excuses not to go to therapy. Now those excuses seem flimsy and childish.

The interesting part is I had recommended and pushed some of my friends into therapy, yet I myself was not willing to go. I did not think I needed it. How wrong I was. I was probably the person who needed it most. I was deep in my depression, I could not see that the suicidal thoughts and desires, the constant state of anger, and just barely surviving each day was not normal. I wonder how many other people survive their lives in the same state. I wonder how many people could be helped to live a more fulfilling and joyous life, if only they would trust psychotherapy and themselves.

November 29, 1996

Yesterday we went skiing. The conditions were perfect! I loved skiing.

During the day, my husband and I were comfortable, like companions. I found I didn't look him in the eye nor initiate any physical contact. It was pleasant, but not loving. I thought I could spend the rest of my life like this, until I got my cup of coffee. That was the true mistake of the day. My husband brought all the lunch stuff back to the van, and I got a cup of coffee while I waited for him. As I was sipping the coffee I happened to look out the window and notice a family of three and an older couple. The mom and dad, from the family, gave each other such a loving and lingering kiss. I used to kiss my husband that way. The way the older couple looked at each other was so full of love. I used to look at my husband that way. My heart and stomach sank to the floor within those two minutes.

I hope I can find a way to fall in love with my husband again. I can't imagine spending the rest of my life married to a man I am not in love with. I guess it isn't so bad spending the rest of my life with a companion, but when I see these other people in love, it is so painful. I want to feel that way again. I feel so guilty. I am afraid my husband is figuring out how I feel.

Yesterday on the lift, I told my husband about taking responsibility for my parent's emotional well-being as a kid. I also told him I have been doing it at home, and that was one of the reasons I don't like being at home. He didn't say anything.

I don't want to deal with all this stuff any more. It is so tempting to jump off the deep end and dissociate. It would be so much easier if there was a part of me who could deal with all this painful stuff. That is precisely what Jim is afraid of. I have to exert every effort to maintain myself as whole. I need to feel like this is all paying off. I don't really know that it is. Maybe I should mention this to Jim on Monday. I have become so dependent on him. I hate the way I feel.

One of the most frightening aspects of this process, was discovering I was not happy in my marriage. Unfortunately, I have several friends who have lost their marriages during the therapeutic process. In discovering the self, they found the current situation too much like their childhood. As a result they wished to cut from their past and run off to another future. Therapists may recommend patience and caution, but in the end, it is clients who must decide to wait for the process to be complete before making the decision to divorce. Do the people I know regret their decisions for divorce? Some do; some do not.

I found an increasing level of marital discomfort. I found I had placed such a high degree of importance on remaining married that I did not try and work with my husband throughout the marriage to keep it a comfortable place for both of us. As far as my husband knew, I was okay with how our marriage was. After all, I had not complained much over the past eleven years, what else was he supposed to think?

Why didn't I confront my husband? I was too afraid of upsetting the status quo. I feared him leaving. I would not tolerate the "failure" of divorce, at any cost, even to myself and my daughter. Does this drive to an end sound a little familiar? It does to me. I was obsessed with the success of my marriage, I placed so much of my self-image and self-esteem into a "successful" marriage; I wanted to keep the marriage in place, at any cost. What I did not see was the damage this obsession was doing to me, my daughter, and my family. I would not allow myself to see what I was doing until my relationship with Jim.

As I began to open my eyes to what I had created within my marriage, I found I questioned my willingness to hold my marriage together. I was beginning to find emotions about my marriage I never would have imagined: ambivalence, despair, unhappiness, sorrow, frustration, and anger, just for starters.

December 4, 1996

I am too tired to think about issues related to my own therapy. I really should cancel my next session, but I would feel lost without seeing Jim next week. It is as though he is my strength right now. I need all the help I can get.

December 7, 1996

Today, I have been fighting off depression. I hope I am successful. I cannot afford the time or energy it takes to deal with depression.

I have been thinking about what I will say to Jim on Monday. I am glad I will be seeing him. I will bring up the fact I had a difficult time answering him when he asked me what I am planning on doing in psychology. I realized I was afraid of what his first reaction would be to me saying I plan on doing clinical work. I was, and still am, afraid he would think to himself, "You have got to be kidding! You are too damaged to do clinical work." I still fear the thought, even from myself.

Although I believed I trusted Jim implicitly, I really did not. I did not trust him enough to feel comfortable in telling him I wanted to become a psychotherapist. I wondered if I would become healthy enough to do it. I knew I had to heal myself, despite not understanding the depth of work that needed to be done. Throughout my life I have found myself in situations in which I would be the helper, not only to friends and family, but also to complete strangers. I had known since the third grade that I wanted to help alleviate the emotional pain and burden from other people. I suppose that choice came from the pain I felt even then.

December 7, 1996 (continued)

I want to bring up what I saw in his eyes last week. I cannot remember what we were talking about. I only remember the slow emergence of pain in his eyes: the recognition of it, the withdrawal, and the composure. It was a raw pain, something he has not dealt with yet. I only know we were talking about my marriage. I wish I could remember what. It was so hard for me not to reach out to him at that moment. I just wanted to touch him gently and say, "Talk to me about it." I know he probably would not have liked that very much, in light of his comment a few weeks ago about therapists sucking each other into taking care of each other. I haven't decided if I will say anything yet, but because I have given it so much thought, I bet I will.

I have given thought to the issue of being mentally healthy. Jim asked me what I thought being mentally healthy would be like. I hate the question because it is so difficult for me. If I thought I had been there before it might be easier, but never really having been there, it is hard to know. At first, I described it in terms of what it wouldn't be. Then I realized this does not answer the question, "What would it be like?" So I have come up with a few ways it might be described.

A. My baseline would be contentment or comfort.
B. I would be able to deal with rejection and anger in a constructive way.
C. I would have several two-way relationships in my life.
D. I would enjoy the company of my family.

> E.　I would have confidence in me, not just what I
>   can do.
> F.　I would be whole.
> G.　I would enjoy life.
> H.　I would take care of myself as a part of my routine
>   life.
> I.　I would be responsible to, but not for, those I
>   love.
> J.　Depression would be something I can deal with.

> There is one last issue I have a difficult time committing to
> paper; I want to feel the interplay of passion and emotion in
> my marriage, and the apprehension I have over the possibility
> of never experiencing it. I know this is one thing I will talk
> about Monday. I am in pain over it.

During the initial sessions of therapy, Jim had asked me several times to describe what I thought my life would be like if I were mentally healthy. I found this to be a very frustrating question. My feeling was that if I knew what it was to be mentally healthy, I would know how to get there. Hearing the thought now, it sounds a little faulty in logic. I suppose it was.

Asking me to imagine being mentally healthy was like asking someone to imagine living in the fourth dimension. In the beginning, there was no way for me to identify with being mentally healthy. I could no longer remember a time when I was not depressed. I could not remember a time I did not constantly think about suicide. I could not remember pure joy. How could I imagine a life other than the one I had known? I could not. It took four months for me to begin to formulate what a mentally healthy life might be like for me.

For some, it is a difficult question to answer? Each person has their own mental quirks and faults. It is difficult to imagine life without them? It is difficult to imagine a mental and emotional life in a way other than what it is now? The prospect of becoming mentally healthy might prompt questions such as: "How will I feel about those closest to me? How will I relate to strangers and strange situations?" Will I function in much the same way, or will my perspective be different? Many would be inclined to say most things would be the same; I did. I just thought I would be happier, in general. In changing the way I viewed myself, even just slightly, it changed the way I viewed the world around me. I was not expecting this, nor was I prepared.

Change is an inherent part of a successful psychotherapeutic process. Many fear change because they fear the negative parts of it. Change is no different from many other things in life. It is not inherently good or evil, it just is. As a result, many clients find they view the world around them differently, as well as their role within it. They discover their relationships have also changed, most frequently for the better. New experiences and emotions await the clients who are willing to strive for a better and more contented life. As with any growth process, whether it be childhood or psychotherapy, there might be some very painful and difficult times, but if given the chance, clients can emerge from the process healthier and happier people.

December 11, 1996

While I was waiting for Jim on Monday, I revised my list of being mentally healthy.

E. delete
G. Life would be worth looking forward to.
K. I would be okay with me.
L. Know what I am feeling and be able to feel it at the time.

Jim seemed very pleased. He mentioned I seemed whole and quite well. I had to agree with him. I have been okay. I did mention I have reservations. I may be just mustering the ability to make it through the last weeks of the semester. I said I was hopeful this feeling I have is permanent, but would not be disappointed if I crashed after finals. While talking about how well I am doing, Jim mentioned something about what a "gift" my being better is. I replied that the way I was feeling was the best gift I had ever received.

The reason I mention this is because I had used the word gift in the same context in my paper for one of my classes. It struck me that throughout the time I have been doing therapy with Jim, he has continually used words I have recently used in my written work, whether it be academically or in my journal. This has felt kind of strange; unnerving almost. I wonder if these are the words Jim uses all the time, or has he selected them because he thinks this is how I talk. In either case, it is still a funny feeling. I think I will bring it up with him the next time I see him.

During our last session, Jim asked about my marriage. I told him I had come to terms with the way it is. I did mention the pain I have concerning the lack of passion and emotional bonding, but said I would have to find a way to deal with it. Instead of helping me find a way of dealing with it, he asked me a peculiar question: "Is it better for your daughter to grow up the way things are now, or would she be better in an environment of affection and intimacy?" I know what I would answer, but to get divorced for that seems a little extreme. I cannot say I would ever find anyone who would be able to put up with me, help me raise my daughter, pay for my house, pay for my graduate school, endure my graduate school, and be all I want in a man. I just don't see it. These past weeks he kept telling me to let things be; now is not the time to make decisions and make changes. Then he asks me this. My head was a swirl with thoughts and emotions. It was very painful. I also had mixed thoughts and feelings about him.

I know I have very confusing feelings about Jim. I know it is natural to have intense feelings about one's therapist. I know this is the first emotionally intimate relationship I have had in thirteen years, even though it is one-way. I am getting all these confusing ideas because of the comfort and familiarity of Jim. It doesn't help that he uses the very words I do; says the things I need to hear at precisely the right time, and seems to be following some unwritten, yet known, script throughout this whole process. I feel we have known each other for so long. I do not feel as though he is a stranger to me, even though I know very little about him. I hate it when his emotions pour through at times; I infer things about his life. I know he said he felt like this relationship was meant to be. That in itself made me feel as though there is something to this relationship which is beyond just therapy. I wish I could put all this to rest. I guess it will have to wait until I am done with therapy, because I am not ready to walk out of therapy. I couldn't if I tried.

I cannot commit to paper the range of feelings I have for Jim. I have not done or said anything which would be inappropriate. I have no intention of ever stepping over the line. I know Jim is very ethical in his practice, and has no intention of stepping over the line either. I have no idea as to how he feels about me either. All I know is I would not have seen my fortieth birthday if I had not met Jim. I now have a lifetime before me. For this, I will be eternally grateful.

In my soul I feel there will always be a relationship between us. I just don't know in what form it will be. Most likely it will be professional. I would like us to be friends, nothing more.

For me, to feel was terrifying. I did not know what I felt. I had been so out of touch with my emotions for so long, I had no idea what feelings I had, nor how to label them. I confused my gratitude and reliance on Jim for something more. Someone else might think this was dangerous or terrible. On the contrary, what better way was there for me to reconnect with my emotional life than through this experience. Had Jim not been as ethical as he was, my feelings might have lead to a relationship which would have been detrimental to my growth and development. This does happen, but not with us.

By feeling my emotions and learning to understand what they were, I began to relearn about myself: what I wanted within my emotional life, and how I really felt about different issues, people, and things. I also opened up my range of expression. Even my journal entries became more emotionally laden, they evolved from being objective and dry to being emotionally expressive and articulate. This had to do more with my increased emotional range than studying the dictionary.

December 12, 1996

At this moment I am so stressed out. I am having great difficulty concentrating on anything. I am a bundle of emotions. I can't even sort out how I feel. I am hoping I will be able to do so with this journal entry. I am feeling angry, sad, overwhelmed, anxious, despondent, depressed, alone, lonely, isolated, and disappointed. Most of all, tired. I need to find a way to work through all this so I can adequately prepare for my final next week. It will be a long one, but I know I must endure. I have such a strong desire to just quit. I want to run away. I must stop running and just face the music and pay the price. If I run now, I will always regret it. I just have to find the courage to stand fast and endure.

I am angry at myself because I turned in a sloppy paper to Dr. Siegal and now he is very disappointed in me. I am very bummed about that. Rick is disappointed in me too. Worst of all, I am disappointed in myself.

I hope I can find the strength somewhere. I only have a week left until the end of the semester. I wish I had the confidence in myself everyone else has in me. This is the first time I have been unable to achieve what I know I am capable of. I am not completely sure why it is I have been unable to do everything I have needed to. I wonder why I have run out of time? Why have I painted myself into a corner throughout the semester? I know part of it is the amount of work and the time allotted. I also know that is not the entire reason. I know that therapy these past four months have taken its toll also. I just wish I knew what was going on. I am confused.

I need every ounce of strength my spiritual essence is able to find. I need to dig deep within myself and my faith to meet the coming challenge. I need to forge ahead even in the face of adversity to meet the pain of what I must do to accomplish my goal. I only have a week to survive. I must center myself. I must find the strength, peace of mind, and internal character I possess to make all I have worked so hard to achieve a reality. I have worked too hard to quit now. I have too much to do in my life to stop now.

I must endure. I have found my limitations in excellence. I must now recognize them and work within the limits I have, or be able to face the consequences of mediocrity. I can only do so much. I am not inexhaustible. I am not perfect. I cannot do it all. I have my limitations. I must accept them and go on accordingly. I hate being mortal.

And now I must work.

"I hate being mortal." What a curious phrase. In writing this, I stopped and thought about this line. At no time did I believe I was immortal. I had not lost touch with reality completely. Throughout my life, I believed there was nothing I could not do, if I truly desired and pursued my goal. I was not perfect in my pursuits, but I did produce quality work consistently. I had not known failure. This was the first time I had to admit I could not attain all I had expected of myself. I had taken on too much, even for me.

My confidence in my ability to perform has been immense. Many possibly felt that I was conceited; I probably was; but not without good reason. I had achieved so much within my short life. Now, I was forced to admit I was just like everyone else; there was only so much I could do, no matter how hard I tried. I was "mortal."

December 13, 1996

I have let my mediocre performance go, for the most part.

This morning I battled a minor bout of depression. I was unable to bring myself to study, but I was not feeling fatally suicidal. I am not sure what the depression is about. I am feeling better tonight. I cannot wait until the semester is over.

I feel like I need to see Jim, but it will have to wait until Thursday. That is just around the corner. I am not sure why I want to see him. I feel as though there is something bubbling just beneath the surface. It is as though it is just out of my reach; it just a little too blurry for me to see, but I feel it there, just out of range.

I have much to do tonight. I guess I should start.

Throughout my time with Jim, I vacillated between enjoying the therapeutic process and wanting to leave. This struggle was linked to my underlying feelings of little self-worth, my threatened self-perception of being independent and capable; my highlighted fear of trust, intimacy and rejection; and my increased apprehensions around change. Objectively, I knew I would have to face all these issues in therapy, but knowing this did not make facing the issues any easier. I fought and struggled with each one just as hard and fearfully as someone who was not aware of the struggles to come. I was ambushed by all my emotions, issues, fears, changes, confrontations, and confusion. In deep intensive therapy, there is no way to be entirely ready for, nor to anticipate all that is to come.

❖

11

The Lull

Many times, I have mentioned the difficulty in pursuing the therapeutic process, but there can be times where there is a feeling of a lull. Areas of concern are being addressed, and new topics are introduced, but somehow there seems to be a quiet, almost sedentary quality to the relationship. The pace, feel, and texture of therapy slows down. As with any other relationship, there are different stages; there are up periods and down ones too.

December 15, 1996

I have spent my free time contemplating the question of what type of environment I would like my daughter to grow up in. I know if it were possible, I would want her to grow up in an environment in which there is emotional intimacy, warmth, affection, and love. At first, I thought giving up my marriage would be impractical and too devastating for my daughter. It took a while for me to be able to respond honestly to the thought of staying in my marriage.

I don't want to leave my marriage for three reasons. First, it would be devastating for my daughter. She is happy in the life she has. She doesn't know anything different; therefore, this is okay. Second, it would be impractical for me to leave. I would not be able to finish my schooling and stay in the only house my daughter has ever known. The third reason is why I am in no hurry to leave. I do not believe I would be able to find someone who would love me the way I want to be loved. I don't believe there is someone out there who will love me for who I am, be emotionally available, a little adventurous, affectionate, warm, patient, and be willing for me to live my life the way I want to live it. I think this is a pipe dream. I don't believe there is such a man; therefore, I will stay with the man who allows me to do what I need to do for now. I imagine there will come a time when I will leave the marriage to live my life. I do not foresee ever getting married again. I think I will spend my life the way I lead it now, alone.

I have met three men who might be what I desire in a man, but they are all married and seem quite committed to their marriages. I just do not see finding a new man happening for me. Not now, not ever. It saddens me to think I will spend the rest of my life devoid of the emotional relationship I so deeply desire. I guess I have come face-to-face with the existential issue of isolation. I know each of us is ultimately alone, but I do believe some of us are lucky enough to have a relationship in which there is an emotional bonding which gives a bridge into the life and love of another person. That is something I do not believe will happen within my life. Why? My past leads me to believe emotionally committed relationships are not meant for me. I would like to change that belief, but I don't know how. I know sitting around and saying "emotionally committed relationships will happen for me" over and over will not change me. I guess someone will just have to prove me wrong, but I don't foresee this either. Oh well.

The previous paragraph clearly illustrates my inability to see the depth of emotional commitment within my therapeutic relationship. If I could not see the emotional commitment there, how would I know when I had an emotional commitment within my marriage or another relationship? I was learning what I wanted, but was having difficulty in seeing where I was within my life. At times, I would be able to see my life clearly. Other times, I would be in a fog.

December 15, 1996 (continued)

I must now find a way to accept with the underlying loneliness I feel. I must find a way to deal with the passion and desire for connectedness. I must channel these feelings and desires in another direction, into my daughter and work. I wish I could find a way to connect with my husband, but I find I do not have the desire. It saddens me deeply. I wish I had some tears left to cry, but it seems I am all out. I just hurt in so many ways. I will bring all this up with Jim on Thursday.

I would like to ask Jim not to bring up my marriage again, but I know I must deal with all I feel. I must bring some resolution to the feelings I have, but I do not know how. I wish there was a quick and easy answer, but there are none, just the hurt.

My heart is so heavy. It seems as though it would just drop to the floor if it were not attached. I have a deep pain within my soul which tells me I must find a way to deal with it or I might just wither away and die. I want to just curl up in the corner and fade away. No, I am not having suicidal thoughts! I just want the hurt, feelings, and thoughts to go away. I wish Jim could take them all away. I know it is not possible, but maybe he will help me find some resolution. For a while, I thought I had nothing left to say to Jim, but now I know I have put myself on hold until finals are over, and basically, they are coming quickly to an end. I see an end in sight and know what I must do to prepare. Unfortunately, the pain of my life is starting to creep back into my consciousness, but I wish it would have stayed away just a little while longer, it was a nice break.

What has been interesting throughout this therapeutic process is that each time I go through a period of intense feelings for Jim, afterward I have a self-revelation. It is an interesting phenomenon. I think it may be due to my trust in Jim. I know he has the ethical strength to handle my feelings. In allowing myself to have these feelings, it is like I am able to allow other feelings to surface. Having the intense feelings for Jim is safe because I know he will not reciprocate; therefore, he is like a roadway for my other feelings to come to the surface on a safe route. At first, I used to be afraid and ashamed of the feelings I had for Jim, but now I no longer feel that way. I know they will come and go, and afterwards, there will be something left which will help me heal. That is what this is all about. If there ever comes a time when I do not return to my baseline of deep affection in an appreciative way, I guess I will worry, but not until then. He has allowed me to find what there is within me. In my way, I will always love him for that. Again, the word love is so inadequate for the feelings I have for him and what he has helped me accomplish these past months. I wish I could find a way to tell him what I feel. I don t suppose it will happen. Maybe one day...

Previously, I wrote about an authentic relationship between the client and the therapist. An authentic relationship can exist within the client about the self. If clients truthfully examine their motivations, desires, emotions, and beliefs, even when they perceive them to be counter to what they would like their "self" to be, they can begin to establish a more authentic relationship with themselves. Without realizing it, this is part and parcel to the therapeutic process. How can change occur if clients are not willing to be honest and open with themselves? A little difficult.

Not only had I begun to know my emotions, but I had also begun to find ways of using them to my benefit. Emotions began to be a vital part of my life, not something to be feared and suppressed. I had not yet learned to verbally express them to Jim very well. Again, I turned to writing an unsent letter.

[An unsent letter]

Dear Jim,   December 15, 1996

Again, I wish there was a way I could tell you all I feel for you and what we have done together. I feel a deep sense of affection which runs to the depth of who I am. You are the one person who has been there. I know this is what I pay for, but I have paid others and they have not allowed me to feel safe. I was not allowed to expose who I am to them, like I can with you. I feel as though you will accept all I am, no matter what it is I say.

So why is it I cannot bring myself to say what it is I feel for you? Maybe it is because I do not really know. Maybe it is because what I feel is so foreign. I am trying to find the words to describe something I have never before experienced. In time, I hope I can bring to words what I feel.

I love you in a way that goes beyond description. It is beyond the feelings I have for anyone else in this world. I love my daughter, but it is in a different way than what I feel for you. I love you in such a way it is okay for you to have a life outside of our time together. When we are together, true living goes on for those few minutes. Those few minutes give me the hope that one day I will live within each and every moment of the day. This is hope I have not had before. Until now, I have only survived my life; now there is a chance I can live my life. When the day comes, I will owe so much of it to you. Without you, there would be no tomorrow for me.

I know all this is possible because of the way I feel about your spiritual presence. I feel we have had a connection before. I know not in what capacity, but there was a deep spiritual connection. If it weren't for that, I would never have been able to feel capable of opening up to you. I know one day I will have to walk away form what we have, and it will kill a part of me. I just do not know where I will find the strength to say good-bye for one last time.

I love you Jim, with deep affection and appreciation for your spiritual essence. I know we will meet again, and spiritually, I look forward to that time and place.

> In Serenity,
> Kathleen

December 16, 1996

I am trying to study for my finals, but find I am very distracted. Jim asks me questions which challenge every aspect of what I believe. The answers can be tormenting. They question what I want for my life. I have such a strange mix of feelings about Jim and therapy.

Jim has been a double-edged sword. He has helped me to become whole and start on my healing process, yet he has opened other wounds from my past, wounds I have long forgotten until now. In some ways, I wish to rediscover myself; in other ways, I fear the resulting changes. I must wait and see.

I am glad I'll be seeing Jim on Thursday. I am ready to jump back into my search again.

One of the purposes of therapy is to challenge and examine the basic core beliefs clients carry within themselves, and to decide if the beliefs are accurate and conducive to a healthy, contented, and productive life. Jim was able to prod me to do this both gently and provocatively. He never led me to one conclusion. After I decided on one course of action, he would challenge my decision to ensure I had considered all aspects of my journey. Jim was able to do this without causing me to become defensive, feel threatened or inadequate. His ability to effectively challenge my beliefs is one of the qualities I appreciate most.

Reopening emotional wounds of the past is not necessarily a bad thing to do. For me, it was quite helpful. Instead of facing my emotional pain, in the past I would neglect and suppress it, hoping it would just go away. In many cases, it seemed this strategy worked. In reality, all the pain was still there, it manifested itself in bodily ailments (e.g. migraines, headaches, neck and back pain, and various general illnesses) and distorted the way in which I viewed the world. Instead of seeing each relationship as a separate event within my life, I saw all relationships as a series of painful events. I saw emotional intimacy as a devastation to be avoided at all costs; destroying my happiness and my desire to live. As much as I would have liked to leave my past in the past, I found I would eventually have to face how I perceived my past and how it colored and distorted the present. I was not yet ready.

December 17, 1996

A long time ago, I used to write poetry and musical lyric. I wasn't so great, but it was a means by which I used to express myself. Tonight, I feel the stirring of that poetic desire returning.

I have been looking for a gift for Jim, when we part our ways. Maybe a poem will do. I think I need to bring up termination again. I know my insurance won't pay the bills forever. To part from Jim's care will be the single most difficult thing I will have done in many years. Somewhere, I must find the strength to say good-bye, when I know my heart wants to stay. It is so safe in his care. I fear being alone again.

The Journey

I have walked this world wide and journeyed every road. I have been within the caverns of Hell and seen the Devil's ire. I have traveled deep within the forests dark and seen the sights of a million lives, safe from within my harbor.

But this journey I could not have trod, without the simple fire. What fire is this I speak of? It is the fire of being. Upon this journey I nearly snuffed the flame from my existence, but was for the kindly touch of a stranger that kept it lit in insistence.

From that moment o'er I flew across the raging rivers. I saw the depth of ocean secrets, climbed the peaks of discovery. All this I did, but not alone, not without my ghost. Ever present, ever strong, it kept me afloat.

Each step I took was taken in stride as though the ghost was knowing. Knowing what, knowing where, or even what was the point. The ghost has promised and has delivered. I have lived to tell.

I mourn the loss of my ghost. I fear the world alone. How will I know? Where will I go? Where is my strength? Who will save me when I drown? I will be alone.

A strange passage indeed, but telling of my journey. It conveys for me a little more than all the words I have written. It sings the flavor of my journey and the fear as yet to come. For now, I am safe. For now, I do not fear, but must prepare for future's dawn.

Termination of the therapeutic relationship is an extremely important part of the process. I can imagine few things more difficult than voluntarily letting go of a relationship in which there is great trust, caring, and love. Why would I want to leave a person who has listened to all that I have had to say, and supported me throughout the relationship? Why would I want to leave a relationship which is about me and my growth? Isn't there always something to be "fixed" within?

There are so many fears and apprehensions in termination. How will I get along without my therapist? Will I find another relationship in which I feel safe and accepted? Will I go back to the way I was before? What if I find I left too soon? Is there ever a good time to leave? When will I know it is time to go?

Although there are many common fears and anxieties about termination, the end of each relationship is unique to that relationship. Accepting the end of the therapeutic relationship is best dealt with throughout the relationship. To ignore the end prior to the last appointment can lead to a feeling of abandonment or confusion on the part of the client.

Life can be viewed as a long string of relationships. Each must have a beginning, a middle, and an end. In the beginning we learns about our new partner. We enjoy the newness of the other person. We enjoy the adventure of exploring a new relationship. We see many commonalities and positive qualities. We hope we are accepted and valued by our partner. There is much uncertainty. In the middle, we enjoy the certainty of what we think the other person is about. We experience life through the sharing of events. Often, we believe the relationship will be "forever." We want the positive aspects of the relationship to remain unchanged. We might even expect the relationship to remain unchanged for all time. The end of the relationship can come about in many ways: no longer a commonality or connection, separation by distance, or change within one or both partners. How the end comes about is not as important as how we deal with the end of the relationship

Few of us have been taught how to say good-bye. Oftentimes, the first time we are faced with good-bye is in our childhood when a friend moves away. We try to avoid the inevitable. We might become angry at their leaving. We might try to hold on to the friend as if for life. In the end, our friend leaves and we hurt. How are we taught to handle the hurt? We are often told, "Don't cry; you will find another friend." Does it sound familiar? Instead of learning to mourn the loss of a significant relationship, we are taught to suppress our feelings. It is as if our childhood relationships are not important. They are. They are the means by which we learn to deal with the rest of the world.

Might it not be more constructive to teach children how to mourn the loss of a treasured relationship? Isn't it important to acknowledge when they hurt and learn how to soothe their feelings of pain using the internal gifts they have? If children learn how to do this, then they might not use food, alcohol, sex, illicit drugs, and cigarettes to ease their pain. If children learn how to acknowledge, accept, and work through their hurts and pains, they might be more satisfied with the lives they have, rather than always running from where they are to find a better place. We must teach children that happiness and contentment are here, not over there somewhere. We just have to learn how to find it.

December 18, 1996

I have noticed I have lost a great deal of my obsessive-compulsive nature. I still want to do well, but perfection is not required. It is nice. It allows me to do more with less time. It is a little disappointing for those who still expect perfection from me, but that is okay. I am no longer placing as much importance on what I do as a measure of my personal worth. This is great, even though I disappointed one of my professors by my performance on a paper. He doesn't hate me. I think he has realized I am as finite as anyone else. It is a relief.

I am still not sure what I am going to talk about with Jim. I hate going to a session unprepared. I suppose I will talk about my marriage and the question from last session. I think I will also bring up my diminished obsessive-compulsive traits. Oh yeah, I do need to bring up termination too. Yuk. I suppose those three items alone will take up most of the time. I hope he is not late tomorrow. Sometimes I feel a little shortchanged on time.

For some reason, tonight I am not as hung up on my therapy and Jim like I was last night. I guess it is because I haven't had any emotional triggers.

I wish I knew where I am. I know it sounds like such a strange question, but I feel like I am still floating around. I feel like I am somewhere in between my old self and my new self. It is a hard feeling to explain.

I am not fragmented anymore, yet I feel a lot of personal self-doubt. I would like to relieve myself of that. I know it is not as bad as it used to be, but it is still there. I still have not come to terms with my underlying feelings of self-worthlessness. In exploring Jim's question, I have come to realize I don't believe I would find anyone who would love me for me and be emotionally available to me. I wonder why. It makes no sense. I feel my husband is as good as it will get for me. It's not that he isn't good; he is great in so many ways, just not emotionally. If I thought he could be, I think it would make all the difference in the world. It is the only thing he is really lacking. I just wish it didn't matter so much now. I need to give him lots of time. As I change further, maybe emotional intimacy won't be quite as important later. I hope that is the case. I am still bummed.

Although I am better and more healed, I still have a ways to go. This process has been intensely gratifying and intensely painful. I am not sure if I would recommend this to anyone. I will have to wait and see how I turn out. The jury is still out, so to speak.

I had an odd notion about how my healing process would progress. From this passage, it occurred to me, I expected I would get better all at once. This is a strange expectation. I expect that healing from a medical ailment may take time and might occur in stages, and yet, I did not have this expectation of my mental healing. I assumed there would come a time when I would feel better all at once.

As if I would wake up one day and say, "Wow! I am cured. I don't have to go back to therapy anymore because I am okay now." It is an unrealistic view at best.

Another observation from this passage is my lack of patience concerning my healing process. Granted I had been in therapy for two and a half years, but I still expected to be healed after twenty years of self-destruction in only four months with a new therapist. Talk about unreasonable expectations. Since each person and situation is different, there is no real way of knowing how long the healing process will take. The healing process continues even after the therapeutic relationship is over. In the age of managed care, I find the notion of healing a lifetime of damage in ten to twenty sessions to be unreasonable and short-sighted. How can insurance companies expect someone to work through a lifetime of issues in less than twenty-four hours of contact with a therapist? Most clients ended up the way they are in more time than that.

December 19, 1996

I am feeling the tip-toe of depression around the corner. I hope it isn't the case. I will just have to wait and see.

My next appointment with Jim is in just a few minutes. I have so much to say, and yet nothing at all. I have a bunch of feelings right now, but don't know what they are. I am sure I will eventually sort them out.

Jim is late as usual.

December 20, 1996

I had an appointment with Jim yesterday. Neither one of us were really present; we did the best we could. We talked about my school stuff.

It turns out he did have a point in asking the question. The point was he wanted me to be completely aware of the choices I am making. He wanted me to understand the depth of the decisions, and did not want me to suffer from depression as a result of my decisions being not well thought out.

I told Jim I thought I wouldn't find a man who would help me provide the environment I wanted. He asked me what if I did meet him? I told Jim it would be the most painful thing, but I wouldn't leave my husband for another man. I don't believe that is the right reason to leave a marriage. He then asked me if I would just have a long-term affair. I told him as long as I was married to my husband I would never cheat on him. I couldn't do it. His reply was he was glad I felt that way.

Before I left, he told me what made him happy right now was he no longer worried if I would be alive the following week. I didn't know how to respond. I was surprised by his comment. I never really believed he worried about me.

If clients and therapist have a truly loving relationship, how can therapists not care about what happens to their clients? The therapists have listened and vicariously experienced the pain, agony, joy, victory, and failures of their client's lives. How can therapists not wonder about their clients even when they are not in session? Not only was my perception of Jim not caring about me a comment on my self-perception of worth, but also my underestimation of Jim as a person.

When we believe others do not care about or love us, not only are we commenting on our beliefs of not being worthy enough to be loved, but we are also judging those around us as being too shallow and base as to not have the capacity to love us, whether or not we are worthy. When we say, "He is so wonderful, how could he love someone like me?" How can we truly view the other person as wonderful? If they are so wonderful, shouldn't they love us for who we are?

Full Circle

Very often as we grow up, we promise ourselves we will not be anything like our parents; and to that end we strive. I am no different. I wanted to make sure my life was totally different from my childhood. I figuratively ran so hard and so fast, I ended up right where I started, and I didn't even know.

Nothing horrendous happened in my childhood. I do not believe I have repressed any memories of abuse. I cannot say for sure why I lived in the pain I felt. I cannot be sure when it all began or why. All I am sure of was my unhappiness. All I have written within these pages are bits and pieces of my reasons, but in looking at them, I find it hard to understand why I was so terribly unhappy. The roots of my unhappiness are no longer of great importance. What is of importance is my ability to learn to let go of the past and recreate a life in which I live, love, and flourish. This is what I choose to dwell on; no longer on the past.

Can we really run from the past? I wanted to, but instead ran back to it. The past is all we really know. How can we do other than what we know? Unless we find a new environment to learn new skills and ways of dealing with life, how can we find a new way of living? The environment of therapy, whether individual or group, allows us to experiment with new ways of facing life's dilemmas. In a safe environment we can try self-expression, assertiveness, tenderness, honesty, and so many things we may have never ventured to try elsewhere.

December 21, 1996

How can I find a way to pretend I love my husband, when I do not? How do I pretend I have a wonderful life when I am in pain? It is funny; at one time it was so easy to pretend. In fact, I did it so well I even fooled myself. I wish I could fool myself again. I have to find a place within myself to where I can

> retreat when I have to be the good wife. I need to find a way
> to make this work. No matter what I do, the price will be
> almost more than I can bear.
>
> I wish I had someone to turn to. I wish I had someone to talk
> to who would be able to talk back to me about this. I wish I
> could find some resolution in this. My heart is breaking. I wish
> Jim could help me, but he can't. In reality, no one can. This I
> must do alone.
>
> I cannot recall a time in which I have ever felt more alone
> than now. I feel as though I am cast out to sea with nothing
> more than my pain. My mood rises and sinks with each
> swelling wave. The islands I see are nothing more than
> mirages. The birds laugh all around me. They know the way to
> shore, but can only call and laugh. I see ocean liners and
> yachts drift by with their happy cargo, and I cry. I am unable
> to hail my own rescue.
>
> The more I think about it, I think I may have to leave Jim.
> Why? Because he reminds me of what I want, but cannot
> have. He is such a stark contrast to my husband. When I think
> of the two of them, it saddens me to tears.

Learning the wonderful connectedness of emotional intimacy was one of the hardest lessons I had to face. The relationship I had with Jim was so opposite to the relationship I had with my husband. I could not see a way in which my marriage could ever be different. I will admit I did not give my husband any room for change. I did not believe he would enter nor allow himself to benefit from psychotherapy. I cannot recall why I felt this way.

Through my relationship with Jim, I was learning the value of emotional intimacy. I had cut away the part of me which remembered what it was like with Ken, my last emotionally intimate relationship. I was so fearful of the pain at the end of the relationship, I would not allow myself to remember how wonderful the intimacy had been. As my relationship with Jim matured, I found I enjoyed the warmth, caring, and comfort of being emotionally intimate with another human being. I did not experience emotional intimacy with anyone for the past thirteen years, until Jim.

It did not occur to me my depression could very well have been in large part due to the emotional isolation I had built for myself throughout my life. How can one experience happiness when emotionally barren within? I cannot imagine how. This is what I was trying to achieve, happiness and contentment while emotionally barren, isolated, and detached. In experiencing the relationship with Jim, I began to see how isolated and barren my life had become. In tasting the emotional intimacy, even if only one way, I began to see how I could find the serenity I so dearly desired. I could find the serenity in accepting myself and others.

December 23, 1996

As has occurred so many times before, after I have cycled through my intense feelings for Jim; I have been able to attain new insight into my life. As with all I have attained throughout this process, my insights are also like a double-edged sword.

I have come to realize, despite all the effort I have put into insuring my adult life is nothing like my childhood, I have done nothing more than recreate it, but in a different shade. Both in my childhood, and now in my present life, I have been tormented by taking responsibility for the emotional happiness and well-being of my family. I therefore exist in emotional isolation and desolation.

I have spent a great deal of time thinking about why it is I do and do not want a divorce. Originally, my reasons to stay seemed so right, so noble, and now so full of shit. I realized what I thought were the reasons for me to stay had more to do with me, than with my daughter. It had to do with my thoughts that I wouldn't be able to find and have a relationship like I truly desire. My getting a divorce was so counter to everything I have worked for, and getting a divorce would mean I have failed. What a novel concept; I have not truly failed at anything I have attempted and worked hard for until now. I have reveled in the "success" of my marriage, but now I am faced with my own "failure" – Ouch!

I also asked myself: "Was it so much the divorce which made me painfully unhappy as a child, or was it that Mom stayed married to my stepfather and her unhappiness?" My mom has admitted to me she didn't think her marriage would last, although it has. Now, they seem comfortable with each other. I think the only reason why she stayed was for me. Isn't it ironic? I sit here and have said to myself the reason why I would stay would be for my daughter. Now I wonder, would I

be doing the same thing to her? Would my staying married
only perpetuate the life cycle I have lived? Emotional isolation
will be one of the things she learns form me and my marriage.
Is that what I want for my daughter's future? No, it is not. If
there is love, intimacy, and affection, life can be fulfilling. So
I ask, why do I stay? I am finding my reasons are running thin.

As a result of years of hearing how horrible divorce can be to children, I
began to believe it was my mother's divorce which had to be the root of my own
unhappiness. Their divorce probably contributed to my unhappiness, but I cannot
believe it was the root cause. I believe this because all my parents and step-par-
ents maintained a cordial atmosphere concerning each other and myself. They
did not convey any feelings of animosity towards each other. After I found out
all divorces were not handled in this manner, I became very appreciative of the
way my parents conducted themselves. Even to this day, when I speak to my
mother or father, they speak well of each other and the past.

If the divorce of my parents was probably not the root of my unhappiness,
then what was? I may never know the reason why I spent so many years terribly
unhappy. At this point in my life, I no longer believe I will ever know. I have also
come to realize there is no real importance in knowing the cause. I have been
learning how to let go of the unhappiness in my life, and allow myself the
courage to live and flourish in my remaining years. My past will always be with
me, but it need not destroy my life ahead.

I would like to address briefly the way in which I speak of the marriage of
my mother and stepfather. The actual flavor and texture of their marriage was
most likely much different than how I perceived it then, and remember it now. I
acknowledge this. What I am addressing in these passages is how I perceived my
environment. My perceptions are what molded my thoughts and reactions to life,
not what really happened. I know I have covered this ground before, but I feel
obligated to return briefly to remind you, what I remember may not have been
what was. Only my mom and stepfather know, and even still, only from their
own respective perspectives. My parents did the best they could. I am okay now,
so that was good enough.

December 23, 1996 (continued)

There are the economic reasons of my graduate work. I need
to ask myself if staying in graduate school isn't a little selfish
now. I want my daughter to grow up in the home and with the
friends she has now. Currently, I cannot do it without being
married to my husband. But other kids move and get along
fine in life. I love this house, and the solace it has brought me.

If there was a way to keep the house and graduate school, I think now I would leave the marriage. I have not figured out a way to do it, so I stay.

I have always told my daughter if she is not happy with something, she should do something about it, and not just gripe about it. Yet here I sit griping about my marriage, unwilling to do anything about it. Am I a hypocrite or what? I hate this. If there is one thing I despise it is a hypocrite.

I cannot believe I am still living in my childhood. I had not realized the emotional life I am leading is so similar to the painful one of my youth. Although my husband is nothing like my stepfather, and I am very little like my mom, the emotional script is still the same. I am frustrated. I see the emotional attachment my stepfather has with my mom, and it is the same my husband has with me. I cringe. I perceive the emotional detachment between my mom and my stepfather, and I see the same barrier between my husband and me. I shudder. I look back and wonder if my mom stayed married to my stepfather because it would give me a better life, and I am thinking of doing the same thing for my daughter. Look how it turned out for me. I ache. I took responsibility for the emotional happiness of my folks, and I had been doing it for my husband and daughter. I am angry. I was intensely unhappy as a child, and I am still. I want to cry. I told myself I would only have to stick out my life at home for "X" amount of years, and I am contemplating doing the same thing with my marriage. It is scary. In the end of my life at my parent's house, I ran out of the house at every opportunity; I am doing the same now. I am saddened.

If I do not change this, I ask myself: "Am I giving the same life to my daughter?" I don t know the answer. What can I do to give her every chance of having a full and happy life with both her experiences and emotions? I don't know. I already know she sees fault in so much of what is around her. I know she got it from me. I am changing and can only hope she too will change by my example. But what of the emotional life I lead now? Will she too inherit the pain if I maintain the pain I live in? I fear she will.

I think this is the first time I have really examined my marriage in true view of what might be best for my daughter and myself. Even still I cannot yet justify divorce. I need not rush into a decision now. There is still much work I need to do before I am justified in coming to a decision. I still need time to understand who I am. I need time to assimilate my newly-found wholeness. I need time to relearn what my emotions are and what I need emotionally. I also need to be able to feel and recognize what I am feeling while I am feeling it. I need time to accept me for me, and to be accepting, caring, and loving of my spiritual being. I am getting there, but am nowhere close to being finished.

I am so thankful Jim is my therapist. I know I frequently mistake my feelings for him. I am safe, because Jim will not allow himself or me to cross the line. He gives me the latitude to feel all I feel and be safe. He allows me to explore all I feel and be okay. If anyone else was my therapist, I do not think I would be this far, nor capable of being any more than what I was. I cannot imagine what my life would have been like without him. I owe Jim so much. I know I will never be able to repay him for the gift of myself he has given me. I only wish I could. Thank you, Jim.

My relationship with Jim was a new and wonderful experience for me. This was the first relationship which I felt was more about me than the other person. I had engaged in relationships in the past which were more about the other person than myself. I selected my relationships this way, yet I felt resentment because they were that way. In the past, I never felt what my life was about was really worthwhile, or of real interest to those around me. I would talk about my life, but not to any real depth. As I expressed my feelings regarding my relationship with Jim, I was learning how to identify, own, and express my inner feelings about both myself and someone else. My comments over time became more descriptive and emotionally-laden.

Another important aspect to this relationship was the balance it provided for my despair and negativity over my marriage. If I did not have the balance, the process of dealing with my marriage might have been more difficult. I might not have been able to identify what was lacking from my marriage, and what I wanted to help me find fulfillment within my life. Although my comments may seem repetitious I could sense the changing quality in what and how I expressed myself.

Of course, this leads me to ask you: "How do you express your emotions about the people around you? How do you describe your relationships? Do you know what you want emotionally from your spouse, friends, and children? And do you know how to let them know?"

December 24, 1996

Today I saw Jim. I read him most of the journal entry from yesterday. We talked about it for a while. He agreed I should tell my husband what is going on. He felt my husband is probably not happy in our marriage either. I came so close to talking to my husband tonight, but decided Christmas Eve was not the time to do it. I think it is only a matter of time before I say something.

Jim asked me why it is I do not have the desire to save my marriage. I told him I was wondering the same thing. I know part of the answer; it has to do with the way I feel when I am with Jim – the emotional intimacy. I don't think my husband is capable of being emotionally intimate. The rest of the answer is still unknown to me. I wish I knew. I know my husband will want to know what happened. I don't want to tell him I changed and that is it. Although I must say to a large extent it is true. I am not the same person he married almost eleven years ago. I feel I have changed so much over time and through therapy. I no longer feel comfortable with what is going on in our house. We no longer have the same philosophy in raising our daughter. What is important to me doesn't seem to be important to him. I don't feel like we are in the same life anymore. We are just cohabitating.

I know my husband still loves me by the way he looks at me. I don't want to hurt him, I don't want to put him through another divorce, but I just don't want to be here anymore. I wish I knew the entire reason why. I need to find and discover the rest of reason why.

I know the life I want now is different from the life I have. I want a life with emotion, risk, and some spontaneity. The only emotion which seems to show up in our house is anger. The only risk seems to be at what restaurant we will eat. Spontaneity seems to come as let's eat out. I feel the desire to have a life. If things are to work out here, many things will have to change.

I think I will have to ask my husband to go to therapy. I need for him to open up and learn how to communicate. I cannot exist in a life in which I get no feedback. I no longer need to live in isolation. I need to live in a life where there is give and take. I need to feel the emotions, dreams, and desires of life from the people I love. I want a multi-dimensional life.

It scares me how close I have come to giving my daughter the same life I have had. I think I will be able to give her a better life. I am on the road to emotional intimacy with her now. I know I have a lot of damage to undue during the next few years, but I think I can do it. I have already started. I am hopeful.

I need to find a way back to dealing with me. I am feeling better about me. I am much more calm. I am far less angry. I am not yet ready to give of myself, as in being a therapist, but I am hopeful I will be ready. I have become so much more patient with my daughter. I am so thankful for that. Sometimes I lose my temper with her, but it is becoming so much less frequent. I feel so much more in touch with her. I enjoy her company like I have never before. I am finally achieving the bond I have wanted all these years. When I think of her, I feel love. I like that a lot. It gives me a sense of peace. It is as it should be. At this moment I feel happy in that thought. I can smile and feel serenity.

I am so thankful I am feeling serenity more and more as time goes by. Maybe it has something to do with why I don't want to be with my husband anymore. When I am with him, I do not feel serenity I feel insecurity, agitation, and uncertainty. I wish I could find a way to convince him to go to therapy. I now realize it is Jim's sense of calmness, security, and inner peace which I find so attractive. Dr. Stephens, our family physician, exudes the same thing. Maybe that is why I do not feel I want to salvage what I have in my marriage, because I do not think my husband will ever achieve inner calmness, peace, and security. Maybe that is why he watches so much TV. I know when I was depressed, I watched a ton of TV. When I am okay, I have little desire to watch TV. Maybe that is why I wish my daughter wouldn't watch so much TV. There is so much more to life. TV is the great American distraction from life. I want to live my life, not watch someone else live theirs. I feel as though my husband is afraid to live his life, so he lives it vicariously through others. I need a man who is willing and wanting to live his own life.

I no longer want to watch life from the sidelines. I want to live my life. I enjoy school for the struggle, achievement, and stimulation. Everything I have done which is out of the ordinary I have done with my daughter. I want someone to join us, once in a while, who isn't going to resist everything.

When I think about what I want out of our marriage, I have a difficult time making it sound attainable. My desires sound so nebulous. How can I explain to him what I want from him without my sounding like a real idiot? How can I tell him his inner qualities need to be worked on for our marriage to last? He will give me a look of "yeah, right." He will think I have been reading too many psychology books. He will never understand it has nothing to do with the psychology books, but more to do with the changes taking place within me. I am returning to me, with or without him. I need to find a way of conveying what I feel without sounding like a dork. I have no idea how to do that. I just need more time.

Although my words do not convey the pain, sorrow, and confusion I was experiencing, this was one of the most difficult periods in my life. Everything I thought I had left behind was still in my own home. All the years I had spent running away from my life were just an illusion. I had only run in place. Not facing my problems and trying to flee from them only left me with them. So many times in my life I thought if I just left this situation and went to the next, everything would be different. No matter how many different jobs, houses, and living conditions I experienced, everything was still the same. I was finally becoming aware that running was not the answer, but not entirely. I had a desire to run from my marriage. Again, I thought divorce might hold the answer to my happiness. Of course it would not, I had to learn to be okay within myself. Whether or not I was married would not change my self-conception or satisfaction.

All too often, many believe they would be happy if they had a different spouse or significant other. They are tired of their marriage. They are tired of the emptiness, frustration, and lack of love. They leave their relationship for a new relationship. All too often, they find they are no happier with a new spouse or significant other. There is no one sure answer. What can be done is to learn from the relationship at hand. By asking the following questions, and truthfully answering them, a deeper insight can be gained about ourselves and our relationships: "How have I contributed to the way things are? Have I done everything for everyone else; therefore letting everyone else feel they are not needed because I will take care of it all? Or have I relinquished my personal self-worth and power to those around me?" Each of us have contributed to the unhappiness of our marriages, the trick is to find out how we have. If we cannot answer that question, then we are setting ourselves up to repeat the same mistake in our next relationship. How many times have you noticed friends or relatives get divorced, only to remarry the same person with a different face? Probably too many times.

One way I found out how I contributed to my own misery was to look at what irritated me most in my marriage. I asked myself: "How did I allow this to happen?" Not only did I consider what I did to contribute to the problem, I also considered what actions I did not take. An often overlooked action is an inaction. By not taking a stand or voicing opinions I made a statement. The unsaid statement is often the loudest. Not saying anything was the most harmful statement I made. Another question I asked was: "Am I also guilty of doing these things?" A long time ago I was told, We dislike in others what we dislike within ourselves. I thought this was probably true, but was unable to see the connection within myself. More accurately, I was unwilling to see how it applied to me. I hated the hypocrites, the liars, the subservient, the overly moral, the condescending, and the disapproving. I hated so many. As I have become better acquainted with who I am, I have found I too am a hypocrite, liar, subservient, overly moral, condescending, disapproving, and so much more. What I found was because I hated these parts of myself, I became one of the people I hated. I do not condone hypocrisy, deceitfulness, or any of the other things listed, instead I see within myself these tendencies and work to expunge them from my behaviors, and have forgiveness for others with the same afflictions.

The Doorway

One of the wonderful experiences in therapy is the feeling of making progress with the self. There is a deep sense of accomplishment and a sense of acceptance in finding out about the self. This sense of accomplishment often feels like the start of a new life or liberation from an old life.

December 26, 1996

If I hadn't found Jim, I know I would not have seen my fortieth birthday. I might not have seen my thirty-sixth. I am finding the parts of me which have lain dormant for over twenty years.

Early in my youth, I was a very patient and spiritual person. I seldom got angry. As things fell apart in my mind, I lost both my patience and my spirituality; both of which I am rediscovering. There was also a time when I wanted to go out and do things, see things, and experience things. As time progressed, that too slowly faded into the background. I can only surmise that there was a time when I had a full set of emotions. As time went on, my emotions became darker, until all that was left was anger and depression. In my youth, I had a zest and drive to pursue and achieve all that was set before me. As time progressed, even that floundered.

So, where am I now? (Again I ask.) I am at the doorway to my renewed life. I am taking the first steps from the depths and darkness of my years of depression into the light of the rest of my life. Again I am finding the patience to give, experience, and live. My spirituality is returning to the everyday moments of existence. The multi-faceted undulations of emotion are slowly returning to my veins. Not only do I now possess anger and frustration, but also happiness, joy, and serenity. I am relearning to feel the moments of my life; experience them for what they are and savor the texture and flavor of each. I am learning to let go of the anger, which once was my constant companion, and walk without its oppression. I am feeling the drive to open myself up to my life. I know I am capable of becoming a doctor and being there for my daughter. The choices will not be impossible, only to be taken one day at a time.

I stand here at the threshold. I see a life of possibility, not probability. The possibilities are infinite. The probabilities used to be whether or not I would live or die. In the future I see energy, life, and love. I envision my daughter to be free of the demon of depression. I see depression as a dark cave. As each day passes we are venturing farther and farther from the shadows and out into the light.

Jim said life is for looking for joy. I say life is serenity decorated with joy. This is my pursuit. I have never failed to achieve any goal I have sought to attain. I anticipate I will be successful in this venture as well.

When I speak with my husband, I must tell him what I have just written. I want to offer him the opportunity to come along, but he must walk with us. I will not drag him. I am not strong enough, nor do I have the desire to carry him. I must make it clear that if he becomes a burden or threatens to drag me back to the pain of depression, I will let him go.

Some would say I am making a very selfish decision. I think not. If I go back to the way my life was, I threaten the happiness and future of myself and my daughter. I cannot and will not tolerate such a loss. For the first time in my life, I know the maternal feelings of saving my child at any cost. And this is exactly what I will do. It may take until I am eighty years old to become a doctor, but I will make it happen. My daughter will not live my life; I hope and pray I can set her free.

I will bring this journal with me on Tuesday. I really want to share with Jim the beginnings of my second life. I know in the past, I have had thoughts and feelings for Jim. I now realize they were part of my healing process. Jim allowed me the safety and freedom to have those feelings so I could remember what love and desire felt like; so I could envision a more fulfilling life for both my daughter and myself. I still love him. I love him in gratitude for his strength, for helping me save my life, for being with me on this journey. Jim is right. I think we have both always known this relationship is meant to be. I know this relationship is the turning point of my life. I am not so sure what, if anything, it will mean to him. Maybe one day a long time from now we will talk about it as old and dear friends. I hope so.

One of the most rewarding aspects of therapy for the therapist is to watch, witness, and encourage the unfolding and maturing of a more healthy and contented client. In some ways, the therapist loves and nurtures the client as a parent does with a child. The love and warmth brings about growth and development. Jim had mentioned several times how good it felt to watch me progress through therapy. I hope I have the opportunity to watch, witness, and encourage a client through this process. If I am given the opportunity even once, then all of this has been worth it.

14

❖

The Bottle and the Box

Not all important issues are divulged in the beginning of therapy. Clients may not mention all the "skeletons" in the closet. Deception through omission may not be the intent; it might be that clients do not see the particular situation or problem to be as great as it later becomes evident. I found this to be the case.

Since my early twenties, I suspected I had a potential problem with my drinking. I was able to drink twice as much alcohol as anyone else I knew. I drank to forget. I drank to hide. My story was no different from many of the hundreds of thousands of stories, with one exception; I had to give up the alcohol because it became too painful. There came a point in my drinking where I would become violently ill after I stopped consuming the alcohol. The pain and nausea would last for hours. The only way I can describe the feeling is that it was as though someone was putting a pitch fork into my stomach and twisting it around.

Before I gave up the alcohol, I started drinking alone. I wanted to drink often, and sometimes I did. I wanted to drink a lot, and sometimes I did. I wanted to drink until I did not care, and sometimes I did. If I was not forced to stop, I know where my drinking would have led. I am thankful I had to stop. I did not stop craving the drink for the past fifteen years. The only difference in 1996 was that I had bought another bottle and started drinking again.

Although I still could drink only a little each time, I still drank. I began drinking again in the summer of 1996. In the beginning, I drank only after everyone was in bed, and I was alone. As time passed, and I was feeling more pain and unhappiness, I would drink with everyone in the house, without anyone knowing. After I was able to give up the bottle, I asked my husband if he knew I had the bottle or that I was drinking again. He never knew.

December 27, 1996

Despite the fact I do seem to feel better, I find I still want to drink. I drank on the 25th and 26th. I really want a drink right now. I have decided to go ahead and write this entry and see how I feel at the end. I hope I won't be in the mood for a drink then. If I am, I am not sure if I will take one or not. I probably will.

This morning, I tried to talk with my husband about what is going on with me. I outlined what I wrote in the journal entry I read to Jim (23 Dec 96) and yesterday's written entry. I told him the parts about relearning my emotions and rediscovering my "former" self. I talked about my relationship with our daughter. The interesting part came when I tried to talk about my relationship with my husband. My daughter was yelling that she was ready to get out of the tub, and after I put her off, the phone rang. I guess my discussion about our relationship was not meant to be at the time.

Knowing that, I made no attempt to rekindle the conversation tonight. I did feel so much better in telling him I am going back to the way I was before. It felt good to tell him how I felt about my daughter's growth and development. I only hope some of what I said sunk in. I am not sure. He seemed to be paying attention, but he may or may not have heard me. I will have to wait and see. Of course, he did not have a word to say.

I can't wait to see Jim. I want to read him yesterday's journal entry. I still feel the same way. That is why I am baffled as to why I want a drink. Maybe it is more out of habit than need.

I have decided to get my own safety deposit box. I will get it in my maiden name. The reason for this is what I have written in my journal is quite honest and could be painful if found and read by my husband or anyone else in my family. I can't risk it. I think I will put a clause on the box stating if I should die within one year of terminating my care with Jim or during my therapy with Jim, then he is the only person allowed into my box. If I die, I want Jim to know how I have felt for him. I am not sure why, but I just want him to know. Also, I want him to know the other half of my story. In a way, I feel he has the

right to know. I just want him to know both sides of what happened between us. It has been a very moving experience for
me. I have changed so much in some ways. I will go and get it
on Tuesday the 31st. I will place all my journals in there.

As I became more expressive, I became more apprehensive over what my
journals contained. I felt it would be painful to my husband if he read my journals. I worried my parents would read what I had written on a visit. I was not
ready to share my inner thoughts with them either. I was afraid of how they
would feel. I was afraid they would not understand my thoughts and feelings. I
was not ready to defend my feelings.

Journals are a wonderful tool in therapy and life in general. They can be both
rewarding and difficult, as well as a liability. I thought that if I wrote exactly
what I felt, I might hurt those whom I love the most. If I did not write what I felt,
I only hurt myself. The safety deposit box was the only place I felt my journals
would be safe from prying eyes and accidental glimpses..

Why have I disclosed my journals now? I have spoken with my husband and
my parents about what is written within these pages. I have hurt them with my
words, at some level, but at another, they know this is my past, and no longer my
present. Having them read these pages will hopefully result in them understanding who I am now.

15

Resolution or No

The beginning of a new year seems to offer hope and renewal. Many are accustomed to making New Year's Resolutions to lose weight, to be more forgiving, or to break an old habit. This year, I actually contemplated making a New Year's Resolution, although I was not one to indulge in this practice in the past. This year was different. I wanted to be able to say I will live, but had not yet been able to say it in good faith. Maybe a resolution would help. Then again, maybe not.

December 31, 1996

I have just had an appointment with Jim. I felt very uncomfortable during the session. At first, I really wasn't sure why. I thought maybe the subject matter was the problem; it wasn't. After thinking about it, the real issue is I am afraid of the end of our relationship. Since I am afraid for it to end, I am withdrawing from our relationship now. I am finding it increasingly difficult to be present with him. I know I have been too attached to him and our relationship.

I wish everything could be okay and over and done with. There is still work to be done. I need to find a way back to being present in therapy and in my marriage. I am not sure how to do either.

I need to find my own strength and my own desire to want. No one else can provide these things for me. It is time to quit hiding within my depression. It is time for me to walk away

114

from it and find out what the consequences are. There may be bad ones, but more than likely, it will be good. I need to let go of my negativity. I have been able to do that with many aspects of my life. I need to find the courage to want to be joyous about living.

Luckily, there have been more times during this past week in which I have enjoyed my life. I feel there is hope for me to attain a baseline state of serenity. I like the notion of my life being at a baseline of serenity, and decorated with joy. This is the true goal towards which I am working. I need to find a way to allow Jim to help me. I think I need to revisit our relationship. I know he feels my discomfort, but it is up to me to address it.

Tomorrow is the beginning of a new year. It is the beginning of a new life, if I want it. I have to want it. My life is up to me. I can keep it or throw it away. If I want to keep it, I need to make it the best life I can. Only I can make it happen, no one else.

I have never made a New Year s Resolution in the past. Right now, I have the desire to make only one. My resolution is to want to live. Within this, there is a subresolution, I will find the courage to walk away from depression.

If I can keep this resolution, then all else will come to pass. I feel so close to being able to make the commitment to myself. It is as though it is within my grasp. I just have to find the strength and courage to want to. I need to challenge myself to that end. I can and will meet the challenge. When I truly want to live, I will be able to tell depression good-bye. Then I will make all things possible for me. I want those endless possibilities available. I need to make it happen. I have the power to make it happen. I must prevail. I must want to live, and then live, I shall.

This has been a tremendous year. So much has happened; it is hard to believe. I hope the coming year will bring better things for me, my family, and all beings. I hope I will find the resolve and desire to live and put depression and suicide behind me

permanently. I am truly curious to see what the coming year
will bring.

The most telling sign of my recovery was my curiosity to see what the
coming year would bring. Even though I could not yet make the commitment to
live, I was no longer fully committed to dying either. I was somewhere in
between.

Unfortunately, there are many silent potential suicide victims out there.
Everyone probably knows at least one without even realizing it. There are so
many people who go to bed each night and pray to God to not wake up in the
morning. When asked why they seem so angry; they respond, "I woke up this
morning." This response may be literally true. It was for me, and I have met
others like myself.

Although people who live in this agony may not be actively planning their
death, there is no reason why anyone should have to exist in a life with this kind
of pain and torture. There is help. To those who contemplate suicide, I say:
"There could be a day in which you would want to wake up and look forward to
that day." Unfortunately, the silence of these passively suicidal people keep them
in hiding. If you are one, there is hope. A loving friend or therapist can help you
find a reason to wake up. I hope you will take the risk of asking for help. How
can your life get any worse than the Hell you live in now?

January 1, 1997

It is the new year. I am hopeful this year will in fact be the best
year of my life. All the possibilities are there. It will be up to
me to make it happen.

As much as I wanted to make the commitment to life yesterday, I was unable to make the New Year's Resolution. I am
not one to make promises I do not know if I can keep. Instead
of making it a resolution, I have put it as #1 on my wish list for
this year. I expect it will come about.

Several good things happened today. We were supposed to
have another couple over for dinner tonight, but they did not
show up. Why was this good? We got a great meal and a clean
house. Most importantly, I wasn't upset by it. I did not take it
as a rejection. I am surprised at my reaction. There was a time
when I would have been livid. I only hope nothing terrible
happened to them. [Nothing did.]

Today I was terribly depressed. What was so great about that? I was able to work through some feelings and come to understand some of why I feel the way I do about therapy and Jim. There is no need to rehash the feelings I have had for Jim. I think I am quite aware of the range. What I have lacked is any understanding of why it is I feel the way I do. There are some reasons for me to be attracted to him, but not enough for me to have the intensity of feelings I have for him at times. So why? I have come to the realization that not only am I afraid of termination, I am terrified to my very soul. I am also angry for letting myself become so dependent on another person, and so vulnerable. I am afraid of being alone again. I am afraid of the pain of losing this relationship. I am angry at my dependency. I know with one sentence, "You can no longer come back to therapy," he could emotionally devastate me.

Over the last few sessions I know I have had an increasingly difficult time being present during therapy. It has been frustrating for me, and I had no real clue as to why. Now I know I have been a torrent of feelings: fear, anger, terror, confusion, insecurity, and loss. I was having a difficult time because I knew there were feelings there, but I didn't know what or how to express them. I can see how I was clutching onto therapy because of the fear of being alone again, knowing I need help, and liking the feeling of comfort with Jim. I was running from therapy because I hated the dependency, vulnerability, and loss of control. I was afraid of therapy because I know it would have to end sooner or later, and I don't want those feelings of loneliness, abandonment, loss, and grief.

I need to bring up these feelings in therapy on Monday. I have to deal with them so I can get back to work on me. I know this is part of the process, but I feel I have lost so much precious time. I am not sure how emotionally charged I will be about the subject. I hope I will be able to bring my emotions into the session. I have not done it in a long time.

During the process of therapy, side issues can be distracting, but they may, in fact, be a central issue. I find it amusing now to think I was not working on myself while I was trying to sort out my desire to leave therapy. Again, I was trying to run from my life without a clear understanding as to why. Detours and distractions are not a waste of time, they can be enlightening and fruitful.

January 1, 1997 (continued)

While reading the book, *The Language of Tears*, by Jeffrey A. Kottler, Ph.D., I realized why I married my husband. A passage in the book talked about dying. I began to cry. I realized my tears were about the loss of my grandmother. It instantly brought the pain of that loss to the forefront. For whatever reason, the latch was made to the idea I married my husband because it would not hurt to lose him the way it had to lose my grandmother, Ken, and Barney. I have never really let go of all three relationships. I hope in my work with Jim I will learn to release these significant relationships, mourn their loss ,and get beyond them. In doing so, maybe I can find a way to connect with my husband. Maybe once I know I can emotionally survive the loss of a significant relationship, I will be able to form a new relationship with my husband. If nothing else, it sounds good.

I did get my own Post Box. I know it is something small, but I needed it for my own independence. I needed something strictly mine and no one else's. It feels good. I think part of my past problem is I lost myself in my family. I had no autonomy. For so many years I had something of my own, and then over the last four years I became a wife and a mother, and lost my sense of individuality. As small as it seems, I feel as though I have part of my personal identity back.

I know I write it almost every time, but I am so thankful Jim is my therapist. Although he may never know the full extent of what I have worked through on my own, he has given me the safety and latitude to explore, feel, and learn so much. He will always be a part of my life, even after therapy is over. Even if all ends up well with my husband, he will still be one of the most influential and important relationships of my life. I am glad I took the opportunity to say it to him directly. I only hope he understands and knows the depth of meaning within that comment. I am sure he does.

The positive tone of the previous passage belies the agony of the day. Throughout the day, I cried whenever alone. Every song I heard and every thought I had, brought tears to my eyes. I cried over the loss of intimacy of my relationship with Jim. I cried over the potential loss of my marriage. I cried to cry.

The transition from my depression of the day to the hopefulness of the evening was an uplifting and hope-instilling experience. This was the first time I was able to work through my depression so quickly, but it did not feel quick at the time.

During the previous session with Jim, I had told him how important our relationship was to me. Again a first. I was finally able to begin telling him how I felt about him as a person, and express my appreciation for our relationship. The importance of this step was my ability to take the risk of expressing my feelings about another person to the person. Previously, I could not even tell a person the good qualities about them I enjoyed or admired. Any disclosure was too much for me. I was making slow gains which were virtually imperceptible to me. This is true of many areas of growth throughout my life. Seldom is growth accomplished in leaps and bounds, generally it is done slowly and quietly. Each small step builds upon the last and almost suddenly, it appears great strides have been made. Not only does this describe early childhood development, it also describes development through the process of psychotherapy.

16

Holding onto Sadness and Snoopy

Many of the physical symptoms which are attended to by physicians overshadow the psychological problems at the root. When help is sought from the medical profession to have the physical symptoms treated; the emotional links which may exist are not usually examined. There are medical doctors who are aware of the mind/body relationship and take note of repeated ailments with nebulous causes. My physician, Dr. Stephens, was one such man. If not for his astute observations, I fear to guess where I might have ended up — six feet under I suppose.

I suffered from repeated physical ailments which had nebulous origins. Repeatedly, I went to Dr. Stephens seeking a cure to my problems. It took me a long time to understand my physical ailments as signs from my body that I needed to examine my life and make some changes. Now, when my body talks, I listen much more carefully.

January 2, 1997

Well, I guess my body finally had enough. Today, my migraine headaches have reappeared. If nothing else, it is a forced rest period. True, I needed one. I still have not learned to take care of myself. It is a good thing my body knows how to tell me it's had enough.

Although I have slept some, I have put my brain on vacation for the most part. I've spent my time thinking of very pleasant things. I know my thoughts are not based in reality, but it's okay. The only part of my thoughts and fantasies which resemble what I anticipate the future to be is the idea I will attain my doctorate.

At least I have not ruminated over all I need to do. This is good. I am finally able to let some of these habits go. I know what needs to be done. I don't need to constantly rehash it all the time. I think today is the first time in a long time I have spent the day thinking of things other than what I need to do. It is good for me to do that now and again.

Things are going better for me in the "being at home with the family" department. I am feeling more at ease, although not totally comfortable; that will come with time.

January 3, 1997

It seems I need to find a way to convince myself I deserve to be happy. At this point, I think I am very close to deciding I want to live, no questions asked. I think I could make the commitment if I could convince myself I deserve to be happy.

Many clients go to therapy because they wish to be happy and pine for a day when all will be glorious and beautiful. What keeps them from their goal is they might secretly believe they do not deserve to be happy. One of the therapeutic goals is to help clients realize they do not believe they deserve the lives they want. Sometimes, it takes a very long time for them to confront themselves with their own truths. Once clients truly believe they can achieve contentment in life, then the goal can be reached.

January 3, 1997 (continued)

It is sad to consider the thought that anyone, let alone myself, would ever arrive at the notion one does not deserve to be happy. Sad indeed. This battle for life and living has taken on some very strange twists and turns. I know where part of the idea gained its foothold. When I was eight or nine years old, I vividly recall a conversation I had with myself. I wanted to know why I was so unhappy; I was so sad and in so much pain. There just had to be a reason. I recall making up the story that I was sent here, to this life, so I could feel every possible hurtful feeling. After I died, I would go and help the Gods[1] understand and help those still living. I also believed once I had experienced all the different types of pain, I would then be allowed to die and tell the Gods what it is like to hurt. This story allowed me to accept the pain and hurt as my burden in life. It made it okay to feel the way I did. In a way, it allowed me to accept the idea I shouldn't be happy.

I haven't thought about this since the time I made up the story. It surprises me to think, as a child, I used this story as a way of coping with my feelings. At the time, it allowed me to survive my emotions, but what I didn't realize is that it set the foundation for a lifetime of hurt, pain, sorrow, and agony. All of which I would accept without argument.

I sit and wonder what could have helped me back then. Would I have let someone help me? Even then, I didn't trust too many people with my emotions. I thought no one believed I hurt, even then.

Making up the story also allowed me to feel special about me, in a sad way. I felt I was chosen to feel all the different kinds of hurt in this world so I could help others later. (Still looking to help others. That is my destiny)

I am saddened by this remembrance. Now I need to find a way to use it to help me to allow myself to be okay and experience happiness and joy without guilt. Is this my first step?

It sounds so foreign to hear myself tell me, "I deserve to be happy at home, work, and with myself." It sounds odd in a nice, strange sort of way. I need to tell myself this until it no longer sounds funny. I will find a way to convince myself I deserve to lead a happy and fulfilling life in which I experience serenity decorated with joy. I have never before said all this to myself until now. It has taken thirty-five years for me to realize I deserve a wonderful life. It is a liberating thought.

If I deserve to be happy, live in serenity, and enjoy each breath I take, then I can live. Also, it allows me to give up the need to die. I am no longer eight years old. I do not have to hold onto my childhood beliefs. It is my life to help others, but I can only do it in this life. Yes, I may have experienced many of the forms of emotional pain, but I must use this knowledge in this lifetime to help others. For if God be true, then God already knows each facet of human agony and doesn't need me to be a source of information. It is I who must allow myself to set myself free. I must release myself from my self-chosen duty of experiencing pain and agony. I must be the one to free myself from my own dark prison.

Go, go, go, into the world of light, for I must live a lifetime of wonder. I have kept my eyes closed to the delights of life for too many years. Let me feast upon daylight. Let me feel the joy of the breath. Let me love and be loved. Let me exist as I should in a life of serenity decorated with joy. For if this is the future to which I can look, then there is no question as to which I must choose. It is life, without question. I deserve serenity. I deserve joy. I deserve love. My life shall be in serenity, and I shall decorate it with joy.

Thank you, Jim.

With these words, I feel contentment and serenity. As though I have finally given myself permission to live.

"Permission to life," what a strange thought for me now. I do not believe anyone needs permission to live. I believe this is a God-given right. Besides, if we need permission to live, who would give it? If God, then has not permission already been given with the birth? I think so. In the end, each of us must take responsibility for allowing ourselves to live, love, and grow. No one else on this earth can do this for us. It is our responsibility; we must take it and exercise it.

I have often wondered why some feel they are less than deserving. Why did I? From where do these ideas originate? Oftentimes, it starts with someone repeatedly saying with words and actions, "You are not good enough." After hearing the words again and again, whether spoken or implied, they become believable. Given enough time the words are believed. To undo the past and become reacquainted with the true self is difficult and may be painful. Some can do it alone, but many need the help of a loving friend or therapist. It can be done.

January 6, 1997

I read through my journal for the last year. It was interesting to read my thoughts during my depressive episodes and therapy. I read things I had forgotten. Some made me smile; most brought tears to my eyes.

Jim was correct when he said I have changed. I enjoy the company of friends more. I enjoy the light of day more. I don't live in a constant state of depression any more. Slowly, I am beginning to learn how to enjoy my life. My life is starting to become enjoyable. In fact, I don't feel so old anymore. I no longer feel in my fifties. I feel somewhere in my mid-forties.

In today's session we skirted around the issue of termination. I told him I knew there would come a point of diminishing returns in our relationship. He told me my insurance company was willing to pay as long as I felt like I needed to come. I guess when an insurance company is told their client is dissociative, has major chronic depression with suicidal thoughts, they'll be a little more lenient. A lawsuit over suicide and not providing care is something they would rather avoid. The insurance people must think I am a real crack-pot. In a way, I guess they're right. Until Jim, I never knew how bad I really was; the funny thing is, neither did anyone else especially the people who should. I guess I insulated myself with emotionally challenged people.

The comfort and warmth of a deeply committed therapeutic relationship is very safe and alluring. Once experienced, it is so difficult to let go. Reasons to relinquish the relationship include: learning to live autonomously, learning how to let go of a significant relationship, learning to build new relationships to replace the one lost, and many other reasons. The pull to stay within the relationship is very strong and very real. Knowing when to depart is hard.

January 6, 1997 (continued)

I have been thinking about why I am unable to let go of my grandmother, Ken, and Barney [my beloved dog]. I think it may be a combination of two things: 1) holding onto the pain to remind myself not to let anyone else in, and 2) pain is comfortable and allows me to remember them. Sad, isn't it.

I told Jim about my coping mechanism of feeling pain for the Gods when I was eight. He thought it was so sad also.

Humans find many creative ways of reminding themselves to avoid pain and suffering. Some are productive and helpful, while others are destructive and hurtful. Unfortunately, I selected the latter. Many people do hold onto the pain in order to remind themselves how much a particular situation hurt. I was one of them. There are many other ways to remember pain, the question is whether or not the method of pain avoidance also causes one to avoid living as well. If so, we have hurt ourselves more than the pain we are trying to avoid.

January 7, 1997

I have been feeling disturbed lately, somewhere between sadness and depression. I think I am depressed, but unwilling to admit it. It would seem like a step in the wrong direction. I must realize at this point, depression will still come and go. I have many of the symptoms.

Starting last night, I have been trying to let my grandmother, Ken, and Barney go. It has been difficult to allow myself to feel the pain. I am hoping in letting them go, I will let go of the pain and more of my depression. I am hoping if I let them go, then I will allow myself to experience the closeness of a true relationship again. I think I have been keeping them around to remind myself how much it hurt when it ended; therefore, I will not to engage in relationships with an emotional twist.

I told Jim how uncomfortable I was with my dependency and vulnerability within our relationship. It felt good to say it. It was very freeing to be able to say how I felt about our relationship. I wonder just how much I can say to Jim.

I know Jim is right when he says I walk away when it gets too emotionally difficult. In fact, he asked if I was going to stay in therapy because I felt uncomfortable about my dependency and vulnerability. I wonder if my feelings for Jim are an effort to justify my leaving to avoid dealing with the dependency and vulnerability. I think so. Using this context, I think I can tell him how I feel, and maybe that will release my secrets and allow me to progress better in therapy. It is so hard to face my emotions, but I must.

Over the last few days I have been feeling very tense. I feel like I am trying to hold myself together. As if I am trying to contain myself. I am trying to figure out if that is the case, and if so, why? I think I may be trying to keep myself from feeling depressed. I say this because of my inability to sleep well, my headaches, my fatigue, and weird feelings. If I have depressive feelings they need to come out and be dealt with. It doesn't matter what Jim or anyone else thinks. I have had depression for most of my life, and it isn't going to stop cold in just four months, which is something I need to accept. I know I want my relationship with Jim to be a miracle cure so he will be pleased and so will I, but I must not fool myself either. That will only result in setbacks in the future, after I am done with therapy. So, depression, if you are there, come on out.

I was caught in a very precarious situation. I needed to release my pain from the loss of previous relationships. Yet I was trying to acknowledge my depression and challenge myself to face it, rather than trying to hide from it. This was proving to be a challenging task. How would I balance all the feelings therapy brought to the surface? There is only one way to learn, by doing it. I learned through experiencing all the emotions which bubbled to the surface and found I could survive them through experience rather than avoidance. Emotions themselves have never killed anyone; it is how they are felt, or avoided, which sometimes results in fatal choices. I found I could experience pain, agony, and pure emotional hell, and remain alive and standing.

January 8, 1997

I find it strange to say, but I fear Jim. Yes, I do. I fear becoming mundane. I fear his rejection. I fear what he thinks of me. I fear his reaction. I fear bringing my emotions to session. It strikes me as odd. At one time, I felt very comfortable with him, and now I fear so much about the relationship.

I wonder if my fears stem from having found meaning within this relationship and fear I will be hurt in the end. I think I fear the end of this relationship. I know the end will come, but I must not brood over the future, and instead enjoy the time we have left.

It had taken two and a half years, to learn how to be honest with myself about how I feel. I finally learned how to own my insecurities and examine the possible origins of my feelings. In being able to do this, I was on the path to knowing myself. In being honest with myself, I could begin to understand my fears, thus releasing the power they had over my thoughts and actions. I no longer needed to run, because I have begun to understand my fears and how to cope with them. Previously, I had only known how to run from my fears, they were not understandable, they seemed to be larger and more powerful than me. I was wrong.

January 8, 1997 (continued)

Enjoying my life now is so difficult for me. I spend far too much time elsewhere in the future. It is hard not to because it is what I am working for. I wonder how I would be if I weren't pursuing my Master's? Would I be different? I guess I won't know. I do know having a goal makes it easier for me. it takes my mind away from the here and now. However, I need to attend to the here and now.

Right now, I am feeling tired. I haven't had much sleep lately. I am feeling relieved; I have got a lot done for school. I am feeling sad, but am not sure of the cause. I have been working very hard at trying to let go of my grandmother, Ken, and Barney. I think I am making progress. I also have been fighting a low-grade depression. I have had it since New Year's Day. Instead of fighting it, maybe I should feel it and try to see what it is about. What is it saying to me? There is probably something I need to deal with. Is it my fear of my relationship with Jim?

Even now, I label my emotions. I am not finished in learning about how I feel. I do not believe I will ever completely finish learning about my emotional life. Why? Emotions are complex and influence every aspect of our lives. They can quietly influence our choices, or they can scream and yell to the point we choose to make them stop. In better understanding my emotions, I hope to better understand the choices I have made and those I have yet to make.

January 8, 1997 (continued)

I have always loved Snoopy®[2], the comic strip character created by Charles M. Schultz. I have often wondered why. I think it is because Snoopy helps me to feel young. So seldom do I feel that way. Through the funny little beagle, I find the happier part of my youth. He is the symbol of the youth I wish I could have been in touch with more. I have never realized it until now. It makes perfect sense why I love Snoopy and refuse to let him go. Why let go of the joys of my youth, especially when the pain so often dominated my existence.

In looking at the pictures of Snoopy, I realize Charles M. Schultz draws him so you know what Snoopy is feeling. Also, Snoopy is quite aware of what he feels. I bet this is another reason why I have loved Snoopy all of these years.

Snoopy is able to feel and do as he pleases. He does what it is he thinks will make him happy. If it doesn't, he is disappointed, but doesn't brood over it. He goes on to something else. Snoopy is so up front, as is; what you see is what you get. I like that and wish I were more that way.

One of my objectives in therapy is to bring my emotions to therapy and be more up front. I am tired of sitting back and wondering. I should be just as positive and proactive in my personal life as I am in my professional life.

I have been a devoted fan of the Peanuts®[3] character Snoopy. Charles M. Schultz created a wonderful character in Snoopy. I have kept my love for the funny little beagle open and above board. I have derived so much pleasure, fun, insight, and comfort from the dog with more imagination than I could possibly imagine. I am grateful to Mr. Schultz for his wonderful comic strip; Snoopy and the gang will always be a special part of my life.

❖

17

Mixed Feelings

To relearn what emotions are and how they feel is a strenuous and confusing process. It is comparable to learning a new language. The basic emotions, which are the easiest to learn, are like the basic words or phrases. Then comes the difficult part, learning the nuances, inflections, and idioms of the language. What is felt and thought can be difficult to express in this new language. Learning the language of emotions can be difficult, confusing, frustrating, and yet rewarding. Through this learning process, some may find they have confused one feeling for another and inadvertently misnamed what is felt. The rush of new emotions can be overwhelming. To learn emotions long forgotten, takes courage.

As I learned new emotions, they seemed much stronger than the emotions which were familiar; it may have had to do with the newness of the feelings. Along with learning new emotions, I also had to learn how to express them in a comprehensible manner. It took a while for me to become comfortable with how they felt and were expressed within my life.

January 9, 1997

I have come to realize that although I have been agonizing over my other relationships during the past month, I have truly neglected dealing with my relationship with Jim.

When the relationship began, I thought it would feel the same as it did with my other therapists: very distant and emotionally detached, and it would be an intellectual exercise of the talking cure. That was the relationship I had expected and was prepared for. I never imagined there would be any emotional intimacy or investment. I never thought I would wonder about the person on the other side of the couch. The safety of the relationship was not an issue for me. I thought safety meant confidentiality and nothing more. Instead, I have been ambushed by my own emotions and feelings.

At the beginning of our relationship, I found Jim to be a very comfortable person to be with and talk to. I assumed it was due to the nature of his experience. I am sure, to a large degree, it is. I didn't feel the same comfort level with my first therapist, who was a very different person.

The comfort I felt with Jim was unlike any other experience I ever had. It gave me a desire to want to open up and reveal myself to him. At the time, I never thought about the emotional consequences of doing so. I needed to connect with and divulge myself to another person with whom I felt a sense of safety, comfort, and understanding. In retrospect, I never noticed how much I wanted to feel emotionally safe with someone.

It didn't take long for me to want to please him in any way. Jim wanted me to bring my emotions to session, and I did. This was how I came to let my Personal Self take control and allow my raw emotions to take control of my life for a while. Once I realized I wanted Jim to take care of me emotionally, I was able to deal with that. What has remained is an emotional dependency, and also my vulnerability.

It is difficult for me to feel my emotions and to know what they are about. At this moment, I know I am having a depressive episode. I also know depression had been with me since New Year's Day. I have masked it with somatic symptoms and my research work. I have paid attention to the somatic symptoms and have been asking myself to deal with the depression, but find it so difficult to get in touch with what it is all about.

It has taken a week for me to realize it has a basis in my relationship with Jim. I fight to get in touch with my feelings and then sort through them. Every time I do, I am interrupted by something or someone. When I do have a few moments like now, it is difficult for me to remain focused. I find I distract myself in a hundred different ways. At least I've finally acknowledged I am having a depressive episode.

I have such mixed feelings about Jim and our relationship. On the one hand, I love the way it feels to be open and to say whatever I can bring myself to say. It's wonderful to have someone listen, seem to be interested, and care. It is such a wondrous experience to feel both my emotions and his, even though I know he doesn't intend to bring them into the session. I feel so emotionally safe and accepted by him. It's comforting and warm to feel the emotional interaction that goes on between us. He makes me feel so accepted and validated by just the way he looks at me. He doesn't have to say a word. He is able to communicate so much with just a look. His eyes tell me who he is. For those few minutes we are together, I feel as though I can be who I am without fear. Well, until a month ago.

Over the last month, I've been waging a dual battle: one I've talked to Jim about, and the other I only hinted at last session. I only told him the tip of the iceberg. I mentioned to him I feel uncomfortable with my dependency and vulnerability. He perceptively knew I had been considering leaving therapy. I wonder if he knows the extent of what I have been feeling? Somehow, I need to find the courage and strength to confront what I have been fighting subconsciously, my mixed feelings about our relationship. So what are the other feelings? As I have written previously, they are basically all based in fear of the future. Every emotionally grounded relationship I have ever had has resulted in pain for me, and I expect this one will also.

Slowly, I began to sense what this relationship had become for me. I started to withdraw. I am so afraid of Jim now. I find it difficult to be present and open in session. I have tortured myself with various thoughts in order to make it easy for me to leave Jim. On several occasions I have almost left. What has kept me in therapy is knowing that he should be able to handle how I feel. If I run from this relationship, I will be losing the one chance I have to heal myself. It has been enormously difficult for me to fight this battle. So far, sanity has prevailed, and I have not left.

As emotionally difficult as this has been, I must stay and fight for myself. I have wanted to leave because I haven't wanted to deal with all the feelings I've had about this relationship. In leaving, I would have only been left with pain and hurt; feelings I know how to suffer with. The torrent of emotions this relationship brings forth and allows is almost more than I can handle; therefore, I want to leave.

This relationship has reminded me of what life can be, but I'm afraid to live. I'm afraid to feel all the emotions life has to offer, so I fend off people who can offer all of life's emotions in an interactive way. I welcome people who only wish to pour out their lives to me. It is safe to experience emotions when they are housed in someone else's life. When the person leaves, they take their emotions with them. If the emotions belong to me, I am stuck with them. It is difficult for me to understand why I am so afraid of the way I feel. Why is it so scary for me to live? I so desperately want to live, and yet, I am so afraid. It is the same with my relationship with Jim. I want to say what I feel and how I feel, and yet I am so afraid.

I am afraid to fully experience the relationship because what I have allowed myself to feel has been so intoxicating and wonderful. I know it can't last forever, and I am afraid I will never find another person with whom I can share this kind of experience again. I don't want to experience it and enjoy it too much because it will hurt even more when it is over. I wish I could take it from the other angle. Enjoy this experience to the fullest because I may never get another chance. Why is it I can't bring myself to do that? I wish I could lose myself in the experience for awhile. Well, I did.

Once I realized what I had done, I began to run away. I have stopped running away, but am not yet going back. I feel like a lost child standing all alone and crying. Jim is standing there telling me he will help me, but I'm too afraid to let him help me. A large part of me wants to reach out and take his hand, but I'm so scared and alone. I just stand there crying. He knows I am hurt, afraid, and need help, but also knows he cannot help me unless I let him. I let him help me once before, and I hope I can allow myself to let him help me again. I must

find a way. This time, being fully aware of what I feel and not
letting the feelings confuse and sabotage our relationship.

Why shouldn't I allow myself to feel the comfort and warmth
of another person, especially a safe person like Jim? I know he
won't hurt me on purpose. I know he won't take advantage of
me in any way. I know he is committed to helping me. I know
he cares for me. He is the one perfect person to help me, and
yet I stand alone.

To question my ability to accept Jim's help may seem as though I was back
to the beginning of establishing a therapeutic relationship again. I feel I was
somewhere in the middle of my therapy. Even though I was not able to accept his
help at the time, I was aware of many of my emotions and where each of us stood
in the relationship. This is more than I could have said for myself a few months
earlier.

Relationships go through many cycles of approach and retreat, a therapeutic
relationship is no different. In fact, there are probably more cycles within a therapeutic relationship than any other type, because the client is learning about the
self, how to interact with others in a new way, and a new way of viewing the
world. All the changes can be scary and overwhelming, making the relationship
an uneasy proposition. To stay in therapy can become challenging.

If clients keep the ultimate goal of therapy in the forefront, then making the
decision to remain in therapy is easier. Leaving therapy too soon can be frustrating for both clients and therapists. Clients may feel the therapeutic experience
was less than expected, and a waste of time and money. Therapists may feel their
client was so close to reaching their goal, but left before the goal could be
achieved. The decision to terminate therapy should be made by both the client
and therapist.

January 10, 1997

Although I'm sorting out my feelings and mental images, I feel
no farther along than a few days ago. I'm trying to figure out
what to say to Jim and what is going on inside me about this
relationship.

Why do I agonize over this relationship? It is because this is a
simple relationship where so many aspects are predefined. This
relationship is simply that Jim and I will meet for 45 minutes
on a specified day at a specified time in a specified place. We
will talk about whatever I want to talk about. He will neither

tell me how to live nor pass judgement. It is up to me to put forth the effort in healing myself. There are few relationships in which an emotional bond can be established and the rules of the relationship are clearly specified and known to all parties involved. This relationship has given me the latitude to have a wide range of feelings about the relationship and Jim. No matter what feelings I have, I know Jim has encountered them before and will act appropriately. In that, I have great faith and trust.

What I want in our next session is for me to talk about our relationship openly. I want to be able to tell him as much as I can about my struggles with remaining in therapy, why I've stayed, what I hope to gain by staying, and any other thoughts which might come up. I hope over the next seven days I can sort some of this out so I can be somewhat coherent and articulate. I hate it when I cannot convey the texture and flavor of what I mean. I get so frustrated when only a part of the message gets through. Also, I would like to bring at least some of my emotions with me to session. Not only do I want him to hear what I've been through, but I also what him to feel it. The only way he'll be able to feel what I've been through is for me to have the courage to bring my feelings with me. In order to do that, I must find a way to get in touch with how I feel. On occasion I can, but it is hard to hold on to. It's like trying to catch a shadow.

I've come to understand why I've liked the song by Brian Adams, "Have You Ever Really Loved a Woman?" This song is able to stir the few positive emotions that rumble around. When I hear the song, I am able to imagine myself in a different and loving relationship with a man I can and do love. A relationship where I'm in touch with how I feel and am able to express the love I feel. The song helps me get in touch with my feelings. I guess that is why I usually have it on when I'm writing in my journal.

So, what do I know about the way I feel about my relationship with Jim?

1. I have enjoyed the emotional intimacy we have shared.

2. I feel he is a safe person with whom I can explore many issues.
3. I fear emotional intimacy because I'm afraid I will be hurt and invalidated when the relationship comes to an end.
4. Although I know the boundaries of our relationship, I still fear the pain and being invalidated.
5. In the beginning, I unknowingly allowed myself to fall into emotional intimacy without reservation.
6. Non-consciously, I realized what had happened and have tried to run from the relationship in a variety of ways.
7. I have withdrawn from our relationship.
8. I have various feelings for Jim. How I feel about him depends on what is going on with me. My feelings range from anger to respect, fear to deep affection, love to frustration.
9. Some of my feelings are driven by my desire to leave the relationship.

At this moment, I hurt. I want to explore where this feeling is coming from. I feel a sense of aloneness, but not being alone. I feel as though I stand alone in a noisy and confused world. I see other people laugh, play, cry, and hurt. It's as if I live in an invisible bubble, or maybe as an animal in a cage. Maybe the latter, because on occasion, people come by and look at me. They unload their life at my cage and then walk away. It's as if they have no realization a living, breathing, and feeling being exists within the cage. When I try to reach out for help and connectedness, all the people turn away, or cannot hear me speak. It is as if I'm talking and nothing is being said. I want to join their world of humanity, but have no idea how. I think just now I looked in a mirror in my vision. What I saw startled me. I saw my image, not as a living breathing being but rather as a statue. So proper, perfect, and unaffected by the trials and tribulations of everyday life. The people come and heap the ailments of everyday life at my feet, as an offering and a relief. It seems no matter what I say or do, they only see the statue of me. It is only when Jim is there that I feel like a living and breathing being with emotions and feelings. When our time is up, I seem to return to stone, no matter how hard I fight the spell. I wonder how I became this way?

Over the years, I have allowed people to put me on a pedestal and have worked very hard to get there when I m not viewed that way initially. It's interesting, many people I know think I'm so "perfect." I have the perfect house, life, child, and marriage. I know many people believe I m so "well-adjusted." What they don't realize is all the turmoil I live with everyday. Is this because I am truly gifted at creating the illusion of the perfect life, or is it that others want to see my life as "perfect?" Maybe it is both.

When I have hinted or even stated portions of my life are less than perfect, it seems as though no one hears what I say. If they do, it seems as though after the conversation is over, it never happened. Even when I have mentioned my suicidal thoughts, it's as if I'm talking about someone else, or I'm talking about a pair of shoes, or everything is now okay. If I hint, allude, or mention it is not, they don't want to hear it at all.

One of the most powerful revelations through the therapeutic process is the self-revelation as to how clients foster or even promote the events in life which cause them pain. There are events which are not provoked by the individual (e.g. rape, child abuse, etc.), but many events are a product of the clients interactions with the environment. If clients can learn how they contribute to what happens around them, they can then take steps to change what they do so the events are altered.

In my case, I allowed and desired others to view my life as "perfect," and it was painful for me to feel as though others did not understand or recognize my pain. Through the process of therapy, I came to realize I was the cause of my own problem. The people around me viewed me as I wanted them to see me, and when I tried to change the picture, my family and friends became uncomfortable. I cannot blame them, and I do not. I set up my own misery. I have had to learn how to dismantle it as well.

January 10, 1997 (continued)

I wonder if I shouldn't resign myself to the thought that I will be in and out of therapy for the rest of my life. Even then, it s no guarantee. Look at my experience with my previous therapists. So what now? I don't know.

By examining the way I feel emotionally and physically, I notice I am unable to get in touch with my feelings for this moment. My shoulders are tense and tight. I remember when I was most open and intimate with Jim, my shoulders were so relaxed. It s as if I'm holding myself together. I need to let go and allow myself to have the relationship I once had with Jim again. I can't force it to happen. I have to allow it to happen, but how?

The first time it happened, it was because I wanted to please Jim. This time, it has to happen because I want the relationship to happen for me. Over the next seven days, I will try to muster the courage to bring myself to the session and want the relationship Jim has to offer. I will use mental imagery to prepare myself as I do for each session, but this time, it is not for an agenda, but rather for a feeling, an openness, and a capability of connectedness. To again go to therapy and truly be present would feel so loving and warm.

Mental imagery is the process of mentally constructing a situation and imagining the process and outcome of the situation. I used mental imagery in preparing for therapy. I rehearsed everything I want to say and do in the session. I tried to imagine myself in therapy with Jim accepting his help, being present in the session, and trying to be open with what I am thinking and feeling. For me, if I can imagine how I want to be, it brings me one step closer to achieving my goals, whether it is for therapy or life in general.

January 10, 1997 (continued)

I need this relationship. No matter what the outcome is, I must accept I will be a better person than when I began. I know I am now. I must not stop the work I have begun, and cannot allow myself to regress to where I was before. I must meet and face the challenge before me. My emotional salvation is at hand. I must accept the help Jim offers me. This is one battle I cannot win alone. I need the help, support, care, and love of another human being to give me the strength. Jim has offered all this, and has shown he is not only capable, but also be able to meet the challenges I present to him. I must allow someone to help me, although I am accustomed to doing most things alone. It is time to let someone in who is safe, trustworthy, and can help me find the way. Jim is the only one who can.

For once in my life, I am begging myself to let me accept the help of another; let me take a chance again. I have my life to gain, and if I lose, I have been there before. In reality, I have everything to gain, and very little to lose. So there is no logical reason not to return to my relationship with Jim. I must allow myself to do it. He is standing there with his hand out. All I have to do is reach out and take it. If I can do it, he will be my strength, not let me drown, and will swim the journey with me.

-later-

At this moment, I feel the strength to accept Jim's help. It wasn't until today did I realize I have never before accepted anyone s help in dealing with my adult life. I must admit, there have been few offers. Oh, I take that back. I did accept Ken's help when I was at the Academy. I recall asking for help along the way, but no one seemed to take me seriously when I asked. Maybe the infrequency of the request has added to the difficulty.

Over the next few days, I need to consider the idea of accepting Jim's help and visualize taking his hand in acceptance. I need to stay away from practicing my in-session speech. I want to preserve some spontaneity. I think the less it is rehearsed, the more emotional content I'll be able to bring. I find if I allow the emotion to surface prior to the session, I cannot bring the emotion to session. It is almost like my emotional reaction is only a one time event. Once expended, it is gone. Knowing I need to keep some of my feelings from surfacing now; I hope to bring them to the surface during my session. I want to be authentic and present to show Jim I am earnest in my acceptance. I don't want to say all the right words, but have an affective state counter to what my words reveal. For once, I want my words and my deeds to be congruent.

Although I am frightened, I look forward to my next session. I want to experience emotional intimacy again for my sake, not to please Jim or anyone else. This may be the first time I am truly jumping into the lake. It's scary not knowing how deep the water is. I m just glad Jim will be with me. I can see this wait will be a long one. I hope I don't use up all my emotions now.

I am pleased I have been able to spend a great deal of time working on me today. I've needed a day like today. It's been a long time since I've been able to devote hours to the pursuit of my sanity. I am pleased with what I am accomplishing this break. I've done a lot of reading, writing, and research work. I've even spent three days in bed with a migraine. OOOHHHH lucky me!

I wish there was more work I could do on me at the moment. It's weird. It seems I can only get so far, and then I have to talk with Jim before I can get any further. I'm just relieved my insurance is willing to help me pay for this work. If they weren't, I'm not sure what I would do? Therapy has been the best thing that has ever happened for me.

January 11, 1997

In reading *The Heart of Psychotherapy*, by Dr. George Weinberg, I read about a technique which aids self-discovery. It's called the "Hunger Illusion." It asks the client to stop any habit and then see what comes forth in thought. I found this intriguing. Since I'm not currently in session, I imagined myself there and imagined stopping my habit of laughing while speaking of something quite serious. It seems my laughing allows the observer to not take me seriously and for me to avoid my own emotions. So far, the technique has not given me insight as to why I want this result. I wish I could understand this. Why am I so afraid of emotional intimacy? I know I have had painful experiences, but so has everyone else. There must be something more fundamental and basic; something associated with my youth, but what? I wish I could figure it out.

Although this technique did not work well for me in this instance, it can still be very powerful. The basic reason it did not work well is that I was not in a situation where I was actually doing the behavior of inappropriate laughing. I did, however, realize how I presented myself to others. Despite wanting to be taken seriously, I found I was not presenting myself in a manner which would let others know I was being serious.

Again, I was the root of my problem, what I was doing was directly contributing to the reaction of those around me. Even though I did not like the way I was being treated, I was the reason why others were acting as they were. I have come to realize this pattern is true in many other areas of my life. Now, when I do not like the way in which I am being treated by others, I try to examine how my behavior has contributed to their reaction.

Very often, when people do not get from others what they want most, it has everything to do with how they are interacting with other people. Instead of conveying the emotion or information they want to convey, they are actually giving an entirely different message than intended. Learning this is a very important step in changing behavior so others will better understand what is wanted from them. Without sending the correct message, others cannot know or understand what is desired.

January 12, 1997

I have been contemplating trying to make a commitment to not leave therapy. I have had the desire to leave therapy for the last six weeks. Why has it been very difficult to stay? Basically, it is the nature of the emotional intimacy which scares me. I know it seems strange; it is what I want most, and yet it terrifies me. I am full of these opposites. The closer it gets to Thursday, the more I find I am thinking of things to help me leave therapy. I cannot let myself sabotage my own healing. Thursday will be difficult, but I must stay the course.

January 15, 1997

This entry is made at the site of the dedication of Rampart Range Road. I finally took the drive to Woodland Park. I've been wanting to do this ever since I moved back to Colorado. It's been fifteen years since the last time. It is still beautiful and peaceful.

Shortly after I got to Woodland Park, I had a desperate desire to leave and go home. For a time, I wished I had gone shopping instead. After reading Dr. Weinberg's book, I decided to fight the impulse and turned around and took the planned route back. I didn't give in to the impulse.

On the drive back, I could see Pikes Peak from a different angle and it was so beautiful. Several times I stopped to just look. The view is magnificent. As I continued the drive, I was able to have fond memories of my relationship with Ken. I realized I have not let Ken, my grandmother, and Barney go, but instead I have released the pain.

There is no sense of liberation, but instead a feeling of calmness. Suddenly I no longer fear termination with Jim. Instead, I expect I will have fond memories of the times we have spent together.

I have a feeling of "okayness." Is there such a word? I feel whole, interconnected, peaceful and serene. I don't feel troubled, pressured, artificially happy or sad. I feel as though I exist in this moment. For the first time in two weeks, I don't have a terrible headache. I haven't taken any pain killers today. Also, my shoulders feel somewhat relaxed. I feel serene. When I was thinking of my daughter coming home this afternoon, I was actually looking forward to seeing her. I will be genuinely happy to see her. This is such a wonderful feeling.

I have been looking forward to seeing Jim for ten days now. I think I am finally ready to see him. If I feel this way tomorrow, I can be open and present during our session.

The only man-made sound is an occasional airplane. The air is cool and crisp. There is no scent of man on the breeze. The sun is strong and warm. The two together make a wonderful feeling. Although I feel good, I do not wish Jim to be here. I am satisfied to be alone in this moment. It is not that I no longer need him; rather, I am okay right now. I wish I could feel like this all the time. Maybe some day.

Dr. Weinberg's technique of fighting the impulse and doing something counter to what you feel you "need" to do is very interesting. I have found I have learned more about myself in doing this. I have found my nebulous fears which desire to do other things are often unfounded. I have found great joy in my life by pursuing things which I might not have previously done due to my unsupported impulses.

Of course, using good judgement as to which impulses to heed and which to ignore is paramount. Therefore, start with something small. Something which really does not matter. Then take the action which would be counter to what you would normally do. It can be liberating. I found it to be so. Some may be surprised by your actions, but do not be dismayed. This is your life; each day is offered as a chance to change the rest of your life. So why not take it?

❖

18

I Want to Die!

The expectation that healing is a smooth and continuous climb to health is far from the truth. Instead, healing travels along a bumpy path laden with set backs. The trick is to endure through the difficult times and to fight the desire to give up in the face of adversity. The process of healing the self is no different, especially when it takes a lifetime to arrive at this moment.

In fighting major depression, it is best to expect episodes of depression to return. To believe depression will completely depart, never to be seen again, could be a very painful and confusing expectation. Many people fight recurrent depression throughout their lifetime. Part of the therapy for the recurrent depressive should be in helping the client to cope with the depression and how to work through it autonomously, or with the help of a friend or relative. If you experience recurrent major depression, it is extremely important to be realistic in your expectations about the healing process. Recurrent major depression seldom walks quietly away, never to be heard from again. It can happen, but seldom does.

January 19, 1997

Today I am plagued by a feeling of depression. I am not quite sure what the depression is about. Then again, I seldom do. I only know I am having negative thoughts and difficulty in concentrating on the task at hand, even writing this journal entry.

I know I need to confront my relationship with Jim because it is so difficult for me to do. I am non-consciously doing everything possible to avoid it. No matter what happens, on the next appointment, I must confront this relationship so I can move on in therapy.

What do I mean by confronting my relationship with Jim? What I felt I had to do was to tell Jim what I thought about him and our relationship. I found it exceedingly difficult to tell him what I was thinking, in terms of our relationship. I was intensely afraid he would reject me because I was too involved in what I was doing within therapy. I was also afraid he would reject me because he did not feel the same way about our relationship. My revelations to Jim would not have been anything more than what I have written within my journal. My anxieties may sound out of proportion to what might have actually happened. I knew this at the time, but I still felt unable to speak freely.

My inability to overcome my irrational beliefs about telling the truth of my own thoughts and feelings was very basic to what I needed to work through. This was true for two reasons. First, I was not able to confront myself and Jim about how I felt about therapy, my fears and feelings consumed my thoughts and held me hostage. My fears gained power over my rational mind as long as I was unwilling to challenge myself. Second, maintaining irrational thoughts and fears despite recognizing the irrational nature of the them is a very common problem many people face in everyday life. It is often expressed as a fear of spiders, snakes, or high places. Many people function in life quite well despite their irrational fears of things which cannot harm them; but for others, these fears become paralyzing.

For me, the fears became obsessive. They seemed to take over my thoughts and actions. They would be the driving force behind what I would do over most of my time in therapy. Since Jim was unaware of most of my fears, he was not in a position to help me until quite late in therapy.

January 19, 1997 (continued)

I wonder if my current bout of depression is a mechanism which I use to avoid the confrontation about our relationship?

Sometimes I feel, at some level, I am still fragmented. I wonder about this because I do have difficulty dealing with depressive episodes, and I have thought patterns which emerge at very predictable situations in my life. I know these two times in themselves do not mean fragmentation, but rather these types of behaviors were very classic manifestations of my Personal Self fragment. I know in the face of an emotional confrontation, in which I feel fearful, I still have the desire to fragment. I have felt it previously and do feel the desire now in the face of my confrontation with Jim.

I think any time at which I risk major rejection, I feel it safer for me to fragment. That way, only part of me is rejected and the Practical Self can find a way to retain her self-esteem.

There must be a basis in emotional abuse in my past. I know physical abuse can result in dissociative episodes. I wonder about emotional abuse. What could have happened to me that would result in this reaction in my adult life? Since I spent so much time with childcare providers, I may never know what triggered my tendency to dissociate. As long as I am aware of this reaction, I should be able to maintain some control over it.

Various symptoms may be attributed to certain events in our past, but there is no definitive guidebook which states if this happens, then this will result psychologically. Sometimes, there is no tangible direct cause. Personalities and lives are so complex it was quite naive for me to think one event would lead me to react in a specific way for the rest of my life. It is possible, but usually there is an intricate web of life events and personality traits which result in adult psychological problems.

January 21, 1997

Tonight is the first time in a very long time I have felt the lethal desire to kill myself. I have been suffering from depression again, and this time it has remained for quite some time. I spend time looking at the TV when I am very depressed. Tonight I sat for 4 hours in front of the TV. When I turned it off, I had such a strong desire to kill myself. The scary part is I possess the means by which to die.

Tonight the Siren's song is so strong. It sounds so soothing, warm, and inviting to die. I have no real reason to want to die. I just do. I know all the reasons not to die. I know if I do, I will take others with me, possibly a friend who also suffers from depression. I know I threaten and jeopardize others as well. In a way, I don't care. The only two people I care about enough to stick around for are my daughter and Jim. I don't want to ruin the rest of her life, and I don't want to disappoint Jim.

I can easily envision swallowing the pills. I hope I have enough to do the job. Dr. Stephens said what I had before might have done the job; therefore, I have no reason to believe what I have wouldn't be enough.

I don't need this depressive bout. I am not stable enough to make it. I don't know why it is I think I can help anyone else, when I can barely keep myself alive. Who am I really fooling? I think the only person I would really be fooling is myself. I feel so much like Dr. Jekyll and Mr. Hyde. It is hard to believe I am the same person I was the last time I saw Jim. I was feeling so well. I could not even begin to imagine suicide, and here I am less than a week later, counting pills.

I feel like such a failure. I really thought I was making progress in defeating my depression, and now I find it isn't really true. I just want to retreat and hide from the world. Sometimes, I think if I could be alone for a long time, I would be okay. I think that is just an escapist story I tell myself. Why can't I get rid of this depression? I had done so well before. Why the serious desire to die? When is all of this going to be over? I can make it be over, but I know I would hurt so many people in doing so. This is what I need to remember. If I can't stay alive for myself, maybe I can stay alive for others. I have always been able to put others before myself. I just don't know if I can this time. All I can really say is I am glad I do not have a handgun. A gun is too simple and there is no return. I just need to hang on until Monday. I know I promised Wil I would live to see my thirty-sixth birthday, but I am ready to throw that promise away. I don't really care about my birthday, nor even tomorrow. I want it all to end.

Jim doesn't really care about me any more than any of his other clients. I am just something to do which is a little out of the ordinary. I have been a source of adventure and challenge at times, but nothing more. I have always known it to some degree, but I prefer to believe there is something more to our relationship than there really is. Why would Jim have any interest in me as a person. I am just a broken, sad, psycho case. He would no more be interested in me than he would an old one dollar bill. [I have a saying about depression. It goes like this: "Depression makes you feel like an old one dollar bill: old, worn out, and nearly worthless."]

I wish something terrible would happen and I would die as a result. Then I would not have to live another day, and not have to burden those I love with my suicide. Maybe I should go for a drive and have my accident. I have the perfect place picked out. It is so beautiful there too. No one would know the truth, only Jim would suspect. Maybe even he would not fully know the truth. All I need to do is have one good entry before the accident, then no one could say one way or the other. It sounds so inviting, something worthwhile to consider. I am afraid the only thing which might give me away is my desire for Jim to have my journal. I must consider all of this carefully. All I need to do is sound okay for a while, then it can be an accident.

I don't want to wait that long. The pills could be taken tonight and then it would be all over. No more of this. I am so tired of it all. Why wait?

I must remember there will be better days. I must remember I might be okay one day. I must remember I may be able to save the life of just one person like me. If I die, then there is no chance. I have to find a way to remember.

Until this time, I had never written a suicide note. Initially, I had not intended to write a one, but as the entry unfolded it seems this was as close as I would get to writing one. If I had killed myself, it would have been a little bit of a challenge for anyone to have read this note. I kept all my computer journal entries locked using a case sensitive password. I know passwords are made to be broken, but it would have taken a little effort.

January 21, 1997 (continued)

Jim, as you sleep this night, I hope life treats you well. I hope one day you find the love and passion you so deeply deserve. I wish you could know just how much I have appreciated all you have done for me, and I regret, through no fault of yours, it might not have been enough. If you could not have been enough to keep me here, there is no one who could have. You are the only person who has ever known me to any real degree.

You are the only person with whom I have ever been close to emotionally or truthfully. You know more about who I am than any other person. I have never felt so accepted since the death of my grandmother. Only you have brought me the chance of living and the few moments of joy I have had over the past few months. For those I thank you.

I would like to take this time to tell you, although you tried to keep yourself from our sessions, you were not as successful as you would like to have been. I know you are an ethical man with deep integrity. I know you have made your "bargain with the devil," but also remember life is far too short to short-change yourself. You have a great capacity for love and passion. I can feel it seething just beneath the surface. My message to you is to listen to the small still voice within, for its message of change may have great meaning for your life. I hope all you wish for is yours in the post positive way. I hope you are successful in your life and love. For you, I wish nothing less than the best of what life has to offer. I love you in the truest sense of the word, beyond romance ad passion, but deeply and with conviction and with certain knowledge that you are a true man in the spiritual sense.

I wish I could make my daughter understand I tried so very hard to stay. Mommies are capable of so much, but this one could not do it. I sincerely tried. If I could have stayed just for her, I would have. I love her so much and want what is best for her too. I want her to have a life which is better than mine. I feel my depression is robbing her of that every time it returns. I am so afraid I am condemning her to the same fate I have known. I don't think anyone should have to suffer what I have. I know there are far more horrible lives out there. I know what I have lived with seems like a "cake walk" to anyone else who would look at it, but what you see is not what I have lived. I cannot begin to describe my internal life, and there are no words which would begin to convey all I live with. I am so afraid my daughter will relive my agony. It is hard for me to believe I can help her, for I can't seem to help myself. I love you my daughter. I am so sorry I have let you down. I am so sorry I wasn't the mother who could have always been there for you. I am sorry I am so broken and can't find the will to remain here. You have been the light of my life these past months. I have finally realized what love is through you. I hate to say this, but love does not conquer all. Sometimes the underdog doesn't win.

My husband, I am sorry I have let you down too. I have neither been a good wife or mother. I thought I loved you when we got married, and maybe I did. I do love you as a person and my friend. I am sorry this hurts you, but I cannot lie and I am sure you will eventually know the truth. I know I burden you with raising our daughter alone, but maybe you can do a better job than I have. I wish I could have brought you the happiness you deserve. I have only failed in the most important parts of my life, being a mother and wife. I was a person who could do every performance task I truly wanted to do, but I could not put my life together. When it came to me, I just wasn't able. I am so sorry I have burdened you with my ailments, depressions, and life. I wish I knew then what I know now. I would never have married you and would have spared you from all these past eleven years.

To my folks, I hope you understand I know you did the best you could. I am not able to find the answer why I turned out like I did. The only true accomplishment of my life was perfecting the art of seeming okay. I know you will say you knew when I wasn't doing well, but I bet you didn't know I have spent most of the last fourteen years looking for ways to kill myself so no one would be traumatized and no one would know it was suicide. In the past, I had three criteria to meet for the perfect method of suicide, but that just doesn't matter any more. I am the only one to blame for this. I am not strong enough, and am too selfish to fight anymore. I know Mom thinks suicide is the most selfish thing a person could do, and yes, you are right. There comes a time when enough is enough. I have had enough. I feel it is time to call it quits, and so I go.

By the end of this entry, it is obvious I had intended to kill myself. Obviously, I did not. I cannot remember much about that night. I do remember making one last bargain with myself. The bargain was simply this, if I still felt like killing myself in two days, I would. Why two days? Then my daughter would be in school all day and my husband was scheduled to pick her up from school. I felt this would be the perfect day to finish my life. I already knew how I would do it in every detail.

I do not talk of my specific plans for suicide purposefully. I do not want to give anyone any ideas as to how to commit suicide in specific terms. I am aware the majority of people know suicide can be achieved through drug overdose; therefore, it is mentioned in general terms. I was very serious in my intentions to die. People who consider suicide and have very specific plans are at very high risk.

I never disclosed my suicidal intentions to Jim. I had a standing agreement with him that I would not tell him how suicidal I was and he would not be legally forced to hospitalize me. I had and still do have a strong need and desire to be in control of my life. I felt hospitalization would take too much control away from me. I feared myself exerting control over my environment. I felt I would successfully kill myself by any means available in the hospital. I did not question my resourcefulness.

In the passage directed to Jim, I talked about his "bargain with the devil." At the time of the writing of this passage, I did not know Jim was actually a newlywed. What he had brought to therapy were his memories of his previous marriage and its dissolution to divorce. Although he never really talked about it directly, he did bring the emotions into session. I incorrectly perceived these emotions to be part of his current marital situation. Had I known he was a newlywed, I am sure I would have wished him much the same: happiness, joy, love and serenity

❖

19

A Failure

I am a person who thinks about and analyzes many of the events of my life; my depression and suicidal thoughts were no different. In looking back on each episode, I had hoped to achieve some understanding as to their origins and any lessons I could learn from them.

Many people will push their more painful events out of sight and "under the rug." This can help for a while, but I believe there are so many lessons that can be learned from life's most painful experiences. I am not advocating searching them out, but rather use them as teaching tools. Reflect back on life's "hellish moments" and answer these questions: "What role did I play in making the situation occur? Is this a pattern of behavior I frequently repeat? Could I have changed the outcome by looking at the situation in another way? Were my beliefs accurate?" This process takes honesty, courage and strength.

January 24, 1997

Well, I did survive my last round of suicidal thoughts. I really hate those.

I know I am not ready to leave therapy because I am still fighting my depression and my self-doubt, but I have nothing to say about it other than it still exists. Maybe that is what I should say. I am tired of talking about my marriage. I know it is over. I suppose I could tell Jim that, but I think he will make some comment about things may change. Maybe he is right, but I am not holding my breath. So, will we sit and stare at each other for forty minutes? I have nothing to say. Maybe I should cancel my appointment, or maybe that is what I should talk about. It might prove to be interesting.

I have not been sleeping well lately. I think I still have a low grade depression going. It is sad I have to depend on my somatic symptoms to know what is going on with me. I guess it is because I have been out of touch with my emotions for so long; it will take a while for them to come back. It is a good thing I have come to better understand my somatic symptoms.

January 27, 1997

In rereading my journal entry of January 21, 1997, there is only one detectable theme, I felt I had failed in my life and I had to apologize. I felt I had not been a good enough patient, mother, wife, and daughter. It is sad for me to think about this. At some level I believe this and yet today, I do not. I feel I have done my best. Granted, I may not be the "best" of all those things, most of all wife, but I am suitably satisfied with what I have done, especially given the circumstances under which I was required to work. Depression is a very difficult condition under which to perform, and at this moment I am proud of what I was able to accomplish under full blown bouts of depression.

Why do I feel I am such a failure at times? I wonder. Maybe it still goes back to the early theory Jim put forth about achieving to be good enough. It must. At this moment I feel as though I have done well, and will do well in the future. So why do I feel a need to return to depression and suicidal thoughts?

I thought about my skiing experience yesterday. I took some lessons. Once I was with my instructor, I found my technique was all wrong. I had to break old habits and learn new ones. In practicing my newly learned skills, I found myself waging the physical battle of old habits versus the new ones. When I did the things I was supposed to, it felt great. I felt more in con-trol of my skiing abilities. When I slipped back into my old habits, I found I would lose my balance and sometimes fall.

How does my skiing adventure relate to my emotional well-being? My emotional ups and downs are very much like my learning new skiing techniques. When I am doing all the things emotionally I should, I feel great. When I lapse into emotional bad habits, I nearly fall and sometimes crash into depression. I think I am learning a new way of living, and it's taking some time to become accustomed to the way it feels, the way I need to live my life, and to make it permanent and automatic. I must work, believe, and continue in my therapy to make the new habits take the place of my old ones.

I love moments like this when I feel as though I am fitting pieces of my new life together. I am thankful I have a journal to document this journey. It is unfortunate I am unable to fully document the emotional aspects I have experienced. I reread various passages from the past; they lack the emotional strength, destruction, passion, and energy that I experienced at the time I wrote them. Even during the periods of greatest depression, my words do not convey my pain and agony. No one else will understand nor comprehend the intensity of all I have experienced. One way in which I can tell I am becoming more in touch with my emotions is that my entries are more and more emotionally charged. I can sense the increase in self-awareness of how I am feeling. I have not yet learned the ways in which I can express my emotional ride in words. I am sure the time will come.

Again, we talked of my marriage. Today, Jim was in the mood for me to let my marriage go. He wasn't well today. He said he was trying to get a cold or something. I think he is finally coming to realize I don't have the desire to keep my marriage together. While we were talking about my marriage, Jim took a moment and went somewhere in his mind. It was someplace painful. I wonder if it was to his own life.

January 31, 1997

I am ending the month on a good note. Emotionally, I am doing much better. I am not deeply depressed like I was on January 1, 1997. I feel good. However, I have not made any headway in my marriage. Everything is still the status quo. I am content to leave it alone.

I have asked Dr. Stephens for a new prescription for anti-depressants because I am still having somatic symptoms. I have made good progress in dealing with my depression. I think I am better able to take anti-depressants and benefit from them. I am hoping it will help temper what depressive episodes I do have and help dampen my somatic symptoms also. I will have to wait and see what he says next week.

In looking back on my journey, one of the most positive signs was my willingness to go back to taking medication. Until this time, I was highly resistant to taking medications for my depression. I suppose part of me did not want to get better nor have to admit the depth of my problem. Whatever the reasons were, it did not really matter. I did not want to take the medications, and I did not feel they accomplished their designed purpose. I am not saying anti-depressant medications do not work, quite to the contrary. Having a belief and desire to get better enhances the potency of the medications. Instead of working against the medications, I was finally ready to work with them.

❖

20

My Perfect World

One method therapists use to measure progress is how the clients overt actions are changing. When clients begin to do things in a positive manner, which they would not have attempted previously, the changes they are making are recognized and acknowledged by the therapist. There are some things clients think silly to bring up which may be the little indicators of progress. When the therapist asks, "How was your week," they really want to know. What initially seems mundane to the client may be of interest to the therapist.

February 1, 1997

Today, I took a leap of faith. I called a friend just to say hello. Even though I did not initially intend to, I told her the truth about my marriage and my depression. The more she listened, the more I said. Even now I am surprised I said as much as I did. It was nice. She didn't say anything about how great I have it, or anything like that. She listened and was caring and supportive. She was as helpful as she could be. It was nice.

It was great to have a friend again, instead of always being the friend. I think for the first time in the ten years I have known her, we finally have a mutual friendship. I haven't really had one of those since I was in high school; it has been a long time, too long.

I think I took a big step today. If someone would have asked me this morning if I would have done it, I would have said no. Sometimes, I surprise myself. I like that.

I truly believe I am finally starting to fly straight. With my overt actions over the last five weeks, I know I am finally internalizing the thoughts I have been trying to instill. I am gaining my life, possibly for the first time. Thanks, Jim. I couldn't have done it without you.

At this moment, I have a terrible headache, but I still feel calm and at ease. Even my shoulders are relaxed. I have a slight grin too. I am well and feel good.

I have so much to talk about with Jim. Right now, I am not sure what I will say first. It is all kind of a blur. I am proud of myself for finally being able to share part of myself with someone else, besides Jim. Jim was the first step, and now I am truly on the road to emotional recovery. I am able to trust again. I never thought I would really ever be able to trust anyone again. I was wrong, and I m glad I was. I wonder what will be next?

In writing this, I was surprised to see I had not written about my sessions with Jim as much as I had thought I had. In the beginning of my journal I did, but as time progressed, I wrote less about the content of the sessions as I did about what I got out of the sessions. The sessions were productive and important; I found the sessions gave me areas to explore and opened up thoughts and ideas which I had not previously considered.

February 3, 1997

I just finished an appointment with Jim. I would have to say I was the most relaxed I had ever been during a session. I also believe our session was very open and authentic, as it should have been.

After the session, I came to realize something. I am wondering if my depression was also a result of emotional and cognitive dissonance or incongruence. I wanted my life to be so perfect to everyone else; therefore I constructed a very stable and sturdy façade. Not only did I want everyone else to believe my life was perfect; I tried to believe it also. I think at some deep level, I knew all the perfection was just smoke and mirrors, and it hurt. I've had tremendous difficulty in reconciling what I want to believe with what I know is true.

Even now, it is hard to believe my marriage and life have been in as much trouble as they have been. I ignored everything and allowed myself to live in a life I wanted to believe was true. I suppose it is all a part of my dissociation. When I allowed myself to be fragmented, I could live in the part of myself which made everything look perfect, and ignore the rest. It got to the point I denied my emotional self even existed.

I think my depression was the only way my emotional self could find a way of manifesting itself. Through my depression, my emotions said, "Don't forget we exist!" I had all but abandoned them. I could not acknowledge them. The chasm between what I wanted to believe and what was true was the foundation of my emotional disturbances.

What has made things worse over the years is I have slowly forgotten how to feel. When I knew my feelings, I was able to be okay. But as I suppressed them, and eventually forgot them, I became more fragmented and depressed. I do not believe my fragmentation and depression were due to any physical or sexual abuse. I truly believe they were a result of my trying to build and maintain the façade of my perfect world.

It was a good session today. Nothing spectacular, just honest, open, and authentic. The way it should be. I look forward to our next session. Part of the reason I can no longer dwell on therapy is I am more open to being spontaneous in session. I am willing to let things come and go as they may.

21

The Devil Within

Progress during therapy may be slow, a few steps forward, a few backward, but progress can be recognized over time.

February 6, 1997

Tonight I felt my suicidal thoughts claw their way into my mind. All the way home from the university I fought the feeling and the thoughts. I knew tonight would be another challenge, but didn't know how difficult. As time wore on, the calling became stronger. As the minutes passed, I could feel my desire to die grow. When I could no longer watch another moment of TV, I turned it off. The call to die was so loud I could hear no other sound within my mind. I kept telling myself I had to fight. I had to find a way to make it through the night. I waged the battle to die or to live. I could feel the pull to call Jim. I knew I had to make the decision to live. I knew all Jim could do was put me in the hospital. I knew I would not stay, nor would I voluntarily consent to stay. I knew I must win here on my own. The desire to die was growing. I was thinking about going to my place and doing it tonight. I was really getting close to calling Jim. I was leaning against the chimney, facing the microwave, trying to muster the strength to fight the desire to die. I could feel the battle rage within my head. And then I started saying I want to live; I repeated it over and over and over. I finally admitted I wanted to live. I started weeping. Like magic the desire to die shrank away. If I allowed it to return, I think it might have. Right now, I feel so weird and light headed, as though my emotions are floating. I know they are there, but I do not know what I am feeling. I feel as though I want to tell the world I want to live. This is such a weird feeling. All I keep hearing within my mind is I want to live.

-later-

My reprieve from the battle did not last long. Again, this night, I wage the battle. Let it be that I win again.

In the end, the suicidal thoughts returned, but this passage does not indicate failure. At the time, I did see it as a small victory. Even though the feeling did not last, I was able to muster something which allowed me to want to live, even for a short time. This gave me hope for a better future. I felt if I was to suffer from suicidal thoughts for the rest of my life, there was still a chance I could conquer them alone.

February 7, 1997

Life these past few days has been a true challenge. It has not only been a challenge to stay alive, but also to remain in my Master's program. I so desperately want to escape from the life I have. It is unfortunate because there is really nothing wrong with my life. Seemingly, I have it all, all except a sound mind. I know I have a troubled mind; if I did not have the self-discipline I have, I would be dead by now. In fact, there is no doubt about it. I suppose there are greater ailments to fight than an imperfect psyche. The unfortunate part is there are no outward signs to prove there is something truly wrong. Also it is unfortunate that mental illness is still considered one of the great hideous sins of this century. Society has forgiven the lepers, but it cannot forgive the insane.

Sadly, having a mental illness is still viewed as shameful and an embarrassment. I find this troubling, not just because I live with one, but because there are so many who do, and do not seek treatment because of the stigma. The treatment of mental illness can have more benefits than just easing the pain of the afflicted. It can also reduce insurance claims for the somatic manifestations of mental illness. If western society would aspire to achieve both a sound mind and a sound body, there would be much less mental and physical suffering in this world. Also, there are those things which are not a mental illness; but are mental distresses such as: divorce, loss of a loved one, or the addition of a new family member, that could be helped through the process of psychotherapy. Frequently, people do not go and seek help because they do not want others to think they are "crazy" because they see a "Shrink." It is unfortunate so many people are needlessly suffering because of an outdated social stigma.

February 7, 1997 (continued)

I suffer from the same fate as those I want to help. Some say the only people who can truly help those afflicted are those who were afflicted. I am not sure I will ever be "cured" of my mental illness. I think it will be a life-long battle. I am just not too sure how long my life will be. At this moment I hope it will be a long one, and yet in the next moment I may be begging myself to die.

At times like this, when I can feel the curse of suicide creeping along the back of my mind it is quite painful. It is as though my mind also belongs to another. I have written of this other presence for years now. It is hard to convey the feeling of not being alone within my own mind. It is hard for me to be with myself. I know the other presence wants to destroy all that I am and have achieved. I am not yet whole. I have not yet conquered my devil within. It still lurks in the darkness. It still wishes for me to die. I feel the agony, anguish, embarrassment, failure, and inadequacy. Where do these feelings come from? I am not sure. I wish I could corner my destructive self and talk to myself. I want to know the truth about myself. I want to know the truth about why I feel the way I do. I want to know why I want to kill myself. I know it can't be possible that I want to die for no good reason. I know I can't feel inferior and inadequate for no reason. There must be a reason. There must be a source to my pain, my agony, my self-hatred, self-loathing, my death-desire. I could not have come into this world this way. I can't just be this way for no reason. There must be something or someone who must own or be the source of my agony. I want to know the truth; I have to know the truth; the truth must set my mind free. I do not deserve this life, this pain, this agony, this horror I live with almost everyday of my life when the depression comes back.

I must set myself free. I cannot live with my life like this too much longer. There is only so much Jim can do and the rest must come from somewhere else. I feel I have done all I can; I need someone else to help set me free. Please, please, please..... I need to be set free. I do not and have not deserved the hell I live with inside my head. No one else can feel the agony of self-destruction. Help me please.... someone... Isn't there someone who can help me? Why is it so quiet? Why doesn't anyone answer me?

I guess I am stuck here all alone with myself. How will I survive?

This passage is probably the one passage which comes closest to touching the agony of my mental illness. Living with a damaged mind is a very scary life. If I had had no concept of reality, I think my life would have been easier because there would not have been anything with which to compare it. Since I had times in which I was very functional both mentally and physically, this made the depressive and dissociative times more difficult. My mental illness became more and more apparent to me. Only late in my personal experience as a client in therapy, did I really acknowledge my mental illness. I thought I was fine, just a little sad now and then, or maybe under too much stress. It took a lot for me to admit my pathology inwardly, and even more for me to admit it outwardly.

22

The Offer

Throughout the therapeutic relationship, the therapist endeavors to create and maintain a therapeutic environment which feels safe for the client. The only time the therapist is sure the client feels safe and secure within the relationship is when the client is able to take risks within the relationship. What are risks? Risks are changes in the client's repertoire of behaviors and thoughts which do not adhere to the client's "old" repertoire. That is to say, when the client does something a little out of the ordinary, or is unexpected; it can be as loud as a tear or as quiet as anger. Each of us has a comfortable set of reactions and behaviors to anticipated situations. Doing something which is not part of the comfortable set is a risk.

As the successful relationship progresses, the client will try new behaviors and explore new areas of the self. Each time a risk is taken, and the client's anticipated adverse reactions are not displayed by the therapist, two things occur. First, the client comes to realize not all people will react as anticipated. Second, there are other ways of behaving or reacting to various situations.

Within the therapeutic relationship, clients might learn that the world can be a different place, and that another person can be trusted. This is no easy task. Even though the world can be an unsafe, learning to trust is a true gift in and of itself.

February 10, 1997

I saw Jim today. I talked about my depression. I mentioned I am again fragmented. I believe he was somewhat disappointed with my regression. I told him about my mentoring relationship with Rick (my prof) and how I believe our relationship has become uncomfortable since November. I think Jim has placed too great an emphasis on my change in my relationship with Rick. He asked me about it twice. What I really wanted to say was: "It is my relationship with you, Jim, which has the most effect on my life." I think it is time I force the issue and write him a letter and make us talk about our relationship. It did feel good to talk to someone about my relationship with Rick.

I believe Jim does not fully understand the torture I live with when I fight the demons of my depression. I think I will include excerpts from my journal. I feel as though Jim is not fully understanding what I am saying to him. It is as though he is no longer in touch with what is going on with me. I am disappointed. Oh well......

Today, Jim asked me what is different about my life now, in contrast to when I was doing better. There are two things. First, is the way I felt about Jim then. Also, I was able to tell Jim things that were going on currently, rather than only about things which had happened weeks before. I think this is part of the message I have to convey in my letter to him. I am not sure what I will say or how.

I also mentioned I am again thinking about leaving therapy. I have mentioned a similar theme repeatedly. He had two comments: "Do you think now is the time to make that decision?" and I hope you will continue therapy. I still do not know if I will go next week. As of right now, I do not think I will go. I will wait until the last minute to cancel the appointment. If nothing else, I suppose I should write the letter to Jim and tell him it is our relationship which has caused me turmoil and I am unable to talk with him about the current things which bother me. Maybe these two topics will give us something to talk about.

Before I left Jim's office, I left him a note offering my journal. It was an impulsive act. I wanted to give myself a chance to force the issue of our relationship, and I wanted one last chance of salvaging this relationship. Again, I feel within this relationship I can give myself a life; but as things stand now, I wonder if I am wrong.

Offering my journal to Jim was the most risky thing I could have done. My journal contained everything I had written about during the previous three years, but I had built enough strength and trust in our relationship to offer him the one thing which would reveal the rest of who I was. I was desperately trying to find my path to real healing. I thought if Jim knew the rest of me, he might find a way of helping me. I had nothing to lose; I was at the edge of living. I only had my life to gain.

I could not talk to Jim about our relationship, not because there was something strange or taboo about it. The relationship had become emotionally important to me, so the most terrifying thing I could imagine was to talk about it. I would have rather done a thousand other things, but this one thing I could not do. The imagined risks of rejection and humiliation were just too great. I knew my fears were not reasonable, but was I still too frightened to prove it to myself.

Many of the fears that maintain a "death grip" on me, were not reasonable. It did not make them any easier to manage or let go. The hope of the therapeutic relationship is to allow clients an opportunity to prove to themselves the unreasonableness of the fears and to work through them. I had hoped to do that through offering my journal.

February 11, 1997

Since Jim did not call yesterday, I assumed he did not want to read my journals. In a way I was relieved.

There was a message waiting for me on the answering machine for me to drop off my journals when convenient. Allowing Jim to read my journal will allow someone into my life to a degree that I have never experienced. No secrets will be left. I never thought I would allow another person to read what I have committed to these pages. Never. And what did I do? I volunteered them. It will be difficult to give them up. The only reason I will is because I believe this relationship will help me to learn how to truly live. I hope I am right. If not, I will know I am crazy for letting him read these pages. I wonder if he will tell me what he thinks, or will he remain silent? I shall see. The silence will be miserable.

If nothing else, he will know more of the truth about me than any other person who has ever known me. Now there's a truly scary thought. My gut reaction is I must have been crazy. In a way I suppose I was, and probably still am. I also know the reason why I did. I have not had the strength to confront the way I have felt about this relationship, and how my feelings have resulted in my separation from it. I have few, if any, secrets now.

February 13, 1997

I am going crazy! Jim probably has my journal by now, if not, he will tomorrow. It is so difficult to know he is reading all the words I have written over the last three years. I never thought anyone else would ever read them. What in the world was I thinking when I offered my journal? I must have been out of my mind! I know I have always wanted him to know the truth about me, but now I want to change my mind. I could call Ruth tomorrow and ask for them back. I know I would just regret that choice later.

I am so afraid to go to therapy on Tuesday, and yet I wish I were going tomorrow. I want to get the first meeting over with. I will be so ticked if I get there and he tells me he hasn't had a chance to read the journal yet. I don't think I can stand another week of agony.

What does Jim think about what I have written? I bet this is one of the few times he will have the opportunity to read someone else's thoughts about his therapeutic style. I did not put in too many negative comments. There are a few, but they are very mild. I wonder how he will feel when he reads I have had very strong feelings for him. I wonder if it will bother him to see this in print. I hope it doesn't make him want to discontinue being my therapist. I don't want to start over. I won't. I wonder if it will end up that there is nothing which surprises him. That is a very strong possibility. He does know me very well.

I wonder what his real motivation was to receive my offer; was it simple personal curiosity or his desire to help me? It was probably both. It must be strange to read the thoughts of someone else, especially when it concerns yourself. I wonder if he wanted to know the truth about how I felt about him. I could ask, but that would be awkward. I wonder if his knowledge of how I feel about him will affect our relationship.

Tomorrow I start back on anti-depressants. I really hate the initial side effects. I don't want to go through them again. Hopefully it won't be as bad as last time. I'll find out soon.

February 15, 1997

Every time I stop for a moment, I imagine Jim reading my journal. In my mind, I can see him turn the printed pages within the purple folder. I see him reading and rereading the passages which pertain to our sessions together and how I feel about him. These past days have been a slow and burning agony. It is embarrassing for me to know he now knows almost everything about me. Granted, there are some things I have thought about that I have not written, but all the significant thoughts are within those pages.

If when I see Jim on Tuesday, he tells me he hasn't read the journal yet, I will just scream (figuratively). I know I will say something. This has been terrible. I wonder what I was thinking to let him read my journal. There isn't anything written within these pages that is so horrendous or unfit for human eyes; it is just that everything I am, to one degree or another, is there. On the other hand, it will be a relief to know there are no more secrets from him. I wonder what his reaction will be. In some ways, I fear it. I wonder if my feelings for him will present a problem for him. Surely he has dealt with this sort of thing before.

Three more days of agony to endure until I see Jim again. I still cannot believe I let him have my journal.

February 17, 1997

Over the past week, I have been regaining attachment with my emotions. During our last session, Jim had asked me what emotions I had been ignoring. At the time I answered that I did not know; I was not lying. It was true. I had separated my emotions from my daily life; therefore, I could not assess them.

I separated my emotions so I could deal with my feelings for Jim. I thought if I could bring my feelings for Jim under control, I would be better able to help myself in therapy. It was faulty to use a destructive strategy to deal with my feelings. I thought I had worked through my feelings, instead I had separated and repressed them.

My depressive mood has lifted over the past week. I believe it is the result of reconnecting with my emotions. My level of productive work has increased, which also helped elevate my mood.

Since leaving my journal with Jim, I have been regaining my feelings and emotions. With them, my feelings for Jim have returned. At this time, I am in a quandary as to what to do. I suppose the only thing left is to talk with Jim about them. I hope Jim will help me learn how to resolve these emotions. I do not know of any nondestructive strategies to do this. I need help.

February 18, 1997

After all the agonizing and the lost nights of sleep, Jim had not looked at my journal. I should have known he would not read it without talking to me first. Today, he was much more present and much more focused on the task at hand. I must say I too was much more present and focused. I wonder if he responds directly to the mood and presence of his client? Sometimes it seems that way. He was fishing for much more insight, or so it seemed. He asked a lot of questions dealing with how and what things would mean to me.

He did make one observation no one else has mentioned to me before. He noted I am generally in control of a relationship, even though I may not be the boss. I wonder if he has tried to regulate the tempo of our relationship in order to withhold entire control of the relationship from me. I know at times when I have wanted to go in one direction, he has prevented me, and he has shoved me towards directions I did not want to go. I also know when I have wanted a particular type of response from him, he has not given it, but he did at a time when I do not expect it. Can he really be that good? I hope so; I want to believe that is so.

Jim asked me if I wanted to read passages from my journal to him. There ain't no way that is going to happen within this lifetime. I told him I could probably read things from prior to our relationship, but I couldn't read anything which pertained to our relationship or how I felt about him.

I told Jim I had been trying, for the past six to eight weeks, to talk about our relationship, but was unable. He returned the comment he felt this relationship was central to my healing process. I know he is right. I believe it, and was unable to risk verbalizing my thoughts and feelings directly to him, but it was just too difficult. That is why I offered the journal to him. I wanted him to know the truth, but could not speak the truth myself.

We talked about so many things today, not in a fluid manner, but rather haltingly. The conversations started and stopped in spurts and bursts. I felt as though I wanted to run from the room at one moment and never leave at the next.

I was finally able to verbalize some of what I have been feeling about our relationship: cost vs benefits; polarity vs the ambivalence of my feelings; discomfort vs comfort with him; fear vs familiarity with him, safety vs risk with him. Today was as close as I have come to being able to tell him what I think of our relationship and what I think of him.

I realize that to express my current feelings and emotions about another person to that person is one of the most terrifying things I have tried to do. I never knew that before.

So now, I return to the agony of waiting until next time. I wonder what will happen then. I have no way of preparing myself. Oh no..... I will have to be spontaneous. Oh dread. Oh dread. I would be okay if the topic were anything but my emotion-related issues. Help!

Neither the client nor therapist can ever be sure as to what part of therapy will be the most beneficial, or for that matter, will backfire. For me, the process of waiting for Jim to read my journal was an interesting learning experience. All my agonizing and imaginings were for naught; it was a waste of time and energy.

If asked at that time, I am sure I would have stated that I was unwilling to let go of it mentally. Learning to let go of worry is a strenuous task at best.

The second week of waiting was easier, compared to the first. I cannot say for sure why. I can only suspect I had learned something from the previous week.

28

Finally

Personal disclosure may be considered a given in psychotherapy, but for many, it can be one of the most difficult aspects of therapy. It takes courage to make the first appointment. It takes resolution to go the first appointment. It takes perseverance to stay in therapy. It takes trust, hope, and strength to honestly talk about the self in therapy.

There are different levels of disclosure, either in therapy or in any other relationship. The first and most shallow level is social disclosure. It happens every day when people tell others safe and socially-acceptable information about how busy they are, or general information about their families. This information does not uncover their vulnerabilities or personal emotional pain and is readily shared with those who are not well-known.

Friendly disclosure happens with friends, but not close friends. People share more detailed information about their lives; they speak about their relationships with other friends or people they do not know well. There is some disclosure of their vulnerabilities, but not enough to put themselves at risk.

The next level of disclosure could be described as risky and intimate, but does not allow full access to the true self; this is intimate disclosure. People talk to their close friends and dear family members about their hopes, fears, and struggles. They risk allowing others into their lives closely enough so they can be hurt, with the hope and trust they will not. On occasion trust maybe broken, and someone may feel hurt, but a true relationship requires this level of disclosure. People who relate to others in this way allow others to influence and change them. Although the risks of intimate disclosure can be great, the rewards of an emotionally intimate relationship far exceed the risk.

The deepest level of disclosure is the disclosure of the self. At this level, people allow others into the very nature of who they are and what makes then who they are. Disclosure of the self allows people to be vulnerable to deep and potentially destructive hurt and pain, as well as the joy of intimacy. In order to achieve this level of disclosure, a rarely reached level of trust must exist between both parties. The association with the other person must be genuine, authentic, and loving. Without these, full disclosure of the self is hard, if not impossible. I believe this is the level of disclosure each therapist attempts to reach with their clients. I believe this true of Jim also.

What people tell their loving partners about their true selves may or may not be earth shattering or intensely embarrassing, generally speaking it is not. Most often the deepest darkest secrets are mundane and common. What makes them secrets is ones own lack of acceptance of one's own thoughts and feelings. When people are able to bring their secrets out into the light of day, they often find, their secrets are not the degrading and humiliating ogres they fear them out to be, but rather the things which make people unique and influence how they live their lives.

February 24, 1997

I saw Jim this morning. He finally read my journal. It is a relief. I'm not exactly sure why. I think it is because there is now someone who knows me for who I am, not what I seem to be. His response is what I logically expected. He was very nice, pleasant, and complimentary too.

He said I should give up psychology and pursue journalism. If I do write professionally, it will be from the profession of psychology. At least that is how I feel for now. I would like to write a novel which takes place completely within therapy.

There is something about psychotherapy which is so interesting to me. I guess it is the journey of the self which intrigues me. There is more than that. It is also the relationship which is built around helping another person. I suppose there is the issue of how it works. Some believe healing is a result of the technique, and I suppose for some people it is. For me, I wonder if it isn't the relationship itself. How many times in one's lifetime is there a relationship built and maintained with the sole purpose of helping just one person?

This relationship has given me room to be myself without rejection. It has allowed me to learn about only myself, in spite of myself. Although I have tried, Jim has not allowed me to take care of him. This is the first relationship I can remember that isn't about me taking care of the other person. It doesn't mean I still don't try to take care of him. He just doesn't let me.

Jim and I talked about his ability to maintain himself separate from me. He felt through his experience there is therapeutic benefit in maintaining a certain distance from the client. This is not the same thing as presence. It is possible to be present with a client without revealing all emotion and without allowing the client to know "all" about the therapist.

Jim stated he had great difficulty in expressing the way he felt about me in my letting him read my journal. He said somehow words didn't seem adequate. I think I know what he means. For words seem inadequate to express my gratitude to him for all he has helped me achieve. I believe giving Jim my journal was a good idea. He now has a better understanding of who I am, how I feel about all facets of my life, and how I feel about him.

During our session today, I felt more relaxed than I ever had before. I feel I don't need to be anyone else but me. I don't have to be the person everyone else knows. I can be me; whoever that is. Maybe now I can be myself. I can find out who I am and learn to be okay with me. If I can do that, I will be a major step closer to being healthy and much farther from depression. I look forward to this day.

I feel a variety of emotions, but what they are, and from whence they come, I'm not sure. It feels good to have these emotions. I'm not as afraid to feel them as I was before. In feeling my own emotions, I feel alive; it feels good today.

I think I was right; my new direction in therapy is to be myself as much as possible. I need to say what is on my mind and forego self-censorship. I doubt there is much I could say which would bother him very much. Maybe now I'm ready to confront our relationship, especially since he already knows the truth. It is one thing to allow someone to read the truth, it is another thing to be able to speak the truth. I hope I can find the strength and self-confidence to do it next time.

-later-

Jim told me I should keep the journal. He referred to the contents as what therapy should be. I should have asked him what that meant. I guess it means all the personal struggles, insights, and reevaluations; the ebb and flow of the relationship itself, and the thoughts about who the therapist is and what the therapist is contributing. I have thought about destroying my journal, but now, it seems I won't. I will instead keep it.

Jim also mentioned he thought he should write an article entitled, "Psychotherapy Isn't for Sissies." It might be interesting for him to write that article, and for me to write an article, "I'm No Sissy." It would make a wonderful set. It might help others to reach out for help to our profession. Maybe we could pursue this thought after our therapeutic relationship is over. I think it would be wonderful.

It never seems to end. My feelings have changed again. It's amazing how the ebb and flow of our relationship molds and changes my feelings about Jim and our relationship. I feel a certain calmness and security in our relationship which I have not felt before. I suppose it comes from knowing he hasn't rejected me even after reading the journal. Also, it comes from the complete trust I have in him and our relationship. There are other feelings I have, but seem unable to pin them down and label each one. It must be part of the journey, to sort and classify feelings I've kept hidden and locked up for so long, but I cannot recognize them at the moment.

Ah! Part of what I feel is a sense of release. It is like confessing a sin. Now that someone knows who I am, virtually uncensored, there are no terrible secrets to hide. It is sad I feel my true self is synonymous with a hideous secret. Now that Jim has met the rest of me and has not left me; maybe I can be as accepting of myself as he is of me. This I need to do, and I hope it will come with time.

In reflecting upon Jim's comments, he conveyed a sense of gratitude for my allowing him to read my journal. It did seem he truly enjoyed the opportunity to find out what the journey is like from my side. I suppose this type of chance doesn't come along too often. There now seems to be a different kind of closeness between us. It seems there is a mutual sense of affection and respect; not that it wasn't there before, but now it seems different somehow. Maybe it comes from knowing I reached out to make this relationship work and help me become healthier.

After Jim had read my journal, it seemed that the ogres I had harbored among my thoughts and feelings were slain on the spot. I can no longer remember why I was so scared to allow Jim or anyone else, for that matter, to read what I had written. There were no hideous secrets or degrading thoughts, only my own thoughts, words, and feelings. In finding I could accept my thoughts, I found I could accept myself. This was something I had been striving towards. I never realized there was a connection between my accepting my own thoughts and me accepting myself. Now, in retrospect, I find it odd I had no inkling of this. I suppose this is just one of the long lessons of life and therapy.

24

Who Is in Control?

During the course of therapy, the therapist will often do what are called interventions; these are therapeutic techniques used to hopefully result in an intended goal. Sometimes they work well, other times they do not work at all. With each client it is hard to tell what will happen. Interventions can be direct, such as teaching a client a method of self-relaxation or they can be subtle, such as controlling therapy. Interventions are not introduced into therapy unless there is an intended purpose. Whether or not the intervention has been successful may not be readily apparent. On one occasion, the client may achieve insight and be awestruck by the skill of the therapist. On another occasion, the client may reject or rebuff the intended intervention, but later see benefit in what occurred. On yet another occasion, the client may miss the attempt completely. There are numerous permutations as to how the client can react to the intervention. The therapist can only wait and see.

February 25, 1997

I can't wait to see Jim again. I just want to sit and chat about my life. I m not searching for answers, I only want to share my experience with someone who's been there and who is willing to listen.

Oh yes, I forgot to mention Jim did admit to keeping control of our relationship, as best he can. He said he felt I needed to be in a relationship in which I did not possess complete control. I guess it wasn't my imagination. It is true, in many ways I have met my match. Part of the reason why I stay, is the challenge he presents to me. I desire not to conquer him, but instead to meet in parity. I respect most those whom I cannot conquer, but by whom I am challenged to the fullest. I know Jim is such a man. In his quiet, patient way he has challenged every facet of my being. He seems to know when and how to bait the trap; some I have dodged, others I have not, and some I have willingly jumped into.

How does he know me so well? No one else has. How can he? Part of it comes from my willingness to allow him to know me; the rest must come from both experience and perception.

I still have a warm, relaxed feeling from Monday's session. I am sure reaching the clinical dosage on my anti-depressant medication is helping quite a bit.

Sometimes it is hard to tell if I m making progress through therapy, but today I know I am. I am finally willing to let the meds help me deal with my symptoms. I've been able to take emotional risks with Jim. I've let go of the hurt of past relationships. I let Jim read my journal. Being less than perfect is not a horrible experience. I am more accepting of myself. My relationship with my daughter is better now than it has ever been in the past. I no longer look forward to getting away from her. I actually enjoy spending time with her. It's wonderful. I don't look at the past as wasted years, but rather as the gift of a lifetime. Today, I am enjoying my life.

When the "right" combination of therapist and client join in the battle to heal the client, there can be an almost unreal quality to the relationship. It is as though the therapist knows the client better than the client knows him/herself. The dance between the therapist and client can be soothing, tumultuous, risky, scary, and even painful, but is never intended to be destructive to the client. The client grows and learns about the self through each interaction and reflection on the interaction. The "right" combination is a gift to both the client and the therapist.

March 2, 1997

This past week has been full of positive signs that I am finally becoming Okay. I met with Jim last Monday about my journal which he had finally read. I have a previous entry in my journal concerning the visit. What I want to write about is the feeling of release I had on Monday night. I felt as though I was free of all my secrets. None of them were hideous or scary or cruel or any of that. My thoughts, worries, fears, depressions, etc. are no longer secrets. Jim's reading of my journal released the negative and restrictive power of my thoughts over me. I now know why confession for the Catholics is such a powerful tool; it frees the soul. It is not the penance that frees the soul, but rather it is sharing the burden of the wicked thoughts and deeds. It steals the power of ruminations. I now understand why it makes sense that women like to talk. Women are prone to rumination and by talking about the things they obsess about, it releases the negative power of the thoughts. I have always known catharsis is a powerful tool; now I have experienced it first hand.

Last Tuesday, during dinner, I had a fond memory of my childhood. It is the first one I can remember. My husband looked at his wrist to see what time it was and then noticed he wasn't wearing a watch. That provoked the memory of my stepfather doing the same thing and then saying: "Oh, it is a freckle past a hair; that means it is time for me to sing." Unfortunately, my stepfather is a terrible singer, and he is very loud. We all would cringe. I told my daughter this story, and she thought it was amusing. As I was relaying this story to her, I realized I felt a sense of warmth. It was a fond memory that made me smile and feel good inside. That had never happened to me before. I now understand why people like to reminisce about the past. It brings a sense of warmth, fondness, comfort, and security. It was truly an enlightening experience.

On Thursday evening, before my Ethics final, I was talking to Monica. Within the conversation I told her my fears about my marriage. She was understanding about it. She didn't try to change the way I felt, discount my feelings, or tell me I was crazy to feel the way I did. She acknowledged my feelings. I had forgotten what it was like to have a friend. It is a wonderful feeling.

Last night I was afraid. I knew I was in one of those depressive episodes in which I want to watch TV so it keeps me from facing my depression until I turn it off. At midnight, I finally found the courage to turn off the TV. Usually, the thoughts of suicide come quickly after the TV is off. I usually feel them come flooding in, slowly at first, and then they become so loud and torturing I want to die so I do not have to deal with them any more. Last night was different, the thoughts never came. I only felt the depression, nothing more. I was so relieved. I asked myself if I wanted to die, just to be sure. I did not. I wanted to live.

Last night I spent quite a while thinking. I came to the conclusion that for the first time in my life, I feel as though I am going to be okay, and I have behavioral evidence that I am changing. I have hope I will have a wonderful life. I don't need to run away from something and hope life will be better. My life will be better within the life I have now.

I need to talk to Jim about this on Wednesday. I want to personally tell him how I feel. I know he already knows, but it is about time I told him myself. I am not sure exactly what I will say, but maybe it is better that I don't know. I want my words to be from the heart. He has given me the greatest gift one person can give another, the hope of life. Maybe I will be able to give this gift to another.

There are few things more comforting than coming to the realization of getting to the point in therapy where mental health is in sight. Of course, there are those who believe there is no such thing, but I feel each of us has a definition of being okay. For me I was finally feeling it for the first time. The realization was slow and sometimes uncertain, but it was beginning to form and becoming a true reality.

March 10, 1997

After not seeing Jim for two weeks, I thought I would have had two hours worth of stuff to talk about. Instead, I barely had 30 minutes of things to say. I wonder why. In fact, I have had very little to write about in my journal. It isn't that I am all fine and dandy. On the contrary, I know I am experiencing some depressive symptoms, but luckily I am not feeling suicidal or down on myself. I just feel intensely sad and almost forlorn. It is as if I have just lost my best friend. In my mind, I wonder if maybe I haven't. I know my time with Jim is almost at an end.

I am seriously considering canceling my next appointment. I
am not completely sure why. I suspect it is my depression
encouraging me to cancel my appointment, but I am not sure.

I am so tired. All I want to do is sleep. I even took a nap this
afternoon, and I am still tired. I don't want to die, quit school,
or leave home, I just want to take a break from all that I have
to do. I am toast and burnt to a crisp. I can't afford to stop yet.
I still have so much to do.

I have noticed something interesting. The closer I have
allowed Jim to get, the farther away I have pulled myself from
him. I find when I am with him, I am unable to be emotionally or mentally present. Maybe that is why I feel like quitting
therapy. I really feel like I am not getting anything out of it,
and yet I am making strides at getting better. I really don't
understand it. Could it be I have made myself so vulnerable to
him, I deeply fear him and therefore am shutting myself off
from him? It could very well be. It would be consistent with
the way I operate. I have done that more than once. Maybe I
should write him a letter and bring it with me on my next
appointment to read to him.

The struggle to stay in therapy had to do with learning to trust and be comfortable with trusting another person. Each time I allowed Jim deeper into my
life, the more I wanted to run and hide from him. In staying within the relationship, I learned to trust more deeply. In the past, I ran away from relationships and
emotional stresses so I would not be hurt. As a result, I was not hurt, so I had no
reason to change my behaviors. With Jim, I was testing my ability to stay within
a relationship in which there was risk. Each time I decided to stay and was not
hurt, I came to realize that I did not have to run away, and that I would not always
be hurt. For me, I was learning a new way to interact with people which is part
of what psychotherapy is about.

This passage introduces the topic of Transference. Basically, transference
describes the process a client goes through in expecting the therapist to act or
behave much like significant people from the past: parents, friends, or lovers. In
placing these expectations on the therapist, the client is able to re-experience
these types of relationships with hopefully more productive and different out-
comes. Very often, clients do not perceive they are doing this until the therapist
asks them to describe significant relationships of their past.

I believe people recycle their past emotional relationships again and again
until they are able to work through the relationship in a satisfactory manner.

Therefore, I believe using transference and examining past relationships are very important parts of therapy. I spent abundant time thinking about my past relationships and how they were being replayed in my adult life. At this point in my therapeutic relationship with Jim, I was replaying the emotional attachment and loss I experienced in my youth. This is why I believed I allowed myself to become emotionally vulnerable to Jim and then tried to sever the relationship before I got hurt. Luckily, I stayed within the relationship long enough to learn that what has been does not have to occur again.

25

Self-Anger and Emotional-Fear

Over the years, I had a feeling of internal turmoil which threatened to kill me. I wanted to die for seemingly no apparent reason. Some part of me wanted to destroy my every achievement as well as my entire existence. At times, this battle made me wonder if I was "crazy." Maybe it sounds like I was, or maybe it just sounds familiar. After almost three years of psychotherapy, I finally came face-to-face with this aspect of myself. Being able to meet the rest of me, and give this part of me form and substance helped me to find a way of releasing the power it had over me. The sources for the accompanying note to the letter written to Jim on October 25, 1996 (See Chapter 3), are the selves talked about in this chapter.

March 15, 1997

I have finally found form for my other selves. It is not as though they are people in and of themselves, but rather more like parts of myself I have compartmentalized and given an element of independence from my ego being. I sense I have done this so I do not have to deal with these two entities and do not have to own or to accept that I have responsibility for them.

I have finally met Self-Anger and Emotional-Fear. They are more than emotional states; they possess distinctive qualities and attributes I can identify when I am them. No, I am not like the multiple personality people so glorified on TV or in popular reading. Self-Anger and Emotional-Fear creep quietly into and out of my daily existence, manifesting themselves in my most brutal depression and emotional withdrawals. On occasion, they can be manifested outwardly, but only rarely. Most usually they reside within my mind, laying waste to my strength, vitality, and serenity.

Self-Anger is the one who wants me to die, to destroy all I have spent my life achieving, to punish me for all I have not been to Self-Anger. What have I not been? I have not been strong enough to defend myself against the emotional battles of my life, with my parents, my friends, and Ken. I allowed them to destroy bits and pieces of who I am within. I did not fight back, instead I allowed it to occur without resistance. Self-Anger does not understand all that I did was an effort to survive and to find some element of existence. Instead, Self-Anger sees these accommodations as personal indiscretions I need to be punished for, to pay the ultimate price for, because I am not good enough and do not deserve either serenity or happiness. Self-Anger sees me as incapable of ever deserving to have the life I want. Self-Anger is vengeful, unforgiving, brutal, and hurt. Self-Anger lives in a world of pain, frustration, and rage. Self-Anger never wants me to forget I am not worthy of the acceptance, caring, and love I so desperately want for who I am, not for what I can do for others.

When I face my depression, I face Self-Anger. When I go to battle to live, I battle Self-Anger. When I win the battle, it is not a victory; it is instead a stalemate. I have not vanquished Self-Anger; I have only insured my survival another day, but I know Self-Anger is still out there, waiting for the time when I no longer have the will to fight. I feel like the prey, and Self-Anger is the hunter. I have not yet found a means of turning the tables and becoming the hunter. I want and need to become the hunter so I may defeat Self-Anger, so I can live the life I want and deserve. Until I find the means, my life will remain a battleground for survival, and I will not truly live.

And what about Emotional-Fear? Unlike Self-Anger, she is small childlike, and nearly helpless. She is the child within who cries out for help, protection, and shelter. She has been alone for so many years she feels no one knows of her existence. She stays huddled in the corner of my mind, balled up in fear of pain, agony, and destruction. She feels as though no

one cares enough to be there for her. She only wants to feel
loved, accepted, and cared for by anyone who would spare her
the time. She wonders why she has been abandoned, and
keeps hoping someone will find her and take her in. She
knows she has so much to offer. She is capable of giving so
much. She wants to give comfort, commitment, caring, and
love to anyone who will have her. She peeks out from her
hiding place, on occasion, and wonders if anyone is out there.
She dreams of the day she will peek out from under her
shielding arms and find there is someone there willing to hold
her, strengthen her, and simply love her.

I know Self-Anger and Emotional-Fear live on two sides of the
same coin, and yet they are miles apart. It is Self-Anger who
seeks to destroy Emotional-Fear, and it is from Self-Anger that
Emotional-Fear cowers and hides herself. I have struggled for
years with the nebulous feelings of what lies within my mind,
and not until now have I been able to label my pain and self-
destruction. Now that I have met them and have come to
know them better, what do I do? How and where do I find the
strength and courage to defeat Self-Anger and the compassion
and love to take care of Emotional-Fear? If I only knew. Maybe
just knowing them will help me find the way.

Just knowing did help me find the way. I did not do anything to integrate or
master Self-Anger and Emotional-Fear. Once they became known, their ability
to drive my life and thoughts quickly began to diminish. I suppose I could compare it to the common story of the young child who fears the closet after dark.
The child imagines horrendous monsters and creatures which threaten to devour
the child with the turn of a doorknob. It is not until the child summons the
courage to actually look in the darkened closet that the truth is known; it is
simply a dark closet. For me, my self-derogation was simply self-derogation.
Once I found the source of my self-destruction, it once again became only self-
derogation; it was no longer the horrendous monster or creature lurking through
the back halls of my mind. This moment was a major victory. This journal entry
gave me freedom, and it gave me a chance to meet myself face-to-face without
being paralyzed by fear.

26

❖

As with Chapter Eleven (The Lull), this period of therapy had a quiet and sedentary quality. There is evidence of progress within these passages, but there does not seem to be any great leaps of insight, only slow plodding progress. I have maintained these passages to provide a more full picture of what therapy can be like. My intent is not to sensationalize psychotherapy, but to provide an honest and authentic picture. As with all things, both the "ups" and "downs" must be endured.

March 17, 1997

Jim is so real, vibrant, and focused. I know this is only how I see him in therapy, yet I know he is to a great extent this way within his own life. When I am with him, there seems to be so much give and take between us. In our relationship I feel he supports me, yet somehow, I know there is something I give back to him. What it is, I am not yet sure, but our relationship has reciprocity.

Today I spoke openly about my fears of being present with him. I think during today's session, I was far more present than I have been in a long time. I did read him my last passage. We didn't talk too much about it.

It seems as though Jim rewards me for my presence and openness by sharing parts of himself and his life with me. He knows I have an intense curiosity about who he really is, and I think he uses my interest as a way of reinforcing my openness. I also believe he wants me to know him.

There is something so powerful about this relationship. I cannot put my feelings into words. There seems to be a connection between us that is not readily apparent, yet makes itself known with such delicate subtlety. I know he feels this connection also.

I wanted to know Jim outside of therapy which is not an uncommon desire. Although what therapists brings to therapy is a part of themselves, the rest of the person may not be what clients imagine. Clients can easily lionize the person on the other side of the "couch." Therapists may seem so intelligent with so many insights and answers and may seem to have perfect lives. Clients often assume their therapists to be "perfect," otherwise how could they be therapists?

In reality, therapists' life may not be what the clients have imagined. This is neither good or bad. What counts is if the therapist is "okay" enough to be present, authentic, and loving enough to help the client heal. Clients who might meet their therapists out in the "real" world, may find them to be mortal human beings. For some clients, this is shocking and horrible. For other clients, it can be helpful. Many therapists have imperfect lives too.

March 18, 1997

I am very relieved I feel as though I am making progress toward a more healthy self. Not only do I feel I am, my behavioral actions seem to agree. Jim's comments seem to mirror these same thoughts. He feels I am more integrated and open. He is no longer overly concerned about my suicidal thoughts nor my dissociative tendencies. He also thinks I am making progress; it is good to hear it from him.

With Jim I feel a sense of certainty, comfort, and familiarity that is beyond words. I feel a gentle strength from him in which I take great comfort. I feel he knows me better than any other person in this world, and that is true. I feel he accepts me and cares for me.

So often, I feel emotionally lonely and isolated. The only time I feel in touch with humanity is with my daughter and with Jim. He has come to mean so much to me. I cannot imagine ever truly letting him go from my life. I will be so alone without him. I do not want to know what my life would be like without him.

There is a subtle and slow transition in how I expressed myself which is evident in each chapter. In the early chapters, the journal consisted of descriptions of events, mostly therapy. In the later journal entries I did not write much of what happened in therapy, instead I write more about how and what I felt.

This shows another way in which my growth occurred. Many in today's society are emotionally challenged. These people can discuss many things of this world, but they are stumped and left speechless when asked how they feel. I would not dare call myself emotionally gifted at this point in my life, I am still growing and heading toward that goal. However, I have come a long way from where I started.

❖

27

Dream of Love

Throughout my life, I have always been a vivid dreamer, in my sleep. In my waking life, I am more of a realist. Because my dreams have been so vivid and dynamic, I have often given them a lot of thought. I wonder about their source and meaning. Many dreams I forget, others I remember for a lifetime. I have found some dreams seem to bring a lesson or message to my life. At the time of the dream, the messages may not be readily apparent. Sometimes I do not see the significance of the dream until many years later.

March 21, 1997

The other day, I thought about a dream I had when I was sixteen which is as clear as if I had dreamt it just last night. The feelings I had in the dream were so real. I still felt them the next day, and even today. In the dream, I went to an island resort with the man I loved with all of my heart and soul. We walked along the beach; it was a small cove where the water was warm and the sand was soft. The island was small and intimate. The resort was on a hill. It was painted white, reminiscent of Greek homes on a hillside. The grass ran from the resort to the edge of the sand. As the man and I walked along the beach we were holding hands. I remember the feeling of love I had for him. I remember turning to kiss him. I couldn't see his face, but our kiss was so passionate and loving. I remember the kiss as though it really happened. I have remembered the dream for the past twenty years. I never want to forget it, because the feeling of love was so deep and intimate. I was with the love of my life. I only wish I could have seen his face, then I would know who the man was. Maybe I will tell Jim about the dream and see what he says.

In session, I mentioned an article I had read about passion and stability in long term relationships. I told Jim the basic premise of the article, which was that long term relationships have stability, but not great passion, and that passionate relationships are short-lived. I asked Jim what he thought. I thought if he agreed with the article it might make it easier for me to accept my marriage as it is. Instead he disagreed right away. He became kind of misty, almost nebulous for just an instant. I think he knew the answer I wanted to hear in order to preserve my marriage, and yet he gave me just the opposite. His response made staying married just that much harder. Every time I come within a breath of making the commitment to stay, Jim goes and says something to disrupt it all. I don't want to leave for all the wrong reasons, but I don't want to stay for all the wrong reasons either. I just don't know what to do.

Jim said what he did for two reasons. First, he actually believed what he said. Second, he did not want me to settle into my marriage for all the wrong reasons. He did not want me to become lazy and stay just to stay. He wanted me to challenge myself to either stay because I wanted to, or go because I needed to.

March 28, 1997

I just got back from a pleasant vacation. The one thing I liked the best was doing nothing and not feeling guilty. The most difficult part of the trip was the distance between my husband and me. We were miles apart even though we rode in the same vehicle. Until the ride home, he just wasn't on the trip. He may have been there, but didn't seem to enjoy the trip very much. On the way home, things were much better. I had a small glimmer of hope. Maybe things might work out, but I'm not sure.

March 30, 1997

I have an appointment with Jim tomorrow, but I really don't have anything to say. I am thinking about talking about my dream of the island. I suppose we will talk about my vacation too. Things seem to be okay, but I know I still have things to work on, but what do I work on now? I know I am far from being where I would like to be emotionally.

I keep thinking about the way I felt in my dream. I want to feel that way in real life. Is it really possible to feel that way, or is such passion only a part of my dream? I have had great difficulty in describing how I felt in the dream. So I will try here. Obviously I was in love with the man in the dream, but it was more. I felt a connectedness, comfort, familiarity, strength, and deep emotional trust with him. I felt so secure in the relationship, it was as though I knew it would last beyond a lifetime. I felt a warmth and love beyond anything I have ever felt in my life since then. The feeling of love seemed to permeate all of my being. There was a depth of feeling which ran through to the core of who I am. Although we shared a sense of connectedness, we remained separate and individual. We did not lose ourselves in each other, instead we were strengthened through our relationship. We did not need to cling to each other, instead we stood together. Again, my words are inadequate.

If I actually thought it were possible to feel that way, I would be so tempted to give up my marriage. I don't know if what I felt is possible, or if it was only a dream? Even though I had the dream almost twenty years ago, I can still remember how I felt. I want to feel that way with a real man. I just wish it could be with my husband.

March 31, 1997

This morning I saw Jim. I don't know why I worry about having nothing to talk about. We talked about my vacation, my dream and the feelings associated with it, my relationship with my daughter, and what I am going to do about my marriage. Today, Jim seemed to accept whatever I said about to my marriage and my future plans. In the past, I have frequently felt he had a definite feeling about what I should do; today I sensed a difference in his feelings, but I can't put my finger on it. The more I talked about what I am going to do about my marriage, the more it sounded as though I have decided to get divorced.

Before I left the session today, Jim told me how well he felt I was doing. He said I seemed so solid. He also commented about how I am changing the things I am doing in my life to make my life better. I told him I felt well. He thought my self-esteem was on the rise because of the way I am treating myself and the things I am doing for myself. I was so pleased to hear he has noticed. I told him I don't get angry like I used to.

I also told Jim I thought I finally have a chance at love within my life. In shock, Jim asked me if there was anyone else in my life. I responded I would never do that. I would get a divorce before having an affair. What I meant had to do with the way I felt about myself: "I am an acceptable human being."

On the way home, I realized I haven't thought of suicide in at least a week and a half. That is such a big deal for me. I need to remember to mention it when I see him next week. I know it will really please him.

Over the last week and a half, I have been doing very well. I feel centered and grounded. Although I am still under a lot of stress, it isn't getting the best of me. I am far more calm than I have been since I can remember. I don't feel the ache of depression just around the corner. I am as close to feeling serenity for a long period of time as I have ever been. I owe Jim so much.

As I look back over my journal entries, I feel this set of entries shows how mentally healthy I was becoming. For the first time in years, I was able to exist without suicidal thoughts as a permanent part of my existence. I had grown to love myself enough to allow myself to believe another person would find me acceptable. Finally, I was able to imagine and want a life of love and emotional intimacy. I was becoming the person I dreamed of being: non-suicidal, self-accepting, self-loving, open to love from others, and able to truly love others.

❖

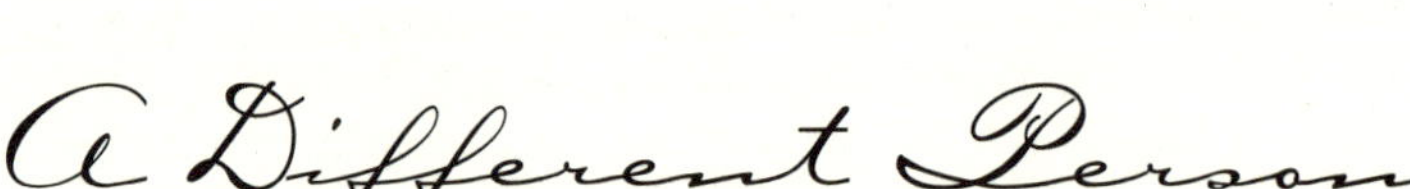

28

A Different Person

Experiencing and feeling personal growth brings a warm and satisfying feeling of accomplishment. I wonder if this is how I felt as an infant when I first learned to walk, the powerful sense of growing independence, autonomy, and development.

Some believe human growth and development stop sometime in adulthood, but I assert that it never really stops. If personal growth and development stop, then I suggest that living stops, not that physical death occurs, but rather the experiencing of life ceases.

April 2, 1997

In a very real sense, I feel my life changing right before my eyes. I know this sounds very strange, but I have a difficult time putting into words what I am feeling. As each day goes by, I feel as though I am becoming a different person. I feel more centered, self-confident, worthy, and serene. Within all of that, I feel as though I am also adopting a new view on things. I know I have always said, What is intended in life, is a product of what we do, what we expect, and what is intended. I feel I am listening to what I am feeling more than ever before. I think that is why I am having difficulty saving my marriage, because it is not something I want to do. I know I "ought" to try, but I don't want to.

For the first time, I think I am actually living my own life. I don't feel as compelled to do everything that ought to be done. I find I am doing more what I want to do and feel is right, and not what I think everyone else will think is right. After all these years, maybe I am finally finding out who I am and what I want. This time, I think it is for real. It is okay if I can't have everything I want, but it is satisfying to know and recognize there is something I want. Over the last five months, I have gone from denying my feelings for Jim, to hating the way I felt, to recognizing my feelings, to admitting I have them, and not feeling guilty. I am okay with the way I feel. They are my feelings, that is what is most important. It is what I want, I don't feel I have to please my mom, dad, husband, friends, daughter, or anyone else. I own these feelings, they are mine and only mine. They are not what I ought to or should feel, only what I do feel. In a very real way, that is totally okay.

It has taken me six years, but I am finally finding a real and true relationship with my daughter. Not one I thought I should have, or what I perceive other people have with their children, but my very own relationship. Through this, I have seen a change in my daughter. She clings to me less often. She is more emotionally independent. I find we don't argue as much. She is becoming a fine young person. I am very proud of what she does and what she accomplishes. I find I am angry with my husband when he does not recognize and praise her for who she is, and instead tells her who she is not.

In my husband, I see my past walking within my house and through my life. I am trying to leave my past, and in doing so, I have realized my relationship with my husband is a re-creation of my past relationships. If I want to free my daughter of the specter of not being good enough, must I leave my husband? I know he truly wants the best for her. He is willing to do some of the work, but does not want to take the responsibility for her. He tells her who she is not, but not how good she really is. I can't stand to listen when he does that. That is how I felt all my life. Such scrutiny laid the foundations of my perfectionism and striving to excel at everything I do, but it laid the very foundation of my pathology. I truly believe happy mediocrity is far better than suicidal excellence. No one should have to live my life, least of all my daughter. It would kill me if I ever found out she has lived any part of my pathology. I know genetically she is prone, but I do not need to foster any environmental factors which will cause depres-

sion or any mental illness to manifest itself in her. Oh God,
please spare her; my daughter does not deserve the pain,
agony, and despair I have lived. I love her too much. Please
spare her, please. If I have only one wish for my life, this is it.

As time has passed, I have come to believe, more and more in what I had
written about happy mediocrity being far better than suicidal excellence. I have
said this to others whom I felt might benefit from this thought. Of course, they
may initially reject this observation, but I hope they come to fully realize the
accuracy of what I have said.

April 2, 1997 (continued)

When I look back over the years, I am so surprised I have
actually made it this far. I am astonished to be alive. I am very
proud of myself. I am amazed how far I have come in my
healing. The last two weeks have been the longest period in
the last fourteen years I have gone without thinking about
killing myself. I noticed this a day or two ago, and I have been
enjoying the feeling. It feels great to drive down the road and
just drive. It feels good to let my mind wonder off, and not go
to suicide. I am not afraid of my thoughts like I used to be.
They no longer wield the negative power they once had. I am
not afraid of that dark place, self-anger, like I used to be. In
fact, I think self-anger is almost gone.

No longer do I capitalize self-anger. I had finally let self-anger return to a
feeling, rather than keep it as an entity within me. As subtle as this may seem,
this was an indication that I was an integrated person. Integration does not mean
I might not attempt to fragment at a later date; it only means I was whole at that
time. Emotional challenges came after my therapy with Jim terminated. I had the
desire to fragment, but I found the emotional strength to resist that desire and to
face what needed to be done.

April 2, 1997 (continued)

For the first time in my life, I feel as though I am good enough.
I don't have anything to prove anymore. I am okay. Tonight is
the first time since graduation from college fourteen years ago
that I have cried for joy. It feels wonderful!

Over these past months, I have cried many tears, mostly due to sadness, loss, anguish, pain, and desperation. To cry tears of joy was an experience I had almost forgotten. With my own growth I have wondered about tears, so I turned to a book entitled, *The Language of Tears*, by Jeffrey A. Kottler, Ph.D. Dr. Kottler describes the importance tears have in the expression of a multitude of emotions, not just sadness. He has learned how to use tears to help him understand his clients and himself. In a response to tears, he asks, "How are your tears trying to be helpful?" My tears have helped me understand my emotions.

❖

29

Beginning of the End

Over the past few chapters, I have omitted entries about my marriage. I did not do this because my marriage was any better than it had been, on the contrary, it was slowly dissolving before my eyes. I omitted the entries because I did not feel they added to the texture and feel of my therapeutic relationship with Jim. Although I am discussing much of my life with you, I want to share my therapy process, not just my marital problems.

April 4, 1997

Today I got my first paying job in psychology. I was so excited. Rick called and asked me if I would do another assessment. It isn't for Alzheimer's; this time it is a personality assessment. Rick said this time I would get paid. After I got off the phone I told my daughter, and we were both so excited. I thought I would share the good news with my husband.

I called my husband and told him about my first paying job, and he sounded like it was no big deal. He didn't even say congratulations. Even my daughter was more excited than he was. She was really thrilled. I felt very disappointed at my husband's reaction. Employment was something I had been working towards for the last three years. I finally took one of my first steps and he acted like he didn't care. I asked him if there was something wrong, and he just said he was working on something. As each day passes, we drift farther and farther apart.

I talked with my mom last night. I told her about our vacation. She asked me if we had a good time. I told her my daughter and I had a great time. She asked me about my husband; I told her I didn't know. She asked me what he did. I said he watched TV and read some magazines. To be honest, I really have no idea if he had a good time or not. I don't think he enjoyed the trip. Later, mom asked me if my husband and I are having the same experience she and dad had. She wanted to know if my husband and I had difficulty communicating. I was honest and told her we had the problem before I started back to school, and he and I have talked about our marital problems a few times.

I think this is the first time I have ever honestly talked about my husband to my mom. I wonder what she thought about the conversation. I suppose over the next year, she will come to realize I am having serious problems with my marriage. I hope she also comes to realize they have been developing for a very long time.

I have to work on my remaining difficult issues relatively quickly. When my husband and I are divorced, I will not be able to afford therapy. I also have to tell Jim so he will understand. If nothing else, it will force me to deal with my marriage and depression and terminate therapy whether I want to or not.

Very often, the length of therapy is not governed by the client or even the therapist, but rather by the managed care administrators. Another source of control over the length of therapy is the client's own financial status. Many clients are now choosing to pay for psychotherapy "out of pocket." If the client pays for the therapy, only the client and therapist determine the length of therapy; the diagnosis and content of therapy remains confidential, as it was originally intended. If the insurance company pays, then they have rights to certain types of information regarding therapy.

Paying for psychotherapy without insurance reimbursement can be very expensive. Some therapists use what is called a "sliding scale" fee format, which means they will charge what the client can most appropriately afford. Since not all therapists do this, it is important to ask about payment options prior to making the first appointment.

April 6, 1997

Last night, once again, I could not sleep. I am tired now, but not terribly so. Today, I have thought a lot about my termination of therapy. I am doing so much better. I am wondering if maybe I shouldn't start putting some distance between myself and Jim. I have wondered if my feelings for Jim stem from the thought he is akin to my future. In him, I see a Ph.D. and what I want for myself professionally. In him, I see emotional connectedness and acknowledgment. In him, I see purposefulness, certainty, empathy, and strength. In him, I see all I want for myself today and throughout my tomorrows.

In my husband, I see none of these things. In him, I see an uncertain future. In him, I see procrastination, indecision, and abdication of responsibility. In him, I see emotional withdrawal, disconnectedness, and reservation. In him, I see isolation, apprehension, and distance. In him, I see aloofness, defensiveness, and subtle sadness. He allows me to do just about anything I want. He does have a charming sense of humor at times, but he generally keeps it in a drawer somewhere. I fully realize he has been hurt in marriage twice before, but I think it is time he does something about it, or lose his third marriage.

Today, I had an appointment with Jim. It was nice to tell him all the positive things that have been happening within my life. I really wanted the opportunity to share with him the good times, and not just the bad times. He seemed genuinely happy and pleased at the progress I am making. I told him for the first time, I was honest with my mom about my marriage. I didn't try to hide my problems by avoiding them. Jim thought it was wonderful that I was able to be more authentic with my mother.

I told Jim I felt I was truly losing the "oughts" and "shoulds" of my life. I told him I turned down a job with the Department of Corrections which I probably would have taken earlier because it was something I "should" do, but I chose what I felt was the right thing for me to do right now.

The conversation reminded me of what happened last Friday, concerning my husband's reaction to my first paying job in psychology. After I described what my husband had said and his reaction, I told Jim: "I can't imagine spending the rest of my life like that!" It was at that moment I voiced my gut level reaction to my marriage in such a way I knew I would probably get a divorce. Jim then said, "That is the real question." Jim seemed genuinely disappointed that my husband had the reaction he did. After I described my husband a little more, he said: "He sounds emotionally detached, maybe that is what brought the two of you together." This was my own conclusion.

I told Jim I thought there was only a ten percent chance I would be married two years from now. I also said I still needed to talk to my husband again and make sure there is nothing we can do to salvage what we have. I told Jim I needed to be sure I had exhausted the last ten percent before I could go through with a divorce. Jim then said it was important to make sure I had done everything I could before I let the marriage go. When he said that, he looked down at his hands with a saddened expression. He seems to thoroughly understand the turmoil and pain I am feeling. I let Jim know before I get divorced, I need to be sure I am through with my work with him. I let him know I could not afford him without my husband's insurance. He did not say much.

Before I left we talked about how well I am doing. He said my healing was purely a result of my courage of working through all the issues and staying the course. I then brought up that I need to start thinking about termination. As I looked him in the eye, I told him, "Leaving this relationship will be very difficult for me to do." We then both continued to look at each other for maybe a half second, just long enough for tears to form in my eyes, but not fall. I could see in his eyes he was not looking forward to our termination either. He then said we had more work to do, and even if I filed for divorce tomorrow, it would take about a year to get through. In that brief moment there was so much emotion, connection, and unspoken words. In the briefest instant we exchanged so much, but said absolutely nothing.

The end of a wonderful relationship has to be one of the most anguishing experiences in life. I entered into this relationship knowing one day it would end. Knowing this did not make what was to come any easier. In the past, I had known only hurt and pain when relationships had ended. I wondered how this one could possibly end any differently. The termination of the therapeutic relationship should be just as carefully done as establishing and maintaining the relationship. If termination is never discussed or dealt with prior to the last visit, the client can be left feeling abandoned, alone, and unsure. If termination is discussed and prepared for prior to the end, the entire therapeutic experience can be a wonderful learning process for the client. Feelings of hurt and loss might still exist, but if appropriately handled they will not be devastating or destructive. Learning how to leave a loving and emotionally intimate relationship with courage and love is the product of a successful termination process.

30

Reasonable Love?

April 12, 1997

Tonight I saw a TV show which brought so many emotions to the surface. What sparked the emotional response in me tonight was the implied love of an older man for his wife who had died. At the end of the show, the parting scene elicited so much emotion within me that I could not contain my tears. I quickly went to bed. Since I have spent most of the past two days in bed, it did not seem strange when I departed. I must have cried for thirty to forty minutes. I cried for the emotional connection and response I wanted from my husband, but did not have. I finally admitted to myself I had to take the chance to find that love. I cannot endure the thought I should never feel that kind of love. If I stay married to my husband, I know it will never happen. I know I have to give him the chance, but now I am truly ready to let him go if he can't, or is unwilling to find an emotional connection within himself. I would rather live alone with the hope of finding the kind of love I want, than living with a man and never feeling the depth of love I know I can have with another man.

For the first time, I feel at peace with these thoughts. I am no longer agonizing over the "what ifs" and "what fors." I finally know this is something I must do for myself. I know it will hurt my husband and daughter, but I can no longer sacrifice myself for everyone else. I know I can show my daughter what love truly is between a man and a woman. I don't want her to grow up with the thought that the relationship my husband and I have is the best that life can be. I want her to know a man and a woman can love each other with an emotional depth and commitment which goes to the edge of eternity. I know some couples have that relationship; I want to be one of them.

I have not craved an alcoholic drink in at least two months. It feels so good to be free of the bottle. I have decided to bring my last bottle to my next session with Jim. I want to celebrate my freedom with someone who will truly understand the importance of this part of my healing. I know he will.

I realize I have not talked much about my drinking. This is not to minimize my relationship with alcohol, but rather to state that I did not place it at the forefront of my therapy or journal writing. There were many times I craved the bottle, but did not write about it. I am not entirely sure why. How was I able to put down the bottle? I am not entirely sure, but once I was able to live with my emotions, I no longer felt I needed the alcohol to deaden what feelings I had. I could live with how I felt, and be okay. All drinkers have their own stories and reasons, but very often a dependency on liquor is a result of emotional pain and agony.

April 12, 1997 (continued)

I have so much to talk about with Jim on Monday. I am so glad he is not yet on vacation. It would be an eternity if I knew I couldn't see him for another three weeks. I sincerely hope he has a good trip.

At this moment I feel so at peace, in serenity. I feel just the way I had hoped I would feel one day; that day is finally here. I feel so serene even though I have a terrible headache. I hope I can feel like this the rest of my life. I know I will have ups and downs, but if this is the way the majority of my days are, my life will be worthwhile. I am so glad I am alive. I seriously thought I would never actually feel this way. I had always hoped, but I never really believed. I am glad I gave myself the chance.

One reason to live that I could give to a potential suicide victim is to give yourself a chance at a better life. I fully understand that someone who wants to die feels there is nothing for which to live, but what I am after is the slightest chance of a better life. If one dies, there is no second chance, only the certain finality of death. There are no guarantees that the pain and agony of life will end, but if one decides to wait and give oneself a chance, then there is a chance to learn how to live in peace. I fully realize this may sound like a flimsy excuse to live, but remember, I have been to the edge. I have survived. I have learned how to live. There is always hope, as long as you remain in this life.

April 14, 1997

I won't be seeing Jim again for three weeks. I think this break will be good for me. Today we talked about my lack of craving for a drink, the emotions I experienced after the last session, and what kind of relationship I want in my life. It was a wonderful session. There were no brilliant insights or revelations. What we did have was an emotionally intimate conversation. There was depth, feeling, and reciprocity. I have to say today's session was by far the most fulfilling one I have had with Jim. I suppose it is a testament to my progress. I hope after this relationship is over I can find someone I can share this kind of relationship with again, not in a therapeutic setting, but in a true interpersonal relationship, friendship or more.

We talked about relationships and love. I told Jim what it is I want in a romantic relationship. I told him I wanted a relationship in which I could feel an emotional depth, warmth, and connectedness. Lovemaking would not be reserved for the bedroom, but would take place in the way in which my partner and I would look at and talk with each other. I asked if my expectations were unrealistic and unreasonable. He told me they were not. He said what I want is a truly loving relationship. He said it may take a few tries to find the relationship, but I will find it. I look forward to the day with a passion and love I can barely contain. I wish I had the relationship now, but I do not.

We talked about the strength I now possess which will enable me to enter into emotionally intimate relationships, lose them, and survive. I think he is right. Even though letting Jim go will be something so sorrowful for me, I know I will survive without him. I will always love him in a deep and affectionate way. How could I ever thank him for all he has given me? I cannot. In our conversation about losing a love, I felt as though he was talking to me about our relationship, and maybe in a way he was. In those words, I found he was right. I do have the strength to let Jim go and be okay. It will still be a most difficult task.

I hope over the next three weeks I will make strides in being able to let Jim go and be okay. I know the pain of termination might bring me to the edge. I have to continue to gain my inner strength so I can withstand and endure our final good-bye. When we do finally part, I know I will be a far happier person than I could have ever imagined eight months ago. I never really thought I could have a life like I have now. I also believe I can further improve my life by adding a warm and loving relationship to it. I hope there will come a day when all of this will be a fond memory, one I can be proud of. I already am.

Jim said our relationship has been therapy at its best. Knowing that makes me want to become a therapist even more. I look forward to experiencing the process from the other side of the "couch." I know I will not remain a therapist for twenty years, as Jim has, but I do know I want to practice therapy for several years. I am finding I also want to do other things within the realm of psychology, to be a part of helping people achieve their full potential. Anything less is not good enough.

Tonight I have a profound sense of sadness and loss. I think it has to do with the possible loss of my marriage and the certain loss of my relationship with Jim. It is unfortunate I have to face both issues at the same time. I wish I only had to deal with one at a time, but I do not have that luxury. Jim seems to think he might be able to persuade my insurance company to transfer funds to continue my therapy. I hope that is the case. I would like to get through the repair or dissolution of my marriage before I walk away from therapy. I think there will be some tough issues and feelings I will have to face over the coming months. I cannot imagine doing it alone without Jim, at least for right now. I suppose I could if I have to, but I don't want to.

I know when I tell my husband about the unhappiness and discontent I feel in our marriage, he will blame my change of perspective on my going to school. What he may fail to realize is school has been my respite. The distraction and challenge of my education has allowed me to endure much of what I have had to deal with. If I did not have my work, I am not sure how I would have dealt with the past three years. I hope I can make him understand school is what has kept our marriage together this long. I am not sure he will believe it, or want to.

I know I will have to have the third conversation with my husband within the next few months. I don t think I can leave it alone for much longer. I need to complete my Master's before our marriage is over, if that is what will happen. If I do, I will at least have some latitude in terms of employment. My paycheck will be miserable, but I should be able to find work somewhere.

I hope I can find a way to finish my Ph.D. I am not ready to let the dream go yet, nor do I believe I ever will. I know I am capable and would be a good psychologist. It is just a matter of money. It is a shame money may stand in the way of my fulfilling one of my most ardent dreams. As the saying goes, Where there is a will, there is a way. I have always found a way to accomplish what I desire most, and I do not plan to let this dream disappear without a fight. If it is meant to be, then it shall be done.

Despite the pain and sorrow I feel, I cannot separate myself from my feelings. I have to feel them and remember I am now strong enough to work through them all. I have to remember part of my new life is my feelings and emotions, no matter how wonderful or painful. If I were to go back to the way I was before, all this work will have been for nothing. I am finally living the life I have always wanted. Now I have to work to keep it. Part of the work will be in learning how to feel my emotions, work through them, and allow my life to develop all the color and splendor of emotions which I am now able to experience. As Jim said, the loss of one relationship allows for the growth of a new one.

My relationship with Jim has been so wonderful that I have great difficulty in imagining a better relationship. I am sure Jim would say there will come a relationship which will be dif-

ferent from the one we have, and it will be even better because
it will be reciprocal and unbounded. I know this is true, but it
is still hard for me to accept. I know that is because my relationship with Jim is the first emotionally intimate relationship
I have ever had. It will be like a first love, something which
will always be special and never forgotten.

I wish I already understood the mechanisms behind the success of this therapeutic relationship as a matter of personal and
professional curiosity. If I could identify all the factors which
have made this relationship work and use them within the
therapeutic relationships I will form in the future, I should be
thrilled. Jim has given me more than his therapeutic skill; his
maturity, strength, caring, patience, empathy, intuition, and
love has been the foundation for my healing. I have learned to
trust, open up, and love over these past eight months. I have
gained so much in such a short amount of time. I wonder what
I could achieve if I had eight more months. I wish I did. I
think Jim does too. I am sure he is curious to know what more
I might achieve.

Without consciously knowing it, I arrived at a point in my therapy where I
was able to work through my emotions and struggles independently. I still craved
each session, but my very existence did not depend on each session as was true
earlier.

Clients may not necessarily be able to identify every victory in therapy, but
it is essential for clients to develop competent mental and emotional tools to
handle life's big and little challenges independently. It is far more important for
clients to attain a sense of personal autonomy than to delineate the many com-
ponents of self-mastery and yet be unable to integrate them.

To see how far I had progressed during the past eight months was a satisfying experience. I saw my improvement, believed in the psychotherapeutic
process, and knew I was pursuing the right course of action for my life. All the
earlier doubts that related to the efficacy of psychotherapy no longer existed. I
knew when the time came, I could begin my psychotherapy internship with confidence in the psychotherapeutic process.

❖

31

Bargain with the Devil

All the gains in therapy are useless if they cannot be brought to life outside the therapist's office. I had begun experimenting with ways to conduct my relationships some months earlier, but had not yet made significant strides in my more significant relationships. Finding the strength and confidence to approach my lifelong relationships differently required more effort.

When I was able to deal with my lifelong relationships in a more loving fashion, I knew I was making real and possibly more permanent change within my life. Although it was not a perfect or highly reliable measure, my behaviors reflected the changes I was making as a result of therapy. For me, this was the only way I was sure I was making real change, and not just intellectually playing the game.

April 16, 1997

Today I saw an old friend of mine. We talked of a great many things. I really enjoyed our conversation. He talked about his divorce, psychologists, and personal commitments. Prior to our conversation, I felt so sure about the course I was taking with my marriage. His version of wive's rationale for seeking divorce was to some degree familiar, and yet, they were not at all the same. Our conversation reminded me that when I got married, I made a commitment to my husband for better or worse .... I had to ask myself if it was right for me to walk away from this commitment just because I was not happy with the way things were right now.

How could I justify destroying a family and forever changing the lives of two or more people because I felt emotionally lonely in my marriage? Why did I ask for more than what I have, when what I have is more than what many people have? My marriage was not terrible, but I am just terribly lonely. Within this loneliness, I also have to realize I am very vulnerable. It is the first time in my life I have felt lonely.

Right now, it is as though my husband has withdrawn from life and only interacts with me and our daughter to maintain the basic elements of a relationship. In a sense he has a warm little place to hide from life. In my gut, I feel like I want to kick him out and tell him: "Get a life, and then come back." Tonight, it was all I could do to not scream out, "ARE YOU REALLY HAPPY WITH THE LIFE YOU HAVE?" I feel as though he is sucking the life out of me.

I am crying. I am crying because I hurt and because I am actually in touch with the way I feel. I am sad because I do not feel about my marriage the way I want to feel. I want to feel love, warmth, empathy, desire, and tenderness toward my husband, but I don t feel these things. When I think of my husband, I feel loneliness, distance, and disappointment. I don't feel disappointment in him; I feel it from him. I think he feels an underlying disappointment with his life. I think the uncertainty and disappointment he feels in his life causes him to withdraw from life more, thus perpetuating his feelings and worsening his situation. He is obviously emotionally detached and may not be able to identify what is going on within himself. I sense his remoteness and withdrawal. This further exacerbates how I feel; and my aloofness from him adds to his disappointment and furthers his own withdrawal.

I know I have changed over the past two and a half years. I know I have saved my own life and the life of my daughter. She might not have been suicidal, but my suicide would have destroyed most of a chance for her to have a fulfilling and happy life. I can no longer live the singular and emotionally-isolated existence that I previously needed in order to survive. I wonder if my need for emotional intimacy has forced my husband to withdraw? Does he sense my new need for emotional commitment and on a level he may be unable to discuss; has he sensed this and withdrawn from confronting the fear generated by our changing relationship?

This is the first time I have thought about my marriage in a way which considers both of us, and particularly my husband. I do not believe I am disengaging from my feelings, I think using this different perspective has helped me to see the dissolution of my marriage impacts not just me. It will take both of us to rebuild a semblance of something we can both live with. For the first time in months, I feel as though I have someplace to start. I am not overly enthusiastic about rebuilding our marriage, but if I make no attempt to do so and simply walk away, I know I will always be disappointed in myself. I have to be able to tell both myself and my daughter that I did everything I knew how to do to save our family. Even though I am not in love with him, I think if there was a greater bond between us, however small, I could endure and thrive within this family. His avoidance of emotional consequences invites another divorce. I cannot take responsibility for his life, emotions, and happiness. I can only be responsible for mine, and help my daughter to learn to be responsible for her own also.

Over the past eleven years of my marriage, I have taken responsibility for everything. I think my husband got very used to that, and now I am again relinquishing those responsibilities back to where they belong. He may feel threatened and uncertain, but I will not keep responsibilities which do not belong to me. I must help my husband feel okay about reclaiming his own responsibilities. The more I try to give them back to him, the more he tries to run away from them. When I did everything, it meant everything was okay; now I do not want to control everything. He is not sure of what that means and what he will have to do now. He might feel adrift in discovering his new role is in our family. He may be waiting for me to explain it to him and to help him establish it. I think he needs to decide what his role is and how to take care of it for himself.

Even though I was not "in love" with my husband, I must admit I had finally found the strength to forge a loving relationship with him. I was finally able to think about what was important and healthy for me, but also what I felt my husband needed to improve his own life, whether or not he was married to me.

April 16, 1997 (continued)

Right now, I feel as though there is a chance to save what we have. That is far more than I would have said a few hours ago. If he is willing to try and find out what his life is about and what is his responsibility, then that would be a beginning. If he decides he is unable or unwilling to do so, then I will have to cross that bridge later. I am willing to work as hard as I can to save my marriage, but I will not work alone; there is no purpose in that. If he is unwilling to change then I will tell him: I will stay married as long as I can stand it, and then I will go.

April 17, 1997

Last night, I asked my husband if he was happy at work. Tonight he asked me why I asked him. That began two and a half hours of real conversation. We finally talked profoundly in a conversation where he actually responded with comments and listened to what I had to say. I told him how close he is to losing this marriage, and I think he finally has realized how serious the situation is. He never became defensive or withdrawn. I was finally able to convey to him that I needed his feelings and emotions; and the problems with our marriage are rooted in my personal growth. He finally understands that his feelings and emotions are what I need. I wonder if he fully understands that without them, this marriage will not survive.

Just before we ended our conversation, I asked him if he was willing to find his emotional life. He told me he wasn't sure. I asked him to think about it. If he says no, at least we will both know the loss of our marriage was neither of our faults. We tried, we did the best we could, and in the end, love was just not enough. We will both be okay.

I am looking forward to seeing Jim when he gets back. I know I have two more weeks to go, but that is okay. I hope to get my husband's answer as to whether or not he is willing to find his emotional life soon. His answer will let me know where my life is headed. I hope he decides to find his emotions. I want to give us one more chance. We deserve it, but it is all up to him. What will he choose?

April 22, 1997

My dad is in town this week. Yesterday, I made a lunch date with him. I was so pleased he responded to my telephone messages. In everyday life, and in everyday things, he seldom has had the time to be a dad. But when I really need him, he finds time to be there. We will be having lunch on Wednesday afternoon. I am very apprehensive about talking to him. It will be difficult to talk about the possibility of my divorce. When I consider my reasons, they sound so trite, but the way I feel and want to feel is so important to me. I hope to convey to him why I want a divorce. If he does not understand, it will be disappointing.

April 23, 1997

Today, I met with my dad to talk about my marriage. I did not know what to expect. We had a wonderful conversation. It is too bad the subject matter had to be divorce. He gave me a lot of perspectives from which to examine my situation better. Interestingly, he knew exactly what I am feeling.

Dad made many interesting and valid points. I didn't know we could have such an in-depth conversation about real life. Of course, divorce is one thing my dad does know a lot about. I made the right decision in talking to him. That was the most intimate conversation my father and I have ever had. It was wonderful. I think it really brought us closer together. Dad reminded me not make any decision based on guilt, which is an extremely good point.

We also talked about life in general. He said we spend the first eighteen years learning everything we know from our parents. Then we spend the next eighteen years undoing it and finding our own lives. That seems to be so true. Look at where I am now. I am finally letting go of my past and rebuilding my life in a way I want to live. At last, I feel I can get on with my life. I will pursue my Ph.D. I will still be the best mom I can be. I will remain a faithful wife. I am not putting my life on hold, instead I am putting a romantic relationship on the back burner, until there comes a time when I can deal with that too.

In the words of Jim Seymour, I guess I too have made my bargain with the devil. I do not know how much I can take, but
I know I can stick this out for a while longer, and I will.

Learning emotional acceptance was a difficult task; discovering emotional
patience was too. After I realized what I felt, I had to learn how to be patient with
my feelings. I had not imagined there could be so much to learn. For so many
years, I thought emotions were something unmanageable, to be avoided at all
costs. Then, I found emotions were something to be felt and experienced, and
were a wonderful part of life. As time progresses, I wonder what the other lessons
will be about how my emotions influence my life.

32

I Need to Talk

One of the more difficult tasks for me to learn was to be myself completely with those around me. I found the thought of others being interested in my life a foreign thought. The idea of making myself vulnerable and taking risks with others was perilous. As I became more used to being open and vulnerable to Jim, I found I wanted to have more authentic relationships in my life, but to take the chance with someone else was still a little too scary.

April 26, 1997

Over the past few days, I have been fighting with a low grade depression. I am not certain what emotions I am suppressing. I only know I must be suppressing my feelings because I have not had many of them lately. Tonight, I reread some of my passages and I could feel the edges of emotion. I think I have been suppressing my feelings so that I might be able to tolerate another couple of years with my husband.

There are two things which scare me about suppressing my feelings. First, if I am able to do it too well, I might forget what it is to feel and settle for the relationship I have had with my husband. Second, my automatic ability to suppress my feelings always results in depression. I must break the habit, or I will end up back where I started. I cannot allow that to occur.

Although I would continue to suppress my emotions on occasion, one of the most healing revelations was learning that my depression was a result of suppressing emotions I was afraid to face. Even now, I sometimes try and suppress my emotions, my depressive reaction is quick to remind me that I must experience what I feel. I must remember the emotions and feelings I have will not kill me, but the depression as a result of their suppression might.

April 26, 1997 (continued)

Even though it may hurt to stay with my husband another couple of years, I must allow myself to feel all I feel. I must stop the compartmentalization and suppression of my emotions. My emotions are a part of my new life. I have to learn it is okay to hurt. It is okay to be confused. I must enjoy every facet of what they bring, happiness or pain. To feel is to live. I have not lived for so many years, I can't give it up so quickly.

It was probably because I did not have connection with my feelings that everything was reduced to intellectual decision-making, where few emotions were involved. Now I have contact with my emotions, and the decision-making process is more difficult. The results of my decisions are more difficult to live with also. Maybe, this is one reason why I wanted to suppress my feelings. In doing so, it would allow me to more easily live with my husband another couple of years. Also, it would make my decision to stay easier to accept.

Instead of this suppression, I need a new means of coping with my feelings. I wish Jim were here so we could talk about it. I have few other tools with which to cope with all I feel. I know this journal is one way I am able to cope with my feelings. I know Jim would say if I would further cultivate non-family relationships so I could talk with others; that would help. I know he is right, but right now, I am not sure what I would say. Based on that, maybe I should just call someone. It is quite late now, but maybe tomorrow. I will wait and see.

Already, I am feeling better. I do not feel as depressed as before. Although, I still have a heavy heart, I know it might remain for a long time. I have a lot to deal with for the next year or two.

This passage shows how I was learning to use my depression to face my emotions. Early in my therapy, Jim had mentioned making a relationship with my depression. At the time, I felt this was the most ludicrous idea. The only reason I did not dismiss this idea entirely was I had heard it before. I could not imagine what type of relationship I could possibly have with a part of me which wanted to kill me. I was beginning to more fully understand my depression, its sources, and how it could be avoided. It took a full seven months for me to begin to see the light.

April 28, 1997

> Last night I spoke with my husband about our marriage. I told him that I would interpret the absence of a response from him about his pursuit of his emotional life as a "No." He said okay. I then told him I would try and stay within the marriage as long as I could, but I could not make any promises. He asked me what that meant. I told him I will stay within the marriage until I couldn't take it any more, and then I would ask for a divorce. He acted like it was a surprise to him that I might ask for a divorce.

> What surprised me was it is a surprise to him that I am considering a divorce. I have told him no less than three times now; I am still not sure whether or not he has heard the message. I feel as though we are treading water. Does he think that just because he says, "Okay, I am listening," that that is enough? I am not sure what to do to make sure he understands just how serious I am about ending our marriage.

> I can't wait for Jim to come back. I really need to talk to someone. I get little response from my husband. I just don't want my therapy with Jim to end any time soon, but I know it must. What will I do without Jim? I just don't know. I will miss him so much; I really do now.

Early in my therapy, Jim had mentioned to me I needed to form emotionally intimate relationships with those around me. In the beginning, I had no idea what this meant. Now that I knew, but I was still too frightened to reach out. Jim's vacation proved to be very good for me. I began to realize how important my other relationships could be if I could find the trust, courage, and strength to just be closer to those around me. I made the effort to reach out to a long-time acquaintance, Mary, who has become my dearest friend, much sooner because of Jim's absence.

April 29, 1997

> I only have six more sessions left with Jim. I am not sure how
> I want to handle them. I keep trying to bring up termination
> in therapy, but Jim doesn't really want to talk about it; neither
> do I, but I know leaving Jim will be tremendously difficult.
> Especially in view of how much I have missed him these past
> weeks.

It may not have been that Jim did not want to talk about termination, but rather he may have felt I should be the one to pursue the topic. Jim was well aware I would avoid topics which were emotionally painful. I may have interpreted his actions as being hesitant when they were not. In any case, his actions forced me to bring up what I dreaded most.

April 29, 1997 (continued)

> I have enjoyed talking with Jim so much. It has felt so good to
> have someone who accepts me for who I am, knows and
> understands where I have been, and keeps me and my healing
> at the center of the relationship.
>
> I know I must have written this a hundred times, but I hope I
> will attain the level of therapeutic acumen that Jim has. I
> know he has been practicing for just short of twenty years, but
> I hope I can get there too.
>
> I imagine my experiences during my internship will tell me a
> lot as to what my actual abilities as a therapist are. I hope I do
> not disappoint myself.

Before my therapy with Jim, I thought I could accomplish anything I tried. There was no room for failure. It was not part of my view of the world. I would have been certain I could be as good a therapist as Jim, given the time. My therapeutic work did not make me doubt my ability; what it allowed me to do was become more accepting of myself, even when I might not succeed. I expect to invest the same effort and energy as before, but now, I am okay with me, no matter what the outcome is. Even though I may not sound as confident and bold as I would have earlier, I feel the change I have made is far more healthy. If I am not successful as a therapist, I will not crumble. What will be important is that I give it my best effort.

❧

❖

Learning to End

Even though clients know therapy has to come to an end sooner or later, it is still difficult to face the final moments. The thought of letting go of an emotionally intimate relationship, which has supported me for months, was not intuitive; holding on for dear life seemed a more natural reaction. I deeply struggled to find a reason to let go. I did not want my therapy to end. I suppose I could have tried to stay longer, but I knew the time was coming for me to learn to let go. There was an element of great safety knowing it was Jim on the other side of this relationship. I knew he would help me to say good-bye.

May 5, 1997

I am not sure what to write. I am feeling quite numb. I have emotions brewing, but am not sure what they are, or from where they originate. I am feeling intensely sad, but not depressed. A part of me wants to cry, but it is as though there are no tears left to cry. I just want to crawl into bed and stay there a while. I know I can't suppress how I feel, but to feel these feelings hurts so much. I can't obsess over how much I hurt. Maybe I should try thinking about how good my relationship with Jim has been about and the good times I had during my marriage.

Today during session, I told Jim a short version of what has been going on. He was a little surprised. He also noticed I really don't want to salvage my marriage. He confronted me about it; I had to admit it was true. I think today is the first time I have admitted aloud that I am ready for my marriage to end.

Jim suggested that I was looking for more excitement. I cut him off right away and told him excitement wasn't a high priority in a long-term relationship. In fact, I'm looking for just the opposite; I want stability, warmth, comfort, strength, gentleness, humor, connectedness, and caring. None of that equals excitement to me.

Jim seems to keep implying I am looking for a change of pace rather than a change to a meaningful relationship. I wonder if that is what he thinks I am after? I should confront him. I thought I made it quite clear as to what I want in a relationship. Maybe he thinks my husband is the right relationship for me. I don't really care what he thinks.

We spent the last fifteen to twenty minutes discussing termination. He is finally willing to discuss it. He told me how he viewed termination. Unfortunately, I was too tearful to hear most of what he said. He talked about keeping the memory of the relationship, and how only a true relationship touches and changes both parties involved. If no change occurs, then it was not a true relationship. I think he is correct. But that insight doesn't lessen the hurt.

Much of my anxiety about termination exists because I still fear emotional pain. I still fear being devoured and overwhelmed by it. Pain in and of itself will not kill me, but I still fear it. With everything else I have endured and learned in these past months, I guess I must experience this in order to fully realize that I am strong enough to survive the loss of the single most influential relationship of my adult life.

I never imagined I would meet someone who would help me change my life to the degree Jim has. I never imagined therapy could bring so powerful a transformation. What has helped me bring about the change? I know it is a combination of technique, personality, gender, metaphysical philosophy, and the relationship. How does this combination of factors bring about change in an individual. I know I have been allowed by Jim and I have allowed myself to feel safe enough to try new things within this relationship and be emotionally rewarded. How does this translate into elevated self-esteem? How have I found a way to break with the dissociation and find a way toward integration and wholeness? I truly believe a key part is Jim's strength, safety, and presence. His promise of those three things, and in the way he promised them to me, allowed me to find the strength to dismantle my defense mechanisms. When I allowed him to see me and he did not reject me, I developed my own sense of being okay. The near total disclosure of all my near-the-edge thoughts and feelings did not scare him away. He remained solid and steadfast. He didn't coddle me, but he still allowed me to lean against him. I also think my own intuitive belief that he was the right man for this task also allowed me to trust him more than I could have trusted anyone else.

Today during the session, Jim said the very words which have passed through my own mind. He has a certain intuition about what to say and how to say it. I will greatly miss that. He talked about the ebb and flow of relationships throughout a lifetime. He said: "Our relationships are never really gone, we leave behind parts of ourselves with those whom we touch, and take a part of others with us when we go." These are some of my very own thoughts about Jim always being with me throughout my life.

Twice he mentioned the extraordinary intuition we have both had about our relationship. I know this feeling we share has had a profound impact on him. I wonder what he has really thought about this. All I know is he has thought about this quite a bit, as I have.

Today he told me he was not ready to let me go. I think he wants to be sure I'll be okay in the long run. After I told him about my decision to leave my marriage, he asked me if I was ready to live with that. He is worried I will spiral back into depression because I feel stuck in my marriage for a while. His concern is absolutely correct. I think he is also concerned about how I will handle our termination. I told him I was still unable to speak of my feelings for our relationship and for him. He seemed concerned by this statement. I reminded him I only have six more sessions.

I know that no matter what happens in the future, I will always love my daughter and will have undying gratitude for all Jim has helped me attain: my life, self-esteem, the ability to truly know love, joy, happiness, and fond memories. There is no greater gift one person can give another. He has given me the ultimate gift – my life and the will to live. How can I adequately thank him for that? I have no idea. Thank you, Jim.

May 6, 1997

I have given some thought to relationship terminations, but I am not any closer to letting our relationship go. I fully realize, conceptually, life is a series of relationships which come and go. I also realize no true relationship is ever completely ended or closed because each person has affected change on the other. What should I do with all that I feel? I know I must acknowledge and experience the feelings, but then what? Or does there have to be a "then what?" Maybe not. I know the feelings in and of themselves will not kill me. I do know the suppression or compartmentalization of them may result in my death. So, maybe the true question should be, "How do I maintain grace and poise even after the loss of a significant relationship?"

Where do I find the strength to feel and not shut down or cut them off? Do I allow myself to feel loss and loneliness and still maintain my life and not let the pain consume all that I am? How do I find perspective?

I think within my relationship with Jim, part of the difficulty in letting go is I feel such an intuitive connection. I know I can't maintain therapy forever, but it will be hard to let go of a relationship which feels as though it was truly meant to be.

Maybe in being able to leave this relationship by choice, it will be the ultimate test of how healed I am. I also know my professional future will consist of numerous relationships and terminations. If I can endure and survive, with strength, this termination, then I can endure the rest.

This is definitely one way of viewing the end of this relationship. It won't make the hurt go away, nor hurt any less. It will

give me something to hold onto. I hope I am headed in the
right direction.

I find as I near the end of this book, my entries speak for themselves. I hope
you will just experience my therapy through my passages.

❖

84

How to End

In retrospect, I think it took me just as long to prepare for termination as it did for me to prepare to engage deeply with the psychotherapeutic relationship. In the beginning, I had to consider all my reasons and feelings about trusting another person. In the end, I had to sift through all my reasons and feeling for letting go of our relationship, but still maintain a sense of trust. I cannot over-emphasize the importance of taking the time to work through the thoughts and feelings associated with termination. I had invested so much of myself in this relationship; its dissolution was not taken lightly.

Preparing for termination is work, because new issues, previously unknown, may surface; sometimes, these issues prolong the experience. Other times, new issues genuinely surface; these result in new insights into the self.

May 7, 1997

In thinking about termination, I feel as though I am starting to make real progress. Part of my fear of termination was founded on the ways in which my three most significant relationships had ended; there was no closure for me and all three were beyond my control. I do know the end of my marriage and the end of my therapy will be directly under my control, so that will make the end of these relationships easier. In ending therapy, I also realize I need to tell Jim all I feel before it is over. If I don't, I will have a sense of "unfinished business."

I am glad I do not have an appointment with Jim any time soon. I am not yet ready to go back. I think I may need the full two weeks to sort through all my feelings and thoughts.

-later-

Throughout the day, I have thought about termination. Tonight I kept telling myself: "I wish I could tell Jim so much, but...." Then I thought: "Why not tell him everything before the end?" What would be the harm? What I tell him will not be anything he probably has not heard before. Also, everything I say will come from my heart and will not have any manipulative undertones. What would I have to lose? Nothing.

I feel so much better knowing I will finally tell Jim my feelings about what has happened in therapy and about him. I really believe I need to do this. It will give me a sense of closure. Right now, it feels like it is the right thing to do. I am not sure when to start. I do not want to start too soon. I have six sessions left. I think during the next session I will talk about my need for closure, and discuss what has happened at the end of my last three major relationships. I want to have fond memories of what we have accomplished. I want to keep the warmth I feel for this relationship with me for the rest of my life. If I can, it will truly be a successful termination.

Deciding to bring closure to this relationship has helped me accept the prospect of termination. I no longer feel the dread and near-panic of a few days ago. I will not be able to control all the endings of all the relationships I have, but for the first time, I will have a say in how this one ends. I know when it ends, there will be no surprises. I know Jim will not intentionally hurt me. Part of me does look forward to the end, because I know when I leave, I will have become a much healthier and happier person than at any other time in my life. The part of me which will miss this relationship is the part which feels the intuitive connection and friendship. Even though our relationship will end, I believe there will always be a bond between us. If nothing else, I will always have my memories of the times we have spent together; these treasures will always be within my heart.

At this moment, I feel I can go through termination without self-destruction; I feel at peace. For the first time I am not afraid nor am I fighting it. It is a natural part of the relation-

ship process. My feelings for Jim and our relationship are the
same, but somehow I have come to terms with the leaving as
a healthy part of the process. This is very interesting. I wonder
how I will feel about all this in a day or two. I hope it will be
much the same.

I hope I will be able to conduct therapy with a client of my
own before I leave Jim's care. I think it would be an interesting
conversation. I look forward to it. Luckily, I will be starting my
internship in June, so this may happen before my sessions are
up. I am sure he is wondering what I will think of my experiences on the other side of the couch.

Maybe, in time, I will write a book entitled, *Both Sides of the
Couch*. There probably isn't a book about being a client and
being a therapist simultaneously. If I ever do write a book
about therapy, I am going to dedicate the book to Jim. I hope
he will get a chance to see it. I will just have to make a point
to send him one. I am sure one day, I will write a book about
therapy, because it is such a powerful a process.

I look forward to my life so much now. Thank you, Jim.

These passages illustrate my increasing ability to work through my emotions
and thoughts autonomously. Even though I was still a client of Jim's, I no longer
hung on to him. I was able to reflect on, experience, and work through very difficult issues independently. The future would show me I was not completely
ready to leave just yet, but for now, I was satisfied that I was headed in the right
direction.

85

I Have Won

During the past nine months, I had grown immensely through my healing process. Unfortunately, I did not feel that I had conquered my depression. Clients who leave therapy should feel as though their core issues have been resolved satisfactorily. This may not always happen, but if at all possible it should be done. Clients who leave without the success of having faced and at least found control over the prevailing issue allows self-doubt to linger. The client may not feel the confidence necessary to face the outside world autonomously for long. Some clients may face serious challenges and feel unsure and scared. Their self-doubts may require them to return to therapy. Although additional therapy might help the client deal with the immediate problem, it might also invite a more long term dependency than might have happened if a few more sessions had concluded the previous round of therapy.

Prolonged client dependency might occur because the client feels anxiety and fear grow when faced with a challenge. If the client goes back into therapy and finds comfort, safety and possibly a solution to the challenge, then the time back in therapy feels good. The next time the client faces a challenge in life, might the client simply repeat this pattern continuously? If clients feel the personal confidence and strength to face life s challenges, then they are more likely to resolve their problems autonomously.

May 8, 1997

Only a day later, and I haven't felt so depressed in a long time, for me. I am not sure what it's about. I am frustrated because I know I felt so good last night. I don't know why I crashed. I hurt so much right at this moment. I feel as though I want to cry, but no tears come and I don't know why I would cry. I feel as though I have lost my best friend. Maybe that is it; losing Jim. He is the best friend I have ever had, and I have to pay for him.

I just asked myself what it is I am suppressing. My only answer is my relationship with Jim. Yes, I am suppressing my desire to not leave therapy. I already feel better. I still hurt, but the sharpness of the pain is already starting to recede. I am not really ready to let him go. At times, I can convince myself I am through with therapy.

Just as quickly as it has come, my depression is lifting. I no longer feel the isolation and internal pain. I know I cannot suppress my feelings of loss and pain with the termination of our relationship, but I keep on trying to suppress them. At least I recognize what is going on within me. I am learning not to ignore the way I feel. If I pay attention, and even if I don't, the feelings of depression let me know there is something I am trying to hide from myself. I still have a heavy heart over the sadness of termination, but I do not have the self-doubt of a moment ago. The suppression of my feelings powerfully impacts the functioning of my psyche. It is startling. I must ask Jim for a reference for an article he mentioned which discusses the suppression of emotions and depression. I have been learning this truth for the last several months, but now it is so obvious. The speed with which the depression has come and gone is phenomenal.

I now feel back to normal. I feel okay with life again. I need to realize I should do nothing with my feelings, but experience them passing by. Why do I believe I must do something with the way I feel. Why is it not okay to just feel? I think that is what I should do. As Jim said, it would be good to just be with someone, and I add also just be with my feelings. I know I will deeply miss Jim. I know these feelings did not arise overnight and they will not leave overnight. It does not matter how I should feel. I simply feel as I do, right, wrong, or neutral. These are my feelings. Let them be. This has been a long hard lesson for me to learn. I am not fully converted in this realization yet. My feelings are what they are, but just being with them and allowing them to be is a little more difficult.

I hadn't fully realized just how much the "oughtness" and "shouldness" of things have ruled my life. I have even let those two words rule the way I feel. I can't continue this pattern; it will kill me if I do. I need to allow the feelings I have to ebb and flow through my mind and through my life. If I understand my feelings and not let them rule me, then I will be okay. I still need this relationship with Jim to help me complete this journey; maybe it will never really be done. I need him to help me complete this part of my journey at least. I wish he could be there for the rest of my journey too.

I have this intuition that once I step into my psychotherapy internship, my life will forever change. I welcome the coming change. It is as though I will truly start the rest of my life. I do not expect any radical changes, but somehow, I think I will not ever return to my former life. I am not sure why I have this feeling. Maybe because when I go to my internship, I will be doing what I think I am meant to do with the rest of my life. This will be one of the steps on my way to my future. My internship is a stepping stone, or an open doorway to a wondrous profession. Let it be so! I am interested to see how my life turns out over the next few months. I am so excited about my future.

Learning how to live with my feelings and emotions has been a most difficult task, I am not accustomed to feeling and acknowledging my emotions. As with learning any new task, I will practice, practice, practice. I have finally learned how to make friends with my depression and use my depression to keep me from suppressing my emotions. Depression is my reminder to live with my emotions and feelings and not cut myself off from any of them. Depression helps me to live with all that I feel. Depression keeps me alive. I never thought I would ever say that. Depression can no longer kill me; it can no longer defeat me. I have finally won the battle and the war.

After I had written these words, I finally felt as though I would do more than survive my life. I knew I had finally found my relationship with my depression. It no longer controlled me. I could use it to enhance myself. One of the most devastating and powerful forces in my life was now at my disposal to help me create the life I so deeply desired.

Although I have not included the letter, I wrote Jim to tell him about this passage. I did not want to wait to tell him; I wanted to share this moment immediately with him. I felt he would know just how important the words would be to the rest of my life.

❖

His Strength and My Tears

As I was reaching the end of my relationship with Jim, I found my thoughts wandering off to other places, not just therapy. I have not placed a good portion of my actual journal in these latter chapters because the entries dealt with issues not relevant to my therapy process.

Even though I speak of termination and the process of my therapy with Jim, the majority of my journal entries dealt with real life. I was more involved with other aspects of my life, such as enjoying my daughter and the world around me. I believe my preoccupation with living was healthy and not a way to deny or forget that termination was coming soon. As my life became more important to me, my ties to therapy and Jim began to loosen. My initial steps to let go of therapy were tentative, but were beginning.

May 10, 1997

Jim, I want a vacation from life for a while. Right now, I am so tired of being a wife and mother. I am tired of not being listened to. I am tired of having to give the world my attention. I am tired of no one appreciating all I do. I am tired of complaining to get what I want. I am just tired.

I love my school-related activities. They fulfill me now. I do enjoy being with my daughter, but that is different. I don't receive the same kind of satisfaction from her that I do from my academic work. Research is okay, but it is the assessment and evaluation I enjoy. Today, I worked with Jason on his case, and I loved it. The mental exercise was wonderful. I felt alive and really doing something worthwhile. It will be interesting to find out what Dr. Bennett's reaction is to my hypothesis about Jason's client. I know it is out there, but it does fit.

I don't care how much managed care destroys the mental health profession. I know this work is what I must do in my life. Psychology is my true calling. I could not have done it earlier, but now is the right time in my life to begin this.

In a way, I was not incorrect in my story to myself when I was a kid. It was not to help God understand humanity that I have suffered through my life. It was so I could understand my own humanity, and therefore, help humanity. Instead of dying to help humanity, I will live to help humanity.

Among the common elements of life, divorce is something to be experienced. If I do get divorced, it will only add to my life's experiences. I will survive that too, and will help others through it. If I would have had the truly perfect life, I would not be adequately equipped to hear the emotions and feelings of others; I would not understand the turmoil and grief of their lives. I would have been an outsider looking in. Now, I have been there. It is not so important for my clients to know where I have been. All that is truly important is that I empathize with where they are today and can give them hope about where they might be tomorrow.

In order to be uniquely effective, a therapist has to be a tremendously strong individual. The strength required is difficult to define and explain. I know this strength is a very central part of why Jim has been so good for me, and also why my other therapists weren't quite enough. I am not saying my other therapists were weak. The type of strength I needed was the type Jim had to offer.

What is this strength? It is partly a centeredness, a certainty about oneself. Many of us walk this earth with false pretenses and try to be what we think we ought to be, rather than who we really are. Most people probably have little true notion as to who they are and what they are about. They live by outside measures and outside evaluations; therefore having no real sense of self-worth. Most of us are afraid to face the real self; the anticipation is too frightening. What if we don't like ourselves? Must we then live with the agony that we are not what we should be? Too often, we fail to ask ourselves: "What if I do like myself?" Wouldn't that be nice? The task of looking at ourselves seems to be as deadly as Medusa looking at her own reflection. I was terrified of what I might find if I took a good hard look at myself. What did I find? Just myself. What I tried to be really wasn't far from who I really was and am. Now, I am just not trying to justify my existence and I am not running from myself. I am being me.

Part of this strength is knowing it is there. It is a sense of self-confidence. It is not knowing one can do anything, but rather anything can be tried. The success or failure of the endeavor is not the ultimate measure, but rather the valiance of the effort. It isn't the fear of failure, but rather the fear of not making the best effort. Failure is not a poor reflection of the self, but rather a badge of life's experience. True strength is not being unyielding, steadfast, or overpowering, it is being malleable, resilient, and patient. Strength is a state of being, and with it comes a presence within which others can find the comfort and safety, which allows them to feel they can unfold themselves. They can try something new, weather the storm, and develop their own self-acceptance. Strength is what Jim offered me; Me is what I offered myself.

This sense of strength is what I have been striving for since I wrote this passage. I am not sure I will ever attain the emotional strength I desire, but I will take every opportunity to do so. This passage helped me to conceptualize what it is I want to bring to my clients in session. I do not want to overpower them; I want to support them until they can support themselves. I also want to have the strength to maintain myself throughout my time as a therapist. This can be difficult; I must take care of myself, and pay close attention to my own life.

May 14, 1997

I know I am supposed to think about termination, and I have been. I vacillate between being ready to go and feeling as though I couldn't live without therapy. At least I have been able to imagine leaving therapy. For me, this is an important step. If I can allow myself to leave in my thoughts, then I am one step closer to leaving in my actions.

I was almost ready to leave therapy. Previously, I had been fearful that I might never reach this point, because I depended on Jim, and I could not imagine being without him. Finally, I was taking the first steps away from our relationship in a healthy way.

May 14, 1997 (continued)

No matter what, I know it will be difficult and I don't believe
I will do it without tears. Tears are okay. If I don't have tears,
I will worry that I am suppressing my feelings or cutting them
off. I wonder what Jim s reaction will be to termination. I
know he will feel better if he sees tears. I wonder if I will?

I had become sensitive to my caretaking instincts, but I did not indulge them. Instead, I wondered what my reactions would be. I had no intention of shedding tears unless they were from the heart, no matter what Jim expected. Leaving therapy was a difficult time; I questioned whether I was really ready to go, or was I running from the relationship? The feelings I was having now about leaving therapy had a different flavor and texture than my previous attempts to leave the relationship. This time, there was no desperation or a desire to leave immediately. I felt comfortable, I was reaching the point where I could leave the relationship and be okay.

My Odyssey

As much as I dislike television, I do occasionally watch. Although the made-for-television version of Homer's great epoch myth strayed far and wide from Homer's original version, I recognized the lessons left for me to learn.

If we keep our minds open to the world around us, there are so many teachers waiting to show us the way through life. The teachers might be our friends, families, strangers, pets, or even a television show. If we shut our minds to exclude the outside world because of bigotry, hatred, ignorance, or self-aggrandizement, we might pass by some of the most precious gifts life has to offer.

All too often, we are so busy making ends meet in our busy lives, we forget to notice the wondrous world out there, just beyond our fingertips. It is up to us to explore and appreciate what is really out there.

May 19, 1997

Today I watched the TV movie, "The Odyssey." It brought back so many feelings I had forgotten. In a way, they were like memories, but different. The movie reminded me of the feelings I had as a child. I remember thinking about my destiny in life, the life the Gods had set before me. As a child, I believed the Gods had a plan for my life. I believed pain was part of what I had to endure so I could perform my duties in my afterlife. I remember the special feelings I had about the Gods. I felt a strong connection and belief they were there for me and guiding me through my life, as Athena did with Odysseus. I believed my patron God was Neptune or Poseidon. Interestingly, the two times in my life I thought that I nearly died were in water. As a child I often felt the presence of the Gods. They did not speak to me directly, but rather I felt their comfortable presence and assistance. As time passed, so did the sense of their presence. Then there came a time in which I thought the Gods had left me. I now realize I too had lessons to learn, just like Odysseus. In my own life, I have had my own odyssey. I am traveling and finding I too, must learn the lessons of life and living before I can have my own life, the life I desire and deserve.

As long as I live, this relationship will remain with me. I will not lose all the wonderful things which have come from this experience. As I have said and thought a thousand times before, Jim will always be with me and be a part of all that I do. In the past, I said those words with the feeling of holding on to what we had. Now, I say those words because I will always remember all that has been, all we have shared, all we have said and not said. This relationship will live within me for all my days to come, and as will all my real relationships to come.

Where are the Gods now? Instead of believing in the Gods of the Greeks and Romans, I believe in the God of my own making, a God which encompasses all, and of which we are all a part. We are still singular beings, but are not isolated. Like drops of water, each drop can be its own entity, but when joined with other drops, no drop can be or do without affecting all the other drops. Like water, each drop alone can be powerful, but united the many drops can be a force which moves mountains.

It is the journey which constitutes my life, not some particular destination. For so long, I have wanted to be not depressed and to feel okay. Like Odysseus, I have endured for twenty years on this journey. Now as I leave my depression behind, I find I could have been okay much sooner if only I could have truly understood that living is the journey. I have learned to appreciate the journey. I have not stopped longing for destinations, but rather I enjoy the journey to each destination, or goal, in my life. When I arrive, I see the next part of the journey, as well as revel in the joy of reaching my present destination.

I see termination as part of my journey. I won't say it will be easy to leave the one relationship in which I feel the most at home. I won't say that walking out of the door for the last time won't be one of the most difficult things I will do. I won't say I'll not miss the relationship or Jim. I won't say I will not cry. All this will be as it will be. What I can say, is that I will survive, I will live, feel and experience all that comes with termination. It will be a part of who I am and who I am becoming. From the other side of that door, a new journey awaits.

May 22, 1997

Yesterday, I saw Jim again. I read him several passages from my journal. The passages had to do with his strength and the entry previous to this one. After I read the passage about strength, I could see in Jim's eyes he was quite moved by what I had written. In fact, he had a few sniffles. He attributed them to allergies or something, but the sniffles left as quickly as they had come. After reading the other passage, again he was visibly moved. He made the comment he is a sucker for anything that moves the spirit. I was pleased he heard what I was feeling when I wrote those passages. Although my writing is primarily for my own exorcism, expression, and consumption, it makes me happy when I share my writing with Jim and he appreciates it. He knows that what I write is from the heart and soul of my existence.

Yesterday's session had a multi-layered quality. There seemed to be so much that was being said behind the words we spoke. I know I expressed myself emotionally without words, and I felt Jim did the same. I know what I was thinking and wishing I could say, I wonder what it was he was thinking and wishing he could say.

Jim said our relationship has been a gift to him. He also repeated his thoughts about the karmic certainty of our relationship. He used the words from my journal. I can only conclude, at the least, our relationship has had a special quality and feel for him.

I am going to ask Jim to make our last session a double session. I know what I want to say to Jim, but it may be an exceedingly difficult session to finish in forty-five minutes. I hope he will consent. I know I am finally ready to go, not because I want to avoid therapy, but because I truly feel I am doing well. I now know how to use my depressive feelings to my advantage, so it is time to leave. If I remain, it will be solely because I want to spend more time with Jim, and that would be counter-productive for both of us.

With those words, I was finally ready to embark on the next odyssey of my life, no matter where it would take me.

The Gift

Gift giving at the end of therapy is not a standard part of therapy. In fact, there are numerous therapists who will refuse a gift from a client. I felt so strongly about what our relationship had done for me that I wanted to give Jim something which might convey to him the importance I attached to the work we had done.

Prior to giving a therapist a gift, the therapist should be asked how they feel about receiving a gift from the client. Some therapists feel receiving a gift from a client is professionally inappropriate rather than a reflection of their personal feelings about their clients. Acceptable gifts are of nominal value, not overly expensive. Something small, yet of sentimental value might be appropriate.

May 25, 1997

My insurance will no longer pay for therapy; therefore, my next session with Jim will be my last. I know there is a reason for this, but it is still hard to believe this is over. There is a very good possibility the next time I see Jim will be my last time ever. It is hard for me to bear the thought. All I can do from this point is hope there comes an occasion in which we will meet again and be friends.

I need to call Jim this week and make arrangements for my last session. I hope Jim will allow me to have a double session. If not, I am not sure what I will say and how. I really think I need a double session.

Some therapists do not feel comfortable with double sessions. Spending time with a client can be very tiring and difficult for the therapist.

May 25, 1997 (continued)

What I really don't know is what and how I am going to say all I need to say on my last visit. I know I should work out the basics here within my journal. I know I want to tell him:

1. I can't believe I am really walking away from this relationship.
2. A good portion of my therapeutic technique will draw heavily on my experience with him.
3. He will always be with me.
4. Thank him for helping me.
5. He kept his promise: being my strength, swimming the journey with me; and not letting me drown.
6. Him - comfortable; familiar; emotive presence; focus of therapy on me; didn't let me control the relationship; gave me what I needed, but not on demand; strength; very intuitive; saying things I had just written or thought.
7. I wish I could know him as a person.
8. I wish him happiness, joy, and love – Dolly Parton's song.

May 26, 1997

I finally figured out what I am going to give Jim as a gift. I am going to give him a book which contains portions of my journal entries which span the time I have been in therapy with him. The last entry will be entitled, "The Gift." It will be a poem-like entry about our relationship. I will keep a copy of the finished piece. This will take a lot of time and effort. I hope I can finish this project in time.

May 30, 1997

I have been suppressing my thoughts and feelings about termination. I suppose I came to this conclusion partly due to the fact I have not had any feelings of sadness over my last session. The afternoon of June 9th will be a most arduous task. Knowing I will be facing the last session I will ever have with Jim is not something I take on lightly. I have been on the grouchy side and distant, all the signs of emotional suppression for me.

-later-

Tonight, I cried. I cried at the sadness I felt over the loss of my relationship with Jim. I am finally getting back in touch with my feelings and emotions. Right now, I feel as though my heart weighs ten pounds. It feels as though it might fall out of my chest and shatter into a thousand pieces.

Over the past few days, I have noticed fleeting thoughts of death; they're quick, quiet, almost unnoticeable, but they did come. What am I not dealing with? I am glad I have learned to listen to myself so I can get back in touch with my feelings.

On the way home, I thought of so many things I will miss about Jim: his eyes, smile, strength, comfort, familiarity, intelligence, intuition, thought provoking questions, silence, voice, patience, caring, and the list goes on. I still have enormous difficulty imagining my life without him. I suppose I better start. I only have ten more days before this relationship is over.

When I think of the warmth, caring, patience, and love which flows within the relationship now, I revel in the wonder of the feelings it all evokes. If this tightly bounded relationship can bring forth these types of feelings, I cannot imagine what an unbounded relationship would be like which possesses all the warmth, caring, patience, and love I feel with Jim. I would certainly like to find out. One reason I am afraid to leave Jim, is I am afraid I will forget the magic and wonder of a truly emotionally intimate relationship. I am afraid I will slump into the convenience of the relationship I have in my marriage. I don't want to forget the wonder and warmth of authentic intimacy. I fear it happening. How do I hold close all I have felt with Jim? If I can remember all this relationship was, maybe I can keep in mind all I desire for my life.

June 4, 1997

I have finally finished transcribing my book for Jim. I am so
tired. I have stayed up until one or two in the morning every
night for the last week. I have decided not to put the poem in
until the night before. I am sure there will be a few things I
will want to add to the book before I am ready to add the
poem. The final version of the poem reads as follows:

The Gift

Each of us receives countless gifts over the years. Sometimes
they come wrapped in beautiful paper and shimmering ribbon.
Other times they come plain and revealed.

The most treasured gift I have ever received was wrapped in
experience and authenticity and tied with a ribbon of hope.
After carefully unwrapping the gift, I found the contents to be
strength, caring, patience, intuition, love, and life.

Oftentimes, the most valuable gifts are not the ones you can
touch and hold, but are instead the ones which touch the soul
and hold the heart.

How can I thank you for such a wondrous gift? I know not. I
only know such a gift is not something to be kept guarded and
secret, but rather shared and given freely.

As the years tumble away, and the luster fades, the value of the
gift remains unchanged. For I will keep it with me always, let
it sustain me, and ever will it bring a smile to my heart.

- Kathleen

I find this poem says so much of what I feel. I hope it adequately conveys my message.

Writing the book for Jim was a good idea in more ways than
one. It is a gift of our relationship, and writing it has allowed
me to review how far I've come over these past ten months. In
many ways, it is unbelievable how far I've come. I don't want
to think about what my life would have been like without this

relationship. After reviewing these past ten months, I feel more ready to leave Jim. I feel as though I am prepared to embark on the rest of my life. Now that I have the book mostly done, it is time to rest.

Reviewing my progress through therapy by writing about it proved to be a wonderful experience. Doing this helped me solidify my confidence in my healing. After reading where I had been and how far I had come, I knew I could travel through my life and enjoy all it has to offer. I would not go back to simply surviving each day, as I had done before.

The Last Time

The last session is both an end and a beginning. It was the end of a wonderful journey with the help of my therapist. It was the beginning of the rest of my life. There have been many momentous occasions in my life; my last day in therapy ranks among them. I cannot begin to explain all this day means to me now.

June 10,1997

Yesterday I had my last session with Jim. It was terribly difficult.

I gave the book to Jim. He was very happy with it. He said the excerpt from the poem, "...wrapped in experience and authenticity, and tied with a ribbon of hope..." was an accurate description of what therapy should be. Based on that comment and Jim's reaction to our therapy, I am currently planning on writing a book about being a therapy client entitled "The Gift." I will place the poem in the book also. Originally, I was going to wait and write a book about both sides of therapy, I have changed my mind. There are lots of books about being a therapist. There are few books which cover being the client and all that goes with it. I want people to understand what therapy can be and demystify the experience. I want people to understand it is a journey of the heart and soul.

In our last session, Jim seemed genuinely thrilled that I had decided to give him the book as a parting gift. I read the opening passage and the closing poem to him. He spent a good amount of time talking about what our relationship meant to him. He mentioned our relationship was very similar to one he had had early in his career. He found that quite interesting. Again, he spoke of the "karmic" connection we seemed to have and how it seemed to play a part within our relationship. He made it quite clear that our relationship and the process of my healing was a wonderful experience for him. He gained satisfaction from knowing I was healing. He felt productive in helping someone regain her life. He felt powerful, in that he was instrumental in facilitating the healing process of a person who needed his help.

It was both satisfying and interesting to hear his comments in regards to our relationship. He admitted it was hard for him to not try and "rescue" me from my pain after our sessions, when I would cry in the car. He said he had feared my therapy would require more help than he could give. He acknowledged his own growth in taking my case, in terms of the challenge I presented over time. He admitted to enjoying the process of my healing and how good it made him feel.

During this session, we spent a lot of time not saying anything. It was extremely hard for me to speak. I had intended to say so much, and ended up saying very little. I do not regret not saying more. I feel what I did say was enough. I really don't remember much of what I said. I remember asking him if he listened to country music. He answered he did. I then asked if he was familiar with Dolly Parton's song, "I Will Always Love You." He asked if it was the same as the Whitney Houston song. I guess he is a late-comer to country music. I told him the story of the origin of the song. I told him our termination was in many ways similar to Dolly leaving Porter Wagner and the Grand Ol' Opry. I said I wanted for him all the things at the end of the song. In response, he said he had felt the same way at the end of his own marriage.

He asked if I was still taking my meds. He then told me I should continue to take them for at least a year, and that it was quite possible I may be taking them for the rest of my life. I told him Dr. Stephens had said the same thing. They had given the same diabetes example too. I was surprised to hear what he had to say next. He admitted he is a daily user of Prozac®[1]. He stated Prozac® alone did nothing to help him deal with his depression, but using Prozac® in conjunction with therapy had worked well. I told him I had the same experience, in our relationship. He then told me he experienced depression as a result of dealing with his divorce. I became quite lost at this point. I stared at his left hand to see if he was still wearing a wedding ring. His emotions indicated his divorce was still a very painful part of his life. It was as though he was still dealing with the divorce. I wondered if the divorce was recent. He was wearing a wedding ring. I was so totally confused.

He mentioned he felt it was important for him to remain as much of a blank slate as possible to me during our relationship. I responded by telling him as hard as he tried, his emotions still surfaced. I wanted him to know how difficult it was for me to not respond. He asked when I started seeing him. Since I really couldn't remember exactly, I told him it was sometime in August. I then asked why? He said he had just got married several weeks before, at the end of July. I am not sure if I was able to hide it, but I was completely surprised and shocked by what I felt. I could have been blown over by a bee's breath. He said he was dealing with the difficulties of the adjustment of living together with his new wife. I would have never guessed he was a newlywed.

Throughout the entire session, Jim's eyes were so red. He also had a terrible case of the sniffles. He did not blame it on an allergy this time. I suppose he remembered I am a little more astute than the average client and decided to drop that line with me. I felt the end of this relationship was nearly as difficult for him as it was for me. After this exchange, I turned to go. As I did, he opened up his arms and said: "How about a hug?" I turned and hugged him.

I had agonized over my last session with Jim. I was so upset when I got home that I called Mary. She wasn't home; however, she called me back later, and we chatted for a few minutes. She could tell I was hurting and needed to talk. She invited me to go to her house at 10:00 p.m. I went. I stayed until 2:30 a.m. We talked about the end of my relationship and what a difficult time I was having. I am so glad I have Mary as my friend. I don't know what I would have done without her. I finally have a living best friend again, and her name is Mary.

Since the beginning of my last session with Jim yesterday, I have cried so many tears. After all of this, I am still a bundle of emotions. I feel so much right at this moment, I am having a terrible time of identifying what I feel.

In the end, I found out the life I thought Jim had was not a mirror of reality. This can happen in therapy. It is usually not a result of deception by therapists, but rather, it is a result of therapists digging deep within to find the emotions and feelings which will allow them to connect, empathize, and understand their clients. Jim's ability to allow me to know he understood how I felt contributed to my assumptions about his life. I did not feel deceived. I was happy for his recent marriage. Since I truly loved him, I took great joy in his happiness. I still hoped for my own marital happiness.

The last session in therapy, outweighs the first. If the first session is a little rocky, amends can be made. If the last session does not go well, the recovery is a little harder. Clients may have to make the recovery alone, unless they return to therapy to try it again. The last session also reinforces the lessons learned throughout the therapeutic experience. It gives clients another chance to exercise all the new skills learned. It gives therapists another chance to reassure their client of their progress and growth. The last session can be so much, and it was with me.

❖

A New Journey

22 June 1997

Last night, I finally started my book about therapy. It will be difficult to fit the book into my schedule with everything else I have to do, but I will. This book is very important to me. I hope it will help change the way people view psychotherapy, and be helpful to those who hurt. I want people to know the truth about therapy and what it is capable of accomplishing; people should know it isn't the garbage depicted on TV and in the movies. Therapy is so much more; it is truly a gift.

Epilogue

As each day passes, my life further unfolds, my healing continues, the lessons present themselves, and my capacity to love grows. I am astonished to see where I am and where I am headed. There was a time I only wished to be where I am now. That time seems like a lifetime ago, and in some ways it was.

My therapy with Jim has been over for quite some time, but while working on this book, I have been asked what I have learned from therapy. Initially, the answer eluded me. I was looking for something profound, instead, it was something more, it was simple. During the ten months with Jim, I learned:

1. Self-love.
2. Self-acceptance.
3. How to love my daughter.
4. How to love another person.
5. How to let go of someone I love.
6. How to live.

Doesn't sound like much, but for me, these have been the most important lessons of my life. Without them, I would not be alive today.

I admit I have experienced a few episodes of depression, but I am not discouraged. I had suppressed my emotions, and the depression reminded me I can not hide from my emotions. I faced my emotions and dispatched the depression quickly. I have not had suicidal thoughts or desires.

I am still working on my marriage. My husband has embarked on his own journey to the self. I wonder what he will experience and what he will find. I have no real expectations about where his therapy will leave us. Only time will tell, and so I wait.

I was concerned about whether or not I should begin practicing psychotherapy. During the second to last session I had with Jim, I asked him if he felt I was healed enough to be therapeutic with others. He responded that if I had asked him several months before, he would have said no. By the end of our work, he said he felt confident I was healed enough to do good work. Also, I worked closely with two supervising psychotherapists to ensure I was delivering the highest quality of care I could provide. If they had felt I was not psychologically fit to practice, they would have been ethically and professionally obligated to remove me from practice. That did not happen.

During my internship in psychotherapy, I found my own therapeutic experience was still my teacher. While I sat with my clients, I found I have brought Jim s strength, caring, patience, and love with me to share my own clients. I am by no means a great therapist; I have just begun. Without Jim, I could have never begun. I desire to give to others what Jim has given to me.

As a result of therapy and this book, many relationships in my life have changed. Some of my relationships have become emotionally intimate, and as a result, I have lost some relationships. Losing relationships still hurts, but I experience the pain and no longer let it overwhelm me or devastate my life. I have established some new relationships which have been interesting and fun. I am living more fully.

I still deeply miss my therapeutic relationship with Jim, and I suspect I always will. Our contact has been limited to the publication of this book. When we have spoken, there has been a gentleness between us. It would not be ethically nor professionally appropriate for us to have a social relationship, either now or any time in the near future. I fully understand this and accept this. Although I was deeply saddened by the termination of our relationship, I was not devastated. I did not experience the emotional pain I had experienced at the end of my previous relationships. When I look back on the overall experience, I remember warmth, fondness, and love. I believe I have healed many areas of pain, and learned so much, there are many more lessons for me to learn, and I eagerly await them.

If you are in therapy, I applaud you. If you have decided to start, I wish you strength and courage. If you have decided against it, I understand. If you are not happy in your life, there is so much out there waiting for you. I hope you will take a chance on life.

In Serenity,

Kathleen

The Gift

Each of us receives countless gifts over the years. Sometimes they come wrapped in beautiful paper and shimmering ribbon. Other times, they come plain and revealed.

The most treasured gift I have ever received was wrapped in experience and authenticity, and tied with a ribbon of hope. After carefully unwrapping the gift, I found the contents to be strength, caring, patience, intuition, love, and life.

Oftentimes, the most valuable gifts are not the ones you can touch and hold, but are instead the ones which touch the soul and hold the heart.

How can I thank you for such a wondrous gift? I know not. I only know such a gift is not to be kept guarded and secret, but rather shared and given freely.

As the years tumble away, and the luster fades, the value of the gift remains unchanged. I will keep it with me always, let it sustain me, and ever will it bring a smile to my heart.

Afterword

When I first read this book, I was immediately struck by how powerful psychotherapy can be. This may sound strange coming from one who has done it for twenty years, but when you are "in it," it is often hard to appreciate the real impact you are having. I was also taken aback by the openness with which Kathleen shared her life and her struggles to become authentic. Reading her journal entries was like peering into her soul. I did not encourage her to write this book. It was part of her journey.

This is a book about what therapy can be – a journey. Kathleen's struggles, growth, and courage are so wonderfully detailed. I hope it will give others the courage to face their most fearful thoughts. To confront the alienation from one's own self is the true source of emotional healing. Her treatment was about healing old wounds and getting in touch with her pain. From the outside, no one would ever guess that it was a struggle of life and death. She was married with a beautiful young daughter. She was a straight "A" graduate student who helped her professors on many research projects. Yet every day, she struggled to choose to live, and some days she came very close to not making that choice.

Some might argue that I did not do intense enough treatment; that she should have been hospitalized or seen at least twice a week. I used my best judgment and intuition based upon twenty years of training and experience. Some may wonder why I was at times so seemingly inconsistent. One moment she saw me as caring, attentive, and providing support; the next moment I could appear to be distracted, or at the least less interested (hopefully never disinterested). This was in part by design and in part by simply being another human being, who even in a therapeutic relationship, can never be totally "on" all the time. When I saw Kathleen as most fragile, I gave her as much support as possible, a type of support she had never known before. When I thought she had the strength to get through it herself, even though she may have been in great pain, I gave her the responsibility. I believed that the only way for her to live was to not become dependent upon me, but for her to make the choice herself. Full responsibility for her life was given to her, and she fortunately took it. For neither a psychologist nor anyone else, even a spouse or best friend, can always be there for another. I wanted to give her internal strength and confidence – a greater gift than kindness and support. There were many times I wondered whether Kathleen would choose to die rather than continue the struggle to live. It is easy to rescue someone, but it takes courage, knowledge, experience, and skill to let someone sail on their own waters. In the end, it was all about discovering that the reason for her depression was a lack of love – love of self and love of others. When she learned to love, she learned to live.

Kathleen taught me, once again, the power of transference (the feeling a patient has for her therapist) and the absolute necessity of establishing professional boundaries. There is no substitute for this in therapy. To violate these boundaries is to violate a sacred trust and to destroy, once again, the hopes and dreams of those who seek out healing. It was through this transference that she could safely begin to explore her feelings and her longing for love. This is the real power of psychotherapy. This is the part you cannot get from a self-help book. One should never underestimate the power of dialog and the power of a relationship.

Kathleen was one of the last patients I saw in psychotherapy. This experience was a wonderful ending for this part of my life. After twenty years of doing "the work," as well as my dissatisfaction with the current managed care environment, I have chosen to use my knowledge and skill in other ways. I want to thank Kathleen for the courage she has shown in sharing her soul with us. I hope *The Gift* will be helpful to patients and providers alike in showing what is possible in healing the human spirit. *The Gift* was given to me as well. Thank you, Kathleen.

Jim Seymour, Ph.D.

Chapter 3

1. According to the *Diagnostic and Statistical Manual for Mental Illness, Fourth Edition*, by the American Psychiatric Association, the essential feature of Dissociative Identity Disorder (DID) is "the presence of two or more distinct identities or personality states. Each with its own relatively enduring pattern of perceiving, relating to, and thinking about the environment and self. These recurrently take control of behavior. There is an inability to recall important personal information, the extent of which is too great to be explained by ordinary forgetfulness. For the Not Otherwise Specified, subcategory One, the clinical presentation is similar to DID but fails to meet full criteria for this disorder. Examples include presentations in which a) there are not two or more distinct personality states, or b) amnesia for important personal information does not occur." In my case, the amnesia did not occur.

2. The Coolidge Axis II Inventory is a personality disorder and mental disorder inventory created by Frederick Coolidge, Ph.D. By answering 225 different questions, it compares the answers selected, against the criteria for the different personality disorders and other mental disorders and with the way in which numerous other purportedly normal people have answered the same questions. A report is generated which tells a therapist what areas might be considered for diagnosis and work.

Chapter 4

1. I highly recommend pages 160 to 180 in *The Road Less Traveled*, by M. Scott Peck, M.D., in order to more fully understand this relationship. I also recommend the entire book. It is a wonderful view of psychotherapy from the perspective of the therapist. There are also many insightful observations about love, spirituality, growth, and potential.

Chapter 5

1. For more readings on classical psychological view on dreams, consider the works of Jung, Freud, Perls, and Coolidge. Although the dream dictionaries may be interesting, only the dreamer can truly know the significance of a dream. After all, sometimes a cigar is just a cigar; and/or the meaning and experience of your dreams might have no significance whatsoever.

Chapter 6

1. I recommend the book, *Wherever You Go, There You Are*, by Jon Kabat-Zin, Ph.D., who talks about ways to experience the here and now within everyday life. This book encourages one to find ways of slowing down life and experience the everyday with greater simplicity and meaning.

Chapter 7

1. In the series, *Power of Myth, Segment II: The Journey Inward*, Joseph Campbell spoke of the idea of heaven being here on Earth within the self, rather than heaven being someplace else.

Chapter 16

1. At this early time in my life, I was very interested in ancient civilizations, which included the Romans, Greeks, and Egyptians. These cultures influenced how I viewed the world. I devoured ancient mythology and the role the Gods played in the orchestration of everyday life of "mortals." Since I could not make sense out of the world I lived in, I found it comforting to turn to the Gods of the ancients to help explain my world.

2. Snoopy is a registered trademark of United Features Syndicate.

3. Peanuts is a registered trademark of United Features Syndicate.

Chapter 39

Prozac is a registered trademark of the Eli Lily and Company.

For Further Reading

Campbell, Joseph. (1988). *The Power of Myth with Bill Moyers*. New York: Doubleday.

Kottler, Jeffrey A. (1996). *The Language of Tears*. San Francisco: Jossey-Bass Publishers.

Miller, Alice. (1994). *The Drama of the Gifted Child: The Search for the True Self*.(Ruth Ward, Trans.) Basic Books.

Peck, M. Scott (1978). The Road Less Traveled: A New Psychology of Love, Traditional Values and Spiritual Growth. New York: Simon and Schuster, Inc.

Weinberg, George. (1984). *The Heart of Psychotherapy: A Journey into the Mind and Office of the Therapist at Work*. New York: St. Martin s Griffin.

Kabat-Zin, Jon. (1994). *Wherever You Go, There You Are: Mindfulness Meditation in Everyday Life*. New York: Hyperion.

Order Form

Fax Orders: (719) 495-3865

Postal Orders:
> Inner Passages Publishing
> Order Department
> P.O. Box 88227
> Colorado Springs, CO 80908-8227
> USA

Please send the following books: I understand that I may return any books for a full refund-for any reason, no questions asked.

Title	Qty	Price Each	Price Total
The Gift: Journey to the Self Through Psychotherapy		$24.95	

Sales tax:
Please add 7.25% for books shipped to California addresses.
Please add 3.00% for books shipped to Colorado addresses.   ________

Shipping:
$4.00 for the first book and $2.00 for each additional book.   ________

Total Payment: ________

❑ Check or Money Order
❑ Credit card: VISA or MasterCard

Card number: ________________________

Name on card: ________________________

Exp. Date: ___/___